The Autonomous City

The Autonomous City

A History of Urban Squatting

Alexander Vasudevan

VERSO
London • New York

First published by Verso 2017
© Alexander Vasudevan 2017

1 3 5 7 9 10 8 6 4 2

Verso
UK: 6 Meard Street, London W1F 0EG
US: 20 Jay Street, Suite 1010, Brooklyn, NY 11201
versobooks.com

Verso is the imprint of New Left Books

ISBN-13: 978-1-78168-786-4 (PB)
ISBN-13: 978-1-78168-785-7 (HB)
ISBN-13: 978-1-78168-787-1 (US EBK)
ISBN-13: 978-1-78168-788-8 (UK EBK)

British Library Cataloguing in Publication Data
A catalogue record for this book is available from the British Library

Library of Congress Cataloging-in-Publication Data
A catalog record for this book is available from the Library of Congress

Typeset in Sabon by MJ & N Gavan, Truro, Cornwall
Printed and bound by CPI Group (UK) Ltd, CR0 4YY

For all the squatters whose struggles to build
a more just and sustainable city continue.

Contents

Introduction

The most intense point of lives, the one where their energy is concentrated is precisely there where they clash with power.

There can be truth only in the form of the other world and the other life.

Michel Foucault[1]

In the early morning hours of 1 March 2007, the Copenhagen police launched a surprise operation to evict the occupants of the Ungdomshuset (The Youth House), a social centre in the district of Nørrebro at Jagtvej 69 that had for many years been run as an autonomous social centre. The house had been established in 1982 after the municipality delegated its running to an undefined group of youth that were connected with a growing squatters' movement in the city. The house soon became the backbone of the movement and, over the years, it served as a key meeting point within a wider alternative scene. The centre hosted concerts and housed a bookshop, a café, a printing press, a recording studio and a weekly vegan soup kitchen. For many, the Ungdomshuset was synonymous with radical autonomous politics in Copenhagen, and meetings between activists routinely took place there.[2]

The police operation was carried out with military precision, personnel and equipment.[3] It began at 7:00 in the morning and was over within an hour. The police cordoned off the area around the Ungdomshuset while an airport crash tender was deployed. It sprayed the doors and windows with a strange foam that hardened on impact, preventing the occupants from opening them from the inside. An elite anti-terrorist unit was then dropped on to the roof of the house using an S-61A Sea King military helicopter. Additional units were able to enter the house from the ground and from a series of containers that had been lifted by two boom cranes, which provided access to the house's upper stories.[4]

The supporters of the centre were able to regroup in the immediate aftermath of the eviction. They were unable, however, to break the police lines that surrounded the houses. Within a couple of hours, barricades had been thrown up on the Nørrebrogade south of the house as the police moved in to arrest the protesters. Across the city, in Christianshavn, another group of supporters were blocking traffic in solidarity with the Ungdomshuset.

Over the course of the day, a series of protest marches were held across Copenhagen. The police adopted an increasingly heavy-handed approach as they attempted to disperse and detain a large group of protesters who had once again congregated on the Nørrebrogade. A series of pitched battles erupted which lasted well into the night. The protesters broke into small groups to evade the police. Others occupied a vacant building on the Blågårdsgade. By the early hours of 2 March, relative calm had finally fallen over the city. A total of 219 arrests had been made by the police, including the thirty-six occupants of the Ungdomshuset.[5]

The repressive tactics adopted by the police did little to quell the anger felt by many activists and young people in Copenhagen. By 3 March, violent protests had once again broken out. In the worst rioting that Copenhagen had seen since the Second World War, Nørrebro was completely overrun as the police were pushed back by the protesters, who coordinated their actions and used burning cars and rubbish bins to barricade streets across the neighbourhood.[6] In response, the police 'accidentally' resorted to the use of lethal Ferret 40 tear gas canisters that are usually used to penetrate doors and walls. 'We made a mistake', one spokesman for the police later admitted.[7]

The following morning, the police launched a major crackdown on alternative spaces across Copenhagen that lasted six days. The (New) Folkets Hus on the Stengade, the squatters' collective on the Baldersgade, as well as the Solidaritetshuset in Griffenfeldtsgade, were all raided as the police searched for foreign activists linked to the protests. Over 140 arrests on the 'presumption of dangerousness' were made, though no crime had been committed by those arrested. In total over 750 people were detained, often illegally and arbitrarily, including a number of minors whose details were entered into the national database. So many arrests were ultimately made that the police did not have enough space in local prisons and had to transport inmates to Jutland. One local prison had to be partially emptied of its normal occupants to make way for the new detainees.[8]

On the morning of 5 March, the demolition of the now empty Ungdomshuset began, with crowds of supporters gathering to watch as a crane went to work on the top floor of the house. The whole demolition was broadcast live via a webcam on the Danish TV-2 website. What remained of the building was later sold as recycling substrate. As solidarity marches against the demolition were held across Europe and North America, the protests in Copenhagen also continued. From 10–19 March, the districts of Nørrebro and Christianshavn became, under police orders, special zones where anyone could be stopped and searched and their details added to the national database.[9]

For many observers, the eviction and the police crackdown that followed in its wake represented an experimental 'laboratory' for a new form of militarised urban policing. A variety of methods, techniques and weapons were deployed by the authorities in Copenhagen in close cooperation with their European counterparts. The Swedish police loaned twenty of their own vehicles for the operation, while five senior officers accompanied the Copenhagen police. There were, in turn, numerous eyewitness reports of plainclothes officers from other European forces operating at the scene. Their presence as active units was denied, though a Copenhagen police spokesperson conceded that they may have been acting as 'observers'.[10]

For the former occupants of the Ungdomshuset, the loss of the centre was the culmination of a long and violent process of repression and vilification that had its origins in the late nineteenth century and in the struggles of Danish workers. The building in which the centre was housed first opened on 12 November 1897, as the fourth headquarters for the Danish labour movement. The Folkets Hus, or People's House as it was known, became a key centre and meeting place for a number of movements. It was from the Folkets Hus that International Woman's Day was first launched in 1910 by Clara Zetkin. The house also played an important role in the storming of the Danish Stock Exchange (Børsen) in February 1918 by a group of unemployed anarcho-syndicalists.[11]

By the 1960s, the building was empty. It was later acquired by local Copenhagen authorities who, in an attempt to neutralise the city's increasingly militant youth movement, donated the use of the house to a group of squatters in October 1982. They quickly transformed the site into an autonomous self-managed social centre, the Ungdomshuset. For the activists running the house, the centre was an opportunity to express their 'right to difference' and their commitment to an alternative set of social relations. Many right-wing politicians saw things differently. In their eyes, the 'pile of rotten stones at Jagtvej 69' was a major source of nuisance and incompatible with the 'respectable' city they envisaged. It was their stated desire to 'tear the shit down' and eradicate the site.[12]

A fire in the house in 1996 was the excuse that they were looking for. Despite the successful renovation of the building, city councillors decided to sell the house in May 1999 against the wishes of its occupants, for whom it represented an autonomous free space in a 'sea of hostility'.[13] The house was sold in November 2000 to a newly formed company, Human A/S, which was headed by a former municipal lawyer. The shares of the company were sold on a year later to an evangelical Christian sect, Faderhuset (Father's House). The leader of the sect later claimed that she was acting in response to a sign from God who requested that she remove this 'abomination' ('*vederstyg-gelighed*') and exorcise the streets of Nørrebro.[14]

Faderhuset immediately terminated the contract with the group running the Ungdomshuset. The activists refused, however, to leave. They organised open houses to raise public awareness of the centre's heritage and history. At the same time, a number of other tactics were deployed including a series of public occupations, protest marches and other happenings. Various efforts to secure a positive legal outcome proved fruitless. An August 2006 ruling by the Danish High Court confirmed a string of earlier court decisions that honoured Faderhuset's claim to private property over the activists' usufructuary rights. The occupants were ordered out of the houses by 14 December 2006. They were refused any further right to appeal.

With all legal avenues exhausted, a number of large demonstrations were organised by users of the Ungdomshuset. While a group was set up to purchase the house on behalf of its current users, the Faderhuset refused to sell and the house was finally cleared on 1 March 2007, and demolished a few days later. The protests that erupted in the immediate aftermath of the eviction continued in various forms for over sixteen months, and testified to the profound sense of loss and trauma felt by many activists and supporters of the Ungdomshuset.[15] In the face of persistent discontent, Copenhagen authorities decided to gift the former occupants two buildings in the city's north-west, at Dortheavej 61. They began to move into the new premises on 1 July 2008. Meanwhile, Faderhuset had already sold the old property to an undisclosed buyer. To this day the site remains empty, a vacant plot of land.

The sheer intensity of the struggle surrounding the eviction of the Ungdomshuset was not unique to Copenhagen, nor were the radical politics of housing and self-organisation that the centre and its supporters embodied. Over the past decade and, in particular, in the years that followed the global financial crisis, a sustained and systematic attack on alternative forms of living and working has taken place in cities across Europe and North

America. Authorities have targeted the often informal and sometimes illegal spaces set up by ordinary people. These were people who became squatters in order to take control of their own lives and respond to basic housing needs, but who found in their actions new political possibilities for collective self-empowerment and autonomous political action.

In a number of European countries, squatting has been criminalised in recent years. In Spain, at the height of the country's own housing crisis, a series of changes were made to the criminal code in 2010. Article 245 of the code which dealt with *usurpació* (or trespass) was modified, and the penalty was increased from a fine to a jail sentence of one to two years.[16] The same year, the Squatting and Vagrancy Act came into force in the Netherlands. It criminalised squatting in all properties and carried a maximum prison sentence of one year. Two years later, in September 2012, a new law came into force in England and Wales that made trespassing in a residential property with the intention of living there a criminal offence. Finally, in June 2015, the French National Assembly unanimously passed a law proposed by the mayor of Calais that clarified the power of authorities (according to Article 226–4 of the Penal Code) to evict squatters.[17] Across the Atlantic, similar legal measures have been rolled out in the states of Michigan and Nevada. Other changes to adverse possession statutes have been proposed in a number of states.[18]

The legal attack against squatting has coincided (perhaps unsurprisingly) with a global housing crisis. In cities in the Global North, the symptoms of this crisis have, as David Madden and Peter Marcuse recently argued, acquired a certain ubiquity. Whether it is Berlin, London, Madrid or New York, households are being 'squeezed by the cost of living. Homelessness is on the rise. Evictions and foreclosures are commonplace.'[19] And yet, at the same time homes are being transformed into commodities. Housing is no longer seen as a basic social need. It has become an instrument of profit-making transforming today's cities into sites of intense displacement and inequality, exploitation and poverty.

It is, in this context, not hard to see the new wave of anti-squatting legislation as an attempt to protect the ongoing commodification of housing at a moment when many people are looking to alternatives that reassert the cultural, social and political value of housing as a universal necessity and as a source of social transformation. These are, in the eyes of many, laws that are driven by ideological motivations. They seek to uphold the sanctity of private property and defend the interests of 'hard-working homeowners' against squatters. They are used as a 'tool' or 'weapon' to perpetuate domination, accentuate inequality and support a system that is increasingly unsustainable.

Ordinary citizens and activists have nevertheless fought back. They point out that, for poor working-class communities, the housing crisis has always been the norm. They find common cause in the words of Friedrich Engels, one of the more astute commentators on the 'housing question'. He noted that 'the so-called housing shortage ... is not something peculiar to the present'. 'All oppressed classes in all periods,' he added, 'suffered more or less uniformly from it.'[20]

While Engels was writing in 1872 with the shock cities of early industrialisation specifically in mind, the injustices of housing have only intensified over the past century or so, taking in cities in both the Global North and South. For the oppressed, the history of housing is a history of insecurity and inequality.[21] But it is also a history of resistance and possibility; one in which squatters occupy an understudied if important place.

Squatting can be defined as 'living in – or using otherwise – a dwelling without the consent of the owner. Squatters take buildings [or land] with the intention of relative (>1 year) long-term use.'[22] For the anarchist and historian Colin Ward, the place of the squatter in the history of housing is far more significant than is usually realised. Not only is this a global history, as Ward is at pains to argue. It also encompasses, on the one hand, a range of customary beliefs, makeshift practices and coping mechanisms that have emerged in the absence of the most basic of necessities. On the other hand, it is equally responsible for the making of new social forms – often radical and militant – that point to a different understanding of the home as a site of cooperation, emancipation and self-organisation.[23]

According to the investigative journalist Robert Neuwirth, it is, in fact, squatters who give 'some reality to Henri Lefebvre's loose concept of the "right to the city"'. 'They are excluded so they take,' he writes, 'but they are not seizing an abstract right, they are taking an actual place: a place to lay their heads. This act – to challenge society's denial of place by taking one of your own – is an assertion of being in a world that routinely denies people the dignity and the validity inherent in a home.'[24]

Neuwirth is one of many writers who have drawn attention to the highly precarious forms of endurance and survival developed by the millions of squatters that continue to live in the cities and towns of the Global South.[25] These are accounts that zoom in on the unjust structures of dispossession, exclusion and violence experienced by many squatters as well as their efforts to eke out a viable life in settings of pervasive marginality.

Set against this backdrop, the squatter movements that first emerged in cities in the Global North in the 1960s and 1970s were admittedly smaller in scale – numbering in the tens of thousands – though they played a decisive role in the development of new forms of grassroots urban politics. Outside of well-established activist communities, these are movements that have, until recently, received little recognition.[26] It is their story – a shared history of political action, community organisation and collective living – that is the main subject of this book.

The book charts the everyday practices and political imaginations of squatters. It examines the composition of alternative collective spaces in cities across Europe and North America. To do so, it explores why thousands of people in cities such as London and Amsterdam, Berlin and New York, suddenly chose to occupy empty flats and other buildings. Were these actions, it asks, dictated by pure necessity or did they represent a new-found desire to imagine other ways of living together? Who were these squatters and in what way did they promote an alternative vision of the city?

To answer these questions, the book highlights how the actions of squatters, from the spaces they occupied to the terms they used, reimagined the city as a space of necessity and refuge, experimentation and resistance. It retraces the major wave of squatting that began in Europe and North America in the late 1960s, and is the first comprehensive attempt to reconstruct this history as the expression of an *autonomous* understanding of shared city life. It does so in three ways.

First, it connects the practices adopted by squatters to a search for autonomy in housing and the built form, and a desire to assemble, organise and sustain their own spaces. As the architect and urbanist John Turner famously argued, housing 'must be autonomous'.[27] The immediate context for Turner's argument was his own practical experience in the 1960s working in the rapidly expanding self-built and self-governing *barridas* of Peru. For Turner, the most important thing about housing, according to his friend Colin Ward, 'is not what it *is* but what it *does* in people's lives'.[28] According to Turner, 'when dwellers control the major decisions and are free to make their own contribution to the design, construction or management of their housing, both the process and the environment produced stimulate individual and social well-being'.[29]

If the work of Turner has been instrumental in rethinking how people learn to house themselves, especially in certain parts of the Global South, the recent history of squatting in Europe and North America may equally be seen as a series of attempts to extend the concept of housing 'autonomy'. For a number of commentators, the veritable explosion of squatting that began in the late 1960s spoke to the emergence of an 'autonomous urban movement' that positioned itself in opposition to the state and as an alternative to capitalism.[30]

The term 'autonomy' is derived, after all, from the Greek *auto-nomos*, which refers to those who 'live by their own rules'.[31] As an autonomous movement, squatting was a political practice, a way of living and a youth subculture. It drew on a range of radical social movements including the Italian Autonomia of the

1970s and the explosive cycle of youth protests that emerged across Northern Europe in the 1980s.[32] In North America, these impulses were more muted, though a strong anarcho-libertarian ethos was certainly present. Taken together, these were movements that shared a radical geographical sensibility that operated at a critical distance from the state. Autonomy was linked, in particular, to the occupation and self-management of urban space. At stake here, was the development of practices that creatively reclaimed the city, often in the face of a specific threat (gentrification, homelessness, police repression, the preservation of public space, urban renewal, etc.).

Finally, as one historian has recently argued, the militancy that often characterised the relationship between urban squatting and 'autonomous' politics in the Global North was itself dependent on a mass of young people who found themselves 'marginal to mainstream society'.[33] Autonomy represented far more, however, than an expression of disaffection or obstinacy, freedom or rebellion. It offered an opportunity to *become a squatter*, to explore new identities and different intimacies, to experience and share feelings and to organise and live collectively. The squat may have been a place that challenged housing precarity, rampant property speculation and the negative effects of urban redevelopment and regeneration. But it was also a place where one could (quite literally) *build* an alternative world. The composition of squatted spaces varied, and spoke to a diversity of positions within a wide range of anti-authoritarian ideas and politics.

As a housing practice, a social movement of sorts and a set of identities, squatting produced complex networks of activism and solidarity that were shared between squats and ultimately stretched across a number of cities. The replication and repetition of ideas and practices, idioms and forms was, in this way, instrumental in the development of squatting in Europe and North America. And yet, at the same time, squatting remained a heterogeneous phenomenon, specific to the local urban context in which it was formed and developed.[34]

The history of squatting developed in these pages cannot therefore be reduced to one neat, seamless story. Rather, the book retraces a series of interlocking episodes that, taken together, highlight the importance of squatting as a radical solution to homelessness and uneven urban development. The book reconstructs the history of squatting movements in London, Berlin, Amsterdam, New York and elsewhere from a period of Fordist decline all the way to our current era of 'austerity'. The main substantive chapters are organised around specific places, with each individual chapter highlighting a particular question or theme connected to the recent history of urban squatting. In so doing, it develops a series of concepts and arguments about the importance of squatting and how we might still come to know and live the city differently.

Each chapter is, in turn, arranged more or less chronologically. The main historical arc of the book retraces the emergence of squatting that coincided with the rise of new social movements across Europe and North America in the late 1960s. It follows the major cycle of militancy that characterised the 1970s and 1980s. This flowed from the actions of Italian Autonomia to the 'countercultural agitprop' and 'streetfighting maximalism' that shaped the practices and tactics adopted in Northern European cities such as Amsterdam, Berlin, Copenhagen, Hamburg and London. These trajectories have, of course, been widely celebrated, and particular attention is also paid to a new set of practices adopted by squatters in more recent decades as a response to long-term capitalist restructuring, the dismantling of the welfare state and the deregulation and financialisation of housing.[35]

The path connecting the events of the late 1960s through to the present is a complex and crooked one, and the actions of squatters must also be seen within broader struggles over the meaning of urban space. As the Marxist geographer David Harvey reminds us, cities have become the key site for a variety of spatial struggles which, for Harvey, speak to the 'intimate connection between the development of capitalism and urbanization'.[36] Local movement histories are invariably embedded within broader cycles of capitalist accumulation and housing inequality, not to mention the different forms of resistance they produced (public occupations, rent strikes, tenant unions). It is with this longer history in mind that the book begins and ends in New York. Along the way, it stops in London, Amsterdam, Copenhagen, Frankfurt, Hamburg, Berlin, Bologna, Milan, Rome, Turin and Vancouver. At the heart of the book is an account of squatting as the political *other* to 'creative destruction', such that we continue to find in the lives, spaces and practices of squatters an alternative vision of the city that grows ever more necessary and urgent in the face of capitalist urbanisation.

This is a book that does not, in the end, seek to posit a blithe romanticism about squatting, nor does it mean to sidestep the sheer precarity and insecurity that many have historically faced in seeking adequate forms of housing and shelter. The book recognises the kind of stealth or deprivation-based squatting most often carried out by or on behalf of homeless people and other desperate would-be squatters.[37] It also acknowledges the 'dark side' of squatting; its fraught relationship to the logics of urban renewal and regeneration not to mention the many disagreements, failures and losses that often punctuated and shaped the experience of squatting. Squatted spaces were sites of liberation and possibility but equally sources of intense conflict and struggle.

It was Colin Ward who, in a small and elegant conspectus, described the history of squatting as a 'hidden history'.[38] The stories gathered together in what follows are an attempt to bring this history into sharper focus. The examples that are drawn here point to the different ways in which new, provisional, often ephemeral and sometimes durable urban worlds are composed in settings of growing inequity. To do so, as the radical history of squatting documented in these pages show, is to reveal the conditions – the counter-archive of practices, sentiments and stories – that point to the potential reorganisation of our cities along more collective, socially just and ecologically sustainable lines. It is these living geographies that hold the promise of the autonomous city.

1

From Shantytown to 'Operation Move-In': Squatter Sovereignty in New York

It's a fine free country, this is, where honest folks can't build a little house to cover their heads on an old rock like this without having the very ground blowed away from under them.

'A Visit to Shantytown'[1]

Landlord, landlord,
My roof has sprung a leak.
Don't you 'member I told you about it
Way last week?

Landlord, landlord,
These steps is broken down.
When you come up yourself
It's a wonder you don't fall down.

Ten Bucks you say I owe you?
Ten Bucks you say is due?
Well, that's Ten Bucks more'n I'll pay you
Till you fix this house up new.

What? You gonna get eviction orders?
You gonna cut off my heat?
You gonna take my furniture and
Throw it in the street?

Um-huh! You talking high and mighty.
Talk on-till you get through.
You ain't gonna be able to say a word
If I land my fist on you.

Langston Hughes, 'Ballad of the Landlord'[2]

In 1970, a forty-two-minute black and white documentary depicting the struggles of a squatters' rights movement in New York's Upper West Side Renewal Area was released by Newsreel, an activist documentary film organisation that had emerged as part of the American New Left in the late 1960s. The film *Rompiendo puertas* (*Break and Entry*) portrays the efforts of over 150 predominantly Puerto Rican families to secure safe and affordable housing against a backdrop of intense inequality, pervasive discrimination and persistent dislocation.

Formed in New York in December 1967 by a group of underground filmmakers, Newsreel was a 'radical news service' that had been initially established to chronicle the various identities, alliances and strategies that characterised the New Left in the United States. It drew particular inspiration, in this respect, from activists rooted in a range of anti-racist and anti-colonial movements. *Rompiendo puertas* was one of a series of films it produced between 1969 and 1972 that focused on New York's communities of colour.[3]

Taking its name from the police shorthand for house burglary, *Rompiendo puertas* details the actions adopted by a group of Latino families who occupied and repaired a series of abandoned buildings on the Upper West Side in the spring and summer of 1970. The families were all part of Operation Move-In, a local anti-poverty and squatters' rights group. The group had been installing low-income families into sound vacant buildings that had been slated for demolition by the city as part of its urban renewal programme. They used crowbars to pry off the tin seals covering doors and windows while helping families to carry their belongings and furniture.[4]

The film combines documentary footage of clashes between the squatters and the police with voice-over analysis exploring the causes of New York's housing shortage. Many of the original organisers of Operation Move-In were old leftists and mavericks of Lyndon Johnson's signature War on Poverty campaign, as well as a group of radical young activists from the Young Lords, a militant Puerto Rican organisation.[5] They were led by William

Price, a former UN correspondent, journalist and Communist who was fired in 1955 from the *New York Daily News* in the wake of his appearance before the US Senate Subcommittee on Internal Security. Price became a housing activist on New York's West Side with loose connections to the Metropolitan Council on Housing (hereafter Met Council), one of the city's most important tenants' rights organisations. As *Rompiendo puertas*, however, shows, this was ultimately a squatters' rights movement that was largely organised and executed by working-class Puerto Rican women. It was their voices and actions that are the main subject of the film.

The film documents the challenges that its predominantly Latino protagonists faced in securing a home in a city where many residents lived in inadequate or unsafe housing while others faced 'removal' to the outer boroughs as part of the city's urban redevelopment plans. As one activist in the film noted, 'wherever the city sets up urban renewal programs, it removes working people and poor people and removes them from their homes and replaces them with rich people and big business'. In one scene, we watch a group of families moving their possessions out of an apartment in sacks and papers bags while a voice-over proclaims that 'hundreds of working people like us are being evicted and forced into the streets'. 'Housing,' another activist concludes, 'is a necessity. Why should we pay for a necessity?'[6]

As *Rompiendo puertas* shows, it was the death of a neighbourhood teen that served as the catalyst for the emergence of Operation Move-In and the seizure of empty vacant buildings across the Upper West Side. The teen had died from carbon monoxide poisoning in a first-floor apartment on West 106th Street. The film follows the funeral march held for the teen as well as the occupation that took place in its immediate aftermath. A day later, another nine buildings around Columbus Avenue and the West 80s were squatted by dozens of families who moved in during the night.[7]

The film places particular emphasis on the actions undertaken by the squatters while foregrounding the role played by middle-aged and elderly Puerto Rican women as leaders of the 'movement'. It depicts the collective formed to organise and undertake building repairs. The squatters created a system to pool their money and labour as part of the effort to renovate apartments. The film also draws attention to the wider infrastructure and network of co-operative services they created within the local neighbourhood (day cares, communal kitchens, apartment registries). In the words of one recent commentator, 'by defining the city as a space built by and thus in a fundamental sense for poor people, by asserting that the seizure of abandoned apartments is a morally justifiable and politically legitimate form of activism ... *Rompiendo puertas* depicts a radical politics of place that challenges the economic and political forces shaping the postwar urban city'.[8]

The squatters were able to secure some modest concessions from the city while salvaging some of the city's low-rent housing stock. These victories were, however, partial and short-lived, and the activism they ultimately depended on was unable to halt the gradual and wholesale gentrification of New York's West Side in the decades that followed. At the same time, the film remains an important document within a rich and expansive history of squatting and tenant-based activism in New York. This is, moreover, a history that challenged traditional social fault lines around class, race and gender. The actions instigated by the squatters of Operation Move-In drew, after all, on a long and varied tradition of resistance rooted in a struggle for a more just and equal urbanism and in opposition to an equally protracted history of destruction, displacement and destitution.

In the end, as David Madden and Peter Marcuse remind us, movements for housing have always assumed a number of different forms. They exhibit 'enormous variety in terms of tactics, strategies, goals, alliances, political calculations, compromises, and ideologies'.[9] New York is no different in this respect, and it is hardly surprising that the city encompassed a vast living *archive* of alternative knowledges, materials and resources that, in the eyes of squatters, tenants and other housing activists, served as a basis for developing a different vision of the city.

This is admittedly a history with a much longer narrative arc, whose origins can be traced back to the seventeenth-century Dutch resettlement of what is now the state of New York. It is also a history that highlights the *exemplary* significance of New York's housing politics and their relationship to national patterns and trends. For historians and radical urbanists alike, New York's lessons derive less from their typicality than their ability to illuminate and speak to developments in other American cities. 'In its tenant history, New York is,' according to the historian Roberta Gold, 'both representative and atypical at different times.' On the one hand, it was largely of a piece with developments in a number of other industrial centres in the United States during the first half of the twentieth century. After the Second World War, on the other hand, it departed from the suburban homeownership model that prevailed nationally. While this led to the destruction of mass movements for affordable housing in most major American cities, activists in New York were able to forge and sustain a tenant infrastructure that supported – sometimes successfully, sometimes less so – many of the city's poorest residents.[10]

If squatting came to occupy an important position within the post-war struggle for decent housing in New York, its relatively recent revival as a radical social movement ultimately belies its place within a more expansive history of occupation, settlement and resistance. Illegal occupations of land and struggles over property were central to what has been described as the 'unjust usurpation of the continent by white settlers'.[11] In the United States, squatting was closely intertwined with the predations of settler colonialism and, on a shifting frontier, it often represented a form of violent displacement through which indigenous communities were dispossessed of their lands and livelihoods.

At the same time, frontier settlers in the late eighteenth and early nineteenth centuries were, in most cases, compelled to become squatters as the distribution of land was largely controlled by speculators and land-grabbers (also known as 'land-jobbers'), and many settlers were simply too poor to enter into credit-debt arrangements. Illegal settlements were vigorously proscribed by Congress, however, though squatters were quick to organise and form 'settler' or 'squatter' associations that lobbied politicians while adopting a range of direct-action tactics. The squatters were, in this way, successful in pushing legislative change through state-level adverse possession statutes as well as a series of pre-emption acts from 1815 to 1841. In 1862, the federal *Homestead Act* was passed which allowed settlers to acquire federal land after living on it for five years and demonstrating that they had 'improved' it.[12]

In the state of New York, the history of land tenure was closely connected to its resettlement by the Dutch in the seventeenth century and the formation of a *patroon* system that bestowed feudal manorial rights rooted in Dutch property law to large landowners. It was English common law, however, which formed the basis for property law in the United States, and while the *Quia Emptores* statute had long-since abolished subinfeudation in England, it was never fully incorporated in the United States, though the 1787 Act Concerning Tenures banned feudal properties and established all real estate as *allodial* – that is, owned absolutely and independently of a lord. Such legal quiddities helped shape the development of New York in the wake of independence and were responsible for the emergence of an Anti-Rent movement in the Hudson Valley in the 1840s that challenged the legalities of manorial tenure. Most landlords chose to sell their interests to the rent-striking tenants, though it was left to returning soldiers from the American Civil War to quash the remnants of the movement and, in so doing, uphold forms of servitude that they had only recently fought against.[13]

In and around New York City, large property-owners had, unlike their upstate counterparts, adopted a system of lease holding in which land was subdivided into small lots that were rented out to workers and artisans. By 1811, a new land-use plan had transformed Manhattan into a rectilinear grid of twelve avenues which ran the length of the island and dozens of streets spanning its width. Property lines were narrowly drawn within city blocks to carve out small parcels of land, twenty-five feet wide by one hundred feet deep. Alleyways, courtyards and rear access streets were left out of the plan. As the city expanded during the first half of the nineteenth century, lease holding allowed land-owners to promote urban expansion and realise large profits without selling their land. A complex web of owners, landlords, sub-landlords, tenant managers, lessees, building operators and speculators soon emerged, however, especially in the Lower East Side were tenement structures were designed and constructed to maximise returns on the twenty-five by one hundred foot lots.[14]

Rapid industrialisation in the latter half of the nineteenth century was accompanied by a new influx of immigrants who crowded into poorly built tenements that had been hastily erected and were packed to capacity. By 1861, 50 per cent or 401,376 inhabitants of the city lived in 12,374 tenements. Tens of thousands more lived in 'rookeries', shacks and informal squatter settlements on pockets of ground that were either too rocky or too swampy for commercial development.[15] An 1867 report by the Citizen's Association Council of Hygiene pointed out that, in 1865, the East Side of Manhattan north of 40th Street contained approximately 1,016 squatter shacks, and that 'the tenant-houses of the city as a whole' were becoming 'rapidly and perilously aggregated'.[16] Another 1867 article in the *New York Times* reported that 'from the Hudson to the East River one can behold at least twenty-five different settlements, some located blocks apart from others, but each bearing a striking resemblance to the sister colony in point of dirt'. The largest was 'Dutch Hill', 'a conglomeration of hovels' that clustered around 41st Street near the East River. There were similar settlements dotted between Fourth and Tenth Avenues as well on the west side of town between 55th and 62nd Streets. As early as 1825, an African American settlement known as 'Seneca Village' had been established on purchased land that stretched from 81st to 89th Street. The only community of African American property owners in nineteenth-century Manhattan, the settlement was finally cleared in the 1850s to make way for Central Park.[17]

Beyond Manhattan, there were also a series of 'shantytowns' in Brooklyn. Many were located on the wasteland and mud-flats adjacent to the docks, including a 'desolate' settlement at Red Hook near the Gowanus Canal on 'an open space of land sunken so far below the city level that all attempts at sewerage have failed'.[18] Others were located nearby including 'Tinkersville', 'Phoenix Park', 'Slab City', 'Smokey Hollow' and 'Darby's Patch'.[19]

While New York's 'shanty dwellers' were widely impugned as 'squatters', they often paid some form of ground rent for their land. The majority were poor migrants employed as manual labourers and factory workers. In Brooklyn, a group of German labourers were living in a 'row of shanties' along Van Brunt Street as early as 1846. Another group of African American workers set up an informal settlement in Brooklyn known as 'Crow Hill'. Many commuted to Manhattan where they worked as domestic servants and in the Fulton and Washington Markets.[20] Other shantytown residents worked within a wider informal economy. Some residents maintained gardens and raised live-stock for sale. Offal boiling and piggeries were also popular businesses. As a retrospective history of squatting in the *New York Times* published in 1880 concluded, the early population of the city's shantytowns was made up of 'rag-pickers, pea-nut vendors, street-peddlers, knife-grinders, labourers, idlers, and vagrants'.[21]

The shantytown and squatter settlements of mid-nineteenth-century New York were nevertheless seen as an obstacle to the further development of the city as a modern metropolis. For city officials, they posed a threat to public health and safety as sites of poverty, pestilence and criminality. In the eyes of the mainstream press, they represented a precarious form of urban existence – a primitive anachronism – that hovered on the edges of 'civilised modern life'. Shantytowns were unsurprisingly por-trayed as 'plague-spots' and their residents as 'strangers': foreign, un-American and, in many cases, inhuman.[22]

Such nativist characterisations provided a justification for the repossession of land occupied by squatters and the demolition of their homes. Shanty dwellers were not the dangerous and degenerate characters portrayed in the mainstream press, however. They were, in most cases, labourers and entrepreneurs who 'took possession of the urban landscape and molded it to their needs'.[23] The self-built (and often informal) communities they created spoke to a 'kind of independent life': makeshift and precarious on the one hand; resilient and resourceful on the other.[24] These were complex and extended communities, a 'landscape of schoolhouses and chapels, work sites and fenced-in yards, pasturage and piggeries'.[25]

And yet, these communities were anathema to the gridded regularity of the nineteenth-century American city. 'The opening of thoroughfares up town,' one reporter concluded,

> Will raze the squatter's huts, and destroy that somewhat unenviable individuality which distinguishes the tenants. By seeking a shelter in tenement houses, the squatter will lose, it is true, the privilege of considering himself the monarch of all he [*sic*] surveys, but his descendants will be afforded some insight in the customs of civilised humanity, and the health and appearance of the metropolis will be benefitted.[26]

Despite fierce resistance, the majority were finally forced out as they gave way to a rapidly expanding city in the 1880s and 1890s. As they disappeared, the everyday experiences of their occupants – the popular working-class culture they produced and nurtured, the experiences of displacement and migration they brought with them – found a new home on New York's musical theatre stage. One of the most popular plays of the 1880s was Edward Harrigan's *Squatter Sovereignty*, a full-length musical comedy which premiered in 1882 at the Theatre Comique on Broadway and ran for over 160 performances.[27]

If mid-nineteenth-century shantytowns were a source of fear and anxiety for New York's middle class, they also brought the city's poor system of tenement housing into sharper focus.

Lawmakers were unwilling to legitimise the feudal model that had been practised in the Hudson Valley. They readily transferred, however, the legal aspects of landlord-tenant obligation to New York's growing urban environment. This was, primarily, a possession–rent relationship in which a landlord turned over 'possession' in exchange for rent.[28] The contractual aspects of this relationship were nevertheless overlooked, at the expense of tenants who had little legal redress when faced with poor living conditions, especially as landlords were not required to maintain the interiors of their apartments. As one expert on the subject therefore concluded, 'for landlords to be held liable there had to be statutes regulating tenement housing, and between 1867 and 1900, these laws either did not exist, or they were weak, unenforced, and largely ignored by landlords, inspectors and the courts alike'.[29]

By the late nineteenth century, New York's weak landlord-tenant laws had combined with an emerging system of leasing and subleasing to produce the severe overcrowding and dangerously unsafe living conditions that was documented by a group of pioneering photographers that included Jacob Riis.[30] These developments were challenged by housing advocates and progressive reformers, though there was little sustained opposition from tenants until the early twentieth century. It was working class immigrant (and mainly Jewish) housewives on the city's Lower East Side who overturned decades of acquiescence and passivity and were ultimately responsible for the city's first large-scale tenant mobilisation. Following a successful boycott of local kosher butchers in 1902, a series of strikes were organised in 1904 by East Side women in protest against crippling rent hikes. The women transformed their own neighbourhood into a staging ground for the emergence of 'tenant unions' (including the New York Rent Protective Association, or NYRPA) that withheld rents and blocked evictions and provided small sums of money to recently displaced tenants. They also formed alliances with neighbourhood socialists who soon seized the reins of the protest.[31]

Despite their efforts, Lower East Side residents were unsuccessful in assembling an infrastructure and institutional base from which they could organise future strikes and other tenant-based activism. While threatened evictions may have failed to materialise and, in some cases, landlords were even forced to roll back rent to pre-strike levels, the fissures within tenant groups prevented them from building on their victories and, if anything, contributed to their rapid dissolution.[32] Within a year landlords were once again raising rents, and by the end of 1907 a new wave of rent strikes had erupted with tenants demanding that landlords 'decrease the rent immediately'.[33] Unlike its predecessor, the 1907 strikes were organised and drew on the leadership, direction and organisational base of the Socialist Party. The political nature of the agitations alarmed many in the city. The strikers were widely criticised by the mainstream press and were, in the eyes of many wealthy New Yorkers, dangerous, unruly and ultimately responsible for fomenting a 'war' and 'uprising'.[34] Few tenants were able, however, to win any real concessions, while municipal court judges issued several thousand eviction notices.[35]

In the decade that followed, tenant action was sporadic at best and spoke to a patchwork of protest rooted in local neighbourhoods and increasingly sedimented histories of dissent. A second intense wave of rent strikes briefly erupted between 1917 and 1920 and was responsible for the 'largest radical housing uprising in New York's history'.[36] Unlike the configuration of its predecessor, the movement had a broader base. It involved Jewish families as well as Italian and Irish tenants in the Lower East Side, Brooklyn and the East and South Bronx, where socialist organising remained a source of direct political action and engagement.[37] A series of tenant unions were set up across the city in Brownsville, Borough Park, Tremont, University Heights and Washington Heights. Most of the unions had strong ties to the Socialist Party, and the prospect of organised tenant power forced the city and state government to pass Emergency Rent laws. The laws imposed controls on rent and provided tenants with some additional protection against eviction.

Tenant militancy waxed and waned in the years that followed as unions fell prey to the Red Scare that swept through the country.[38] It was soon revived, however, during the Depression, assuming forms that reflected the emergence of new organisational structures and tactics. The expiration of Emergency Rent laws in September 1920 provided the most immediate source of contention as controls on apartments renting for either fifteen dollars or ten dollars per month were scheduled to end in December 1928 and June 1929 respectively. In Harlem, where the black community faced rigid segregation, local Communists came together and formed the Harlem Tenants League to resist and agitate against impending rent hikes. The League became one of the most important early sites of black Communist activism in New York. It organised demonstrations and rent strikes, blocked evictions and demanded the enforcement of existing housing regulations. While the League worked locally, it also adopted a radically transnational outlook that linked housing insecurity to wider struggles against 'global white supremacy, capitalism and imperialism'.[39]

The efforts of the Harlem Tenants League pointed to the many problems faced by blacks living in New York, where they remained barred from renting most apartments. As a radical housing movement, it also anticipated a new wave of activism in which Communists played a central role. With the onset of the Depression, New York tenants faced growing immiseration and unemployment and were forced to scramble to retain or find affordable housing. Hundreds of thousands moved, became lodgers or joined the growing ranks of the homeless that lived on the city's streets.

Many others found shelter in squatted shanty towns known as Hoovervilles (after then President Herbert Hoover). The most notable encampments could be found on the Great Lawn at Central Park ('Hoover Valley'), on Houston Street ('Packing Box City') and in Riverside Park ('Camp Thomas Paine') along the Hudson River at 72nd Street, though the largest Hooverville in New York was actually in the East Village on the East River between 8th and 10th Streets ('Hard Luck Town') on a site that later became the Jacob Riis public housing project.[40] There were countless other Hoovervilles across the country, from Seattle to Washington, DC, where thousands of veterans erected a vast informal settlement along the Anacostia River and in full view of the Capitol.[41]

Tenant organisations active in early struggles were largely unresponsive to the new housing crisis. It was left to members of the Communist Party to fill the vacuum. They formed 'unemployed councils' that resisted evictions and organised rent strikes in Harlem, the Lower East Side, Brooklyn and, in particular, the Bronx, where large protests inspired widespread neighbourhood militancy. Violent confrontations with the police were commonplace, though mass evictions and heavy-handed policing combined with legal injunctions against the 'picketing of apartment houses in rent strike demonstrations' prompted activists to shift tactics. City Home Relief Bureaus were soon occupied by tenants who refused to leave until they received funds to pay their rents. The occupations often proved successful, and the *Daily Worker* reported in May 1933 that:

> half a dozen workers who refused to leave the Bureau ... forced the Home Relief Bureau to pay the rent in spite of previous repeated refusals. In Coney Island, over 30 families secured their rent by similar actions. In Manhattan and the Bronx, the Home Relief Bureaus were forced to revoke the 'no rent' order in cases of workers participating in these militant actions.

A few weeks later, the *Daily Worker* claimed that 'Rent checks [were] ... being issued to nearly 500 unemployed families in the Bronx by the Home Relief Bureau ... as a direct result of picketing, demonstrations, and anti-eviction fights led by the Unemployed Councils.'[42]

In the end, the most significant legacy of housing-based activism in New York during the 1930s and early 1940s was not the repertoire of contention that it produced but the wider politics of action and solidarity that it summoned into being. Depression politics fuelled new political alliances and networks that brought radicals into contact with liberals, progressives and professionals. In 1936, they formed the City-Wide Tenants Council which adopted a less confrontational approach to housing advocacy. The Council balanced political lobbying for public housing – the New York City Housing Authority (NYCHA) was formed in 1934 – with direct action tactics (picketing and strikes) that were only adopted when more moderate appeals had failed.[43] The Council was, in this way, able to provide a tenant 'perspective' to wider public deliberations on issues including low-income housing, rent controls and code enforcement. Where earlier tenant groups were largely tethered to local neighbourhoods, the Council chose a more scaled-up approach to its activism, sending tenant delegations to the city council, state legislature and US Congress. It also played a significant role as a member of the Citizen's Housing Council, an alliance of New Deal progressives that was formed in 1937 and became a leading advocate for public housing and improved housing for African Americans.[44]

The tenant movement that emerged in the 1930s not only provided a much thicker web of organising than its predecessors, it also helped to shape the terrain of tenant struggle in the immediate post-war period. This was a framework with a complex interlocking infrastructure that combined building councils and leagues that thrived in highly politicised neighbourhoods with a broad mainstream labour-left alliance that supplied resources, professional expertise and 'lobbying muscle'. Post-war tenants thus inherited a rich assemblage of ideas, institutions and tactics that were in many ways responsible for an *exceptionalism* that set New York apart from other American cities during a period where rapid suburbanisation and home ownership had acquired a new social and ideological legitimacy.[45]

While New York tenants were faced with a major housing shortage at the end of the Second World War, they were nevertheless able to draw on successful alliances and strategies developed in the years before and during the war. Economic exigencies during this period had created possibilities that were hitherto unforeseen and, as such, paved the way for new policies such as public housing and a rent cap which was implemented by the Federal Office of Price Administration (OPA) in November 1943. With the end of the war, these policies came under sharp attack across the country in a climate shaped by rising anti-Communist feelings, longstanding racial divisions and a pro-business and housing lobby unwilling to tolerate further regulations and controls. In response, tenant activists across New York turned to the networks and structures that they had only recently created, and were able to retain – even institutionalise – the 'signal achievements of rent control and public housing'.[46]

These achievements came at a cost, as rent caps were withdrawn in May 1947 when the OPA was finally wound down.[47] Post-war tenant groups in New York were able, however, to convince state lawmakers to extend rent control through the passing of new rent regulations in 1950.[48] The new law was largely concessionary, though in national terms it represented a victory of sorts as New York tenants were able to secure rights and protections that had been largely obliterated across the country. In the wake of the 1949 Federal Housing Act, many of the same alliances were also mobilised to extend public housing provision in the city. In a country gripped by a wave of intense red-baiting, tensions erupted between leftists and liberals and were responsible for the fracturing of solidarities and the dissolution of countless public housing initiatives. In New York, however, the broad liberal consensus assembled in the 1930s was able to stay the course and, through the NYCHA, the city's low-rent public housing stock actually grew and, by 1950, it was able to provide decent and affordable shelter for over 100,000 residents.[49]

The 1949 Housing Act was conceived as a response to post-war housing scarcity and clearly stated that the health and living standards of [the Nation's] ... people require housing production and related community development sufficient to remedy the serious housing shortage, the elimination of substandard and other inadequate housing through the clearance of slums and blighted areas and the realisation ... of a decent home and a suitable environment for every American family.[50]

In practical terms, the implementation of the Housing Act proved controversial, especially its Title I provision which provided federal funds for the redevelopment of so-called blighted urban neighbourhoods, a policy that came to be famously known as 'urban renewal'. Despite new legislation in 1954 that expanded federal housing support to urban renewal projects, the Title I programme was predominantly used for 'slum clearance'. This, unsurprisingly, had a significant impact on cities across the country, and New York in particular. As one historian of the subject concluded, 'under New York's urban-renewal program, federal money and local officials dramatically redrew the city's map, razing and rebuilding neighbourhoods, uprooting hundreds of thousands of people, intensifying racial segregation, and galvanising the tenant movement in the process'.[51]

As Title I of the 1949 Housing Act took effect in the early 1950s, housing activists in New York were gearing up to challenge the city's plans for slum clearance and urban renewal. The expansion of public housing also opened up a new arena in the struggle by New York's black community against discrimination and segregation. Once again, it was a broad coalition of tenant organisations that challenged entrenched racial iniquities and, in the case of Stuyvesant Town, was able to overturn its strict segregation policy. The vast private complex of apartment towers on the East Side of Manhattan covered eighteen blocks along the East River and was built by the insurance company Metropolitan Life in the late 1940s as a whites-only 'suburb in a city'.[52] While the campaign against the project highlighted the development's planned displacement of low-income tenants, it also found support from within the housing project itself as a group of residents mobilised to form a committee to end discrimination. The committee conducted a poll of 105 Stuyvesant Town residents, 62 per cent of whom favoured integration. The results were published in the local independent newspaper, *Town and Village*, who, in facing a torrent of abuse and outrage, published their own poll of 551 residents which showed a two-to-one majority in favour of admitting blacks.[53] At the same time, residents tapped into the city's nascent civil rights movement while linking up with other progressive housing activists to form the New York State Committee Against Discrimination in Housing (NYSCDH) in 1948. The NYSCDH provided crucial support for two new landmark bills, the Wicks–Austin Bill (1950) and the Brown–Isaacs Bill (1951), which outlawed racial discrimination in all tax-subsidised housing.[54]

The struggle over Stuyvesant Town marked a significant moment in the history of tenant mobilisation in post-war New York. Not only was it responsible for the nation's first fair-housing legislation, in the eyes of many activists it also represented a key touchstone in the fight for racial equality. As one activist later recalled, 'integration [was] as important as affordability'.[55] And yet, the movement's gains were, more often than not, incremental, piecemeal and even pyrrhic in some cases. New statutes, on the one hand, lacked any real means of enforcement. On the other hand, initial liberal support and tolerance for slum clearance in Stuyvesant Town and elsewhere did little to forestall the eviction of thousands of working-class residents. The failure by local activists to generate any resistance to these displacements or seek public housing alternatives for low-income tenants was a key issue that underpinned later opposition to clearance projects which, in most cases, were obliged to organise from scratch.[56] These were, in turn, challenges located within a political climate characterised by a virulent anti-Communism that placed immense pressure on alliances and solidarities that ranged across the progressive spectrum. Finally, in economic terms, this was a period of restructuring in the labour market in which the disparities between well-paid unionised employment in primary industries and precarious work in smaller secondary enterprises widened. These divergences only served to consolidate the recomposition of the city's workforce while reinforcing existing class and racial divisions and their impact on local communities. While some workers were, in other words, able to afford new public housing, many others were quite literally (and paradoxically) displaced by it.

For many poor New Yorkers, the 1950s and 1960s were thus a time of profound social and physical dislocation as over 500,000 residents were displaced from mainly working-class neighbourhoods, all in the name of Title I slum clearances.[57] And yet, dispossession also brought with it new forms of resistance. Tenants rediscovered idioms and patterns of working-class sociability in their neighbourhoods, which offered a vibrant alternative to the suburban society and home ownership model coursing ideologically through the 1949 Federal Housing Act. The fight against urban renewal, in particular, triggered a revival of an intense local model of tenant activism. Such new tenant mobilisations across New York (in Lincoln Square, Chelsea, Gramercy Park, the Lower East Side, etc.) also brought veteran organisers and old leftists together with a new generation of activists who were, in turn, supported by a number of critical urbanists including Lewis Mumford and Jane Jacobs. In May 1959 they formed the Metropolitan Council on Housing, pledging to resist Title I clearances in a fight for 'decent housing at rentals people can afford to pay'.[58]

The Met Council represented one of the most important citywide tenant organisations in a struggle which, by the early 1960s, combined well-honed tactics with increasingly radical political trajectories. While activists were, in this way, able to defend rent control and push for public housing, many of the new units were aimed at middle-income tenants. The challenges facing low-income residents, in contrast, reflected New York's changing social and economic geography. As manufacturing and industry declined and shifted across the Hudson River, hundreds of thousands of blue-collar jobs disappeared and were replaced by a new service-based economy.[59] These changes were also profoundly racialised, as white New Yorkers moved out of the city to the suburbs while hundreds of thousands of African Americans and Puerto Ricans moved in. The new residents faced bleak prospects in both the workplace and at home. Many were trapped in precarious, poorly paid service work, and Gotham's low-income rental stock was 'scarce, expensive and ill-maintained'. Ghettoisation became the common default experience for the city's non-whites, 30 per cent of whom were, by 1960, living in dilapidated housing. Over half of all apartments in Central Harlem were unsound according to a 1964 report.[60]

Housing, unsurprisingly, became the site where radical political energies in 1960s New York converged, representing, in the words of one historian, a 'local wave of the rising nationwide tide of civil-rights activity'.[61] Facing deteriorating conditions, a series of small rent strikes and informal housing inspections in the late 1950s and early 1960s were organised by blacks and Puerto Ricans living in Harlem.[62] These initiatives won minor concessions and paved the way for a major rent strike in the neighbourhood that erupted in August 1963 and later expanded to other parts of New York including Brooklyn, where the local chapter of the Congress of Racial Equality began supporting rent strikes in Bedford-Stuyvesant. Tenants in Red Hook also began to withhold their rent. The strikes drew on the expertise of veteran housing activists as well as a new generation of campaigners including Jesse Gray, a military veteran and Communist Party member who formed the Community Council on Housing.[63] They depended increasingly, however, on the work of young mothers, including Inocencia Flores whose 'Diary of a Rent Striker – Life Amidst Rats and Junkies' was serialised in the *Herald Tribune*.[64] They also found support in a growing, ever-radicalising civil rights movement. The strikers increasingly eschewed the pragmatic reformism of earlier tenant struggles favouring, in its place, a more ambitious and militant approach. While they extended existing alliances with predominantly white liberal activists and organisations, they also articulated a new language of black and Latino empowerment. As these political vectors overlapped, an emboldened commitment to community autonomy and self-reliance, and an assertion of a right to do so on its own terms, slowly took hold.

As in the case of countless earlier housing struggles in New York, the protests were only able, however, to eke out a series of minor improvements for striking residents. When a group of striking Harlem tenants appeared in court on charges of rent non-payment, they argued that they were withholding rent in protest again their buildings' combined 129 building violations. They drew attention to 'dark and littered' hallways, 'crumbly ceilings', a lack of water, electricity and heat, and produced three dead rats as evidence of the 'subhuman' living conditions that they faced.[65] While the rats were inadmissible as evidence, the tenants scored a victory in the courts as Judge Guy Gilbert Ribaudo legalised the rent strike and 'upheld the right of 13 tenants to refuse to pay to a landlord for apartments where hazardous violations exist'. The judge directed the tenants to deposit their rent 'to the court'.[66] A few days later, at a hearing in Brooklyn, Judge Fred Moritt went even further, ruling that 'tenants could live rent-free for as long as landlords failed to correct housing evils that menaced health or safety'. 'Some of the buildings,' Moritt added, 'aren't fit for pigs to live in. If it takes the landlord two years to make the repairs, he gets no rent for two years. Period.'[67] In the end, despite securing some modest repairs, little effort was made by the city to systematically reha-bilitate low-income housing. If anything, citywide inaction served to further radicalise activists who, in the wake of riots in 1964 and an ongoing crisis in schooling, gravitated towards a more contentious repertoire of practices and tactics.

New radical impulses were, of course, shaped by the con-tours of local political geographies. In Harlem, the influence of Black Power – housing was part of their ten-point programme – encouraged activists to recast the neighbourhood as the 'prop-erty' of African Americans. A Harlem chapter of the Black Panthers was set up in the summer of 1968 offering the kind of free breakfast programmes and health clinics popularised by the group on the West Coast.[68] New neighbourhood initiatives also drew on a range of occupation-based practices (squatting, street actions, takeovers, etc.) as a means of 'decolonising' the 'ghetto' and reclaiming tenant territory. At the same time, other forms of radical proprietorship were mobilised in neighbourhoods such as Morningside Heights, where multiracial tenant coalitions turned to direct action and community control. Activists drew particular attention to the process of 'warehousing', as landlords (individual or otherwise) left apartments deliberately vacant with a view to their eventual and profitable redevelopment.[69]

As the 1970s began, the tactics adopted by housing activists became increasingly militant. It was in the spring of 1970 that a new squatter movement sprung up, spontaneously so it seemed, across the City of New York. It was called Operation Move-In, and by the summer of 1970 it had successfully placed 150 working-class families in new homes, most of whom were African American or Latino with long experiences of housing insecurity. 'We knew what we were getting into', one of the new occupiers explained to a reporter with the *New York Times*. 'But we've been living,' she continued, 'in horrible places with horrible people for a year. This is nice because it's a nice community and you know the people can't mess over you like they mess over you in other places.' In the last year, she, her husband and their two children were forced to move from the Lower East Side to a hotel, and finally to three rooms on 84th street. 'It was horrible', she added. 'There was rats, the plaster was bad, holes in the floor ... I hated that place.'[70] Another large Puerto Rican family, the Marcanos, described how they had been forced to stay with relatives for over seven years as they could not find a landlord who would accept them. Operation Move-In installed them in a twelve-room walk-up, which they painstakingly restored as the plumbing and wiring had been wrecked by city crews in an attempt to drive away would-be occupants. Several large holes in the roof were repaired by Mr Marcano. 'I knew it was illegal,' his wife explained, 'but I felt something right would come out of it.' 'Operation Move-In,' she added, 'is negotiating with the city to let us stay. We won't have to leave.'[71]

Operation Move-In had its origins in longstanding struggles over housing on the Upper West Side. It was the establishment of the West Side Urban Renewal Area (WSURA) in 1959 that became a major source of grassroots organising by local tenants and housing groups. Activists drew particular attention to the lack of provision in the WSURA plan for the renovation of salvageable, abandoned buildings as an alternative and legitimate source of housing for low-income tenants. The plan focused, in contrast, on the redevelopment of the neighbourhood through the demolition of thousands of housing units and the construction of subsidised high-rise apartments for upper- and middle-income families paying income-adjusted rents. While 30 per cent of the new units were 'officially' reserved for low-income residents, the experience of previous Title I clearances on the West Side cast doubt on the city's commitment to rehouse displaced tenants, the majority of whom were unable to afford the rents in the newly constructed apartments. The renewal plans were thus received as a form of 'urban removal' that not only reinforced existing local grievances surrounding poor, inadequate housing and unresponsive slumlords, but also exacerbated racial and class divisions as long-time tenants were forced out of salvageable buildings and 'decanted' to the city's outer boroughs. Those who remained were, more often than not, left to live in overcrowded, unsafe tenements and saw little hope in the city's redevelopment plans.[72]

It is in this context that groups of West Side residents began to seize, occupy and claim empty buildings in the neighbourhood. The first actions were largely spontaneous, though after the death of a local boy from carbon monoxide poisoning they escalated in size and scale and were increasingly part of a planned strategy. What became known as Operation Move-In soon spread to other parts of New York as activists took up the cause and orchestrated a series of similar occupations across the city. Jane Benedict, a veteran housing activist and member of the Met Council, set up a 'We Won't Move' committee to support tenants resisting eviction. The Met Council Office was also used to help connect squatters with 'holdout tenants' in half-empty buildings across the city.[73] In Chelsea, a vacant building on West 15th Street was briefly squatted in July, while a number of buildings were occupied in the Lower East Side with the help of Frances Goldin, another key member of the Met Council. A few blocks further north, another four families of squatters moved into two buildings on East 19th Street only to be evicted by the police. One of the organisers later described how there were 'as many as 20 policemen [*sic*] in one of the squatters' apartments' and that the corridors in his building were 'lined with police elbow to elbow'.[74]

The relative success of the new squatter movement played a decisive role in fostering new solidarities with militant groups of colour including the Black Panthers, the Young Lords and I Wor Kuen, a radical youth organisation based in Chinatown which began to place squatters in recently vacated buildings in the neighbourhood.[75]

Operation Move-In thus spoke to a conspicuously *multiracial* form of direct action that, in New York, was shaped by an array of increasingly radical organisations that gave 'practical expression to several strands of late sixties liberatory thought'.[76] Tenant activism also helped to promote interest in housing-related issues among young, predominantly white women who were involved in the women's liberation movement. Such 'squatter-sister interactions', as the historian Roberta Gold has argued, were instrumental in connecting the city's tenant struggles with a new tide of feminist organising.[77]

The city responded to the squatters with threats of forced eviction. Maintenance crews, as depicted in the 1970 documentary film, *Rompiendo puertas*, were dispatched to other vacant apartments across the city where they proceeded to smash fixtures, remove stoves and sinks, and wreck the plumbing and wiring. These actions only served to strengthen the resolve of the squatter movement which, if anything, gained momentum over the course of the summer. The city was forced to reverse course.

It allowed the squatters to stay, though officials insisted that any further actions would not be tolerated. This did little, however, to stop the squatters, and on 25 July 1970, fifty-four families including 120 children occupied two condemned buildings in Morningside Heights at the corner of West 112th Street and Amsterdam Avenue.[78] The action was coordinated by activists from Operation Move-In and a group of young Latinos who had earlier squatted a storefront on 588 Columbia Avenue and West 88th Street and were now called El Comité.[79] They were also supported by Latino students in the 'Urban Brigade', who were based at Columbia and Barnard College as well as forty-seven citywide community organisations.[80]

The two occupied buildings as well as other four others on the same street were owned by the Episcopal Church. They were slated for demolition in order to make way for a luxury nursing home to be built by a non-profit subsidiary of the Cathedral of St John the Divine, which stood directly across the street from the buildings. The church officially denounced the new occupants, though many of its parishioners supported the action.[81] The squatters quickly became a *cause célèbre* across the city. They also undertook extensive repairs on the buildings and created an elected council to represent their demands. The squatters' public relations campaign culminated in December 1970 with the Housing Crimes Trial, a People's Court tribunal that brought a new wave of young radicals together alongside an older generation of housing activists from a range of citywide groups that included the Met Council, the Cooper Square Committee and ARCH (Architects' Renewal Committee in Harlem), a civil rights organisation formed by a group of radical architects based in Harlem.[82]

The Housing Crimes Trial was presided over by a judicial panel made up of Jane Benedict of the Metropolitan Council on Housing, Durie Bethea from the Black Panthers and Iris Morales of the Young Lords. Representatives from two other Puerto Rican organisations and from I Wor Kuen also joined Benedict, Bethea and Morales on the bench. A small group of seasoned housing campaigners served as prosecutors while the named defendants – Mayor Lindsay, city housing officials and bank executives – were conspicuously absent and held in contempt. The trial took place before an audience of over 1,500 spectators in Columbia University's Wollmann Auditorium. The panel heard testimony from a number of squatters and tenants as well as several housing professionals who, according to the *New Yorker*, provided 'stories of crumbling ceilings, broken fixtures, injuries, lack of hot water and illness caused by heatless winters'. There were also reports of rat bites, lead poisoning and beatings dished out by landlords and their hired thugs. Given the sheer weight of evidence, the defendants were found guilty of 'criminal neglect, racism and harassment'. Judge Benedict read out the sentence to an approving audience: 'all rental housing in the city should pass into public ownership under tenant control'.[83]

The Housing Crimes Trial was, in the end, much more than a carefully calibrated theatre of protest. On the one hand, it pointed to a long and unresolved history of housing struggles in New York and the various actors, alliances and strategies that it encompassed. But the trial also played a constructive role in the emergence and development of new ways of thinking about and inhabiting the city as a space of political action and self-organisation. Racial inclusiveness and cross-generational collaboration and solidarity were, after all, key features of the trial and Operation Move-In, more generally. These were, moreover, features that pointed to an arena of struggle where local living conditions combined with increasingly militant tactics and an existing infrastructure of tenant-based activism to produce some genuine gains. While many squatters across New York were evicted by the police in a matter of days, the Episcopal Church decided, in the wake of the occupations, to scale back its plans allowing over 400 residents to remain.[84] A further 200 families on the city's West Side were able to secure major concessions more than a year after the start of Operation Move-In. City officials conceded that they could stay as long as they paid rent, while a further 946 low-income housing income units were added to the original WSURA plan.[85] Some squatters in the Lower East Side were also able to reach agreements with their landlords, though the occupants of properties owned by individuals, hospitals and schools were, more often than not, quickly and forcibly cleared.

The story behind the Housing Crimes Trial and Operation Move-In thus brings together a number of themes that are central to the history of the housing movement in New York: the longstanding importance of squatting, and of the occupation of empty buildings and land, to the wide repertoire of practices taken up by local residents, activists, students and workers in the struggle for affordable housing; the recognition of uneven development and urban renewal as an enduring source of political mobilisation; the formation of new identities and intimacies and the cultivation of solidarities that cut across class, race and gender lines; and finally, the widespread desire to reimagine and live the city differently and to reclaim an alternative 'right to a city'. For Richard Sennett, writing in *The Uses of Disorder*, published in the same year as the Housing Crimes Trial and Operation Move-In, it was indeed the dense, disorderly and overwhelming nature of American inner cities out of which, in his view, a radically 'new social space' would ultimately emerge.[86]

The 'social space' Sennett imagined never materialised. While housing activists were able to connect the 'housing question' to larger struggles around race, class and inequality, their successes, however real and substantive, were short-lived and concessionary. Residential abandonment continued unabated. Public housing and rent control received little support. 'In the end', as the historian Joel Schwartz, has argued, 'it was hundreds of thousands of low-income tenants who found themselves out in the cold'.[87]

In the decades that followed, housing insecurity and neighbourhood gentrification only intensified as the city 'yielded to a neoliberal growth model'.[88] Still, the tactics adopted by squatters and other radical housing activists had some constructive and lasting effects. Low-income housing *was* saved, new networks were established and a broad albeit fragile infrastructure of tenant activism survived. It was this infrastructure and the fierce opposition from squatters, in particular, that paved the way for a new wave of protests in the 1980s and 1990s and a new generation of activists who were ready to protect and seize their right to housing.

2

'Who are the Squatters?':
London's Hidden History

Asses, swine, have litter spread,
And with fitting food are fed,
All things have a home but one,
Thou, Oh Englishman hast none!
                    Shelley, 'The Mask of Anarchy'[1]

I was homeless, pissed off, had nowhere to stay
Half of fucking London tinned up and grey
It was then that I noticed every flat in the block
Had a squatters legal warning and a newly fitted lock.
Goodbye bed and breakfast, farewell rent
Why not force a window and take up residence.
                              Squatters' song[2]

In 1994, the artist and photographer Tom Hunter began to construct a model of the street in Hackney that had been his London
home since 1991. Hunter was part of a community of over a
hundred squatters who had occupied a series of Victorian terraced houses on Ellingfort Road, a narrow side street that ran
under the Great Eastern Railway line and connected Mare Street
with the eastern edge of London Fields. By the early 1970s,
many of the houses on the street were run down and in need of
serious repair. The London Borough of Hackney (LBH) elected
to purchase many of the houses as part of a plan to create an
Industrial Improvement Area. Existing residents and businesses
were evicted.[3]

Squatters soon moved into some of the empty buildings. A
group of travellers occupied the yards. While some houses on

neighbouring Martello Street were converted into studios with the help of the artist-run organisation Acme, the majority of houses on Ellingfort Road remained empty. Between 1985 and 1992, they were occupied by squatters who transformed the street into a vibrant community. Garden walls were knocked down to create a community garden while a former motorcycle repair shop became a café. There was even a city farm with chickens and goats. As Hunter later recalled, 'It was all very varied...Two doors down the guys were motorbike dispatch riders – they'd save up enough money and go off to the Far East for a few months. Next door to me there was a builder, and a girl who worked in a casino as a croupier. There were charity workers, people doing hardcore labouring jobs, and others who were saving up. It was a really good mixture.'[4]

The threat of eviction only served to galvanise the community. In 1994, the LBH unveiled new plans to demolish the houses in order to make way for a new industrial zone that included a frozen chicken warehouse. The squatters as well as other local residents and businesses resisted. They formed the London Fields Renewal Partnership and drew up an alternative plan for the neighbourhood.[5] In the case of Tom Hunter, resistance also assumed a decidedly aesthetic form. He was in the midst of constructing his final submission for the degree show at the London College of Printing. With his friend, James MacKinnon, Hunter constructed an exact replica model of the street he lived on.

Hunter began by producing a series of 5 × 4 transparencies using a large-format camera. The transparencies as well as other photographs were combined with wood and cardboard to make the final model. *The Ghetto, as it was known*, painstakingly recreated the exteriors of the squats as well as the lit-up interiors of the rooms, complete with the people who lived there. In Hunter's own words, 'I wanted to make a document of the area before it was bulldozed, that was the idea. Because I wanted to represent everyone's houses before they were all destroyed so that in generations to come they could see what was there.'[6] 'I was trying,' Hunter added, 'to get people to look at the urban landscape, for people to look at my friends and the way they live and see that it was quite beautiful and worth having a look at.'

The final model quickly became a *cause célèbre* attracting attention from *The Guardian* and *Time Out*, as well as the Museum of London. With the media spotlight on the local neighbourhood, the LBH backed down and initiated negotiations with the squatters. It was agreed that the squatters would form a co-operative to purchase and rehabilitate the houses using borrowed money from a housing association. Hunter's own life took a different turn as he set off across Europe in a repurposed double decker bus named *Le Crowbar* as part of a touring convoy that organised free gigs, raves and festivals.[7] His model neighbourhood, in turn, became part of the official exhibition at the Museum of London and is currently on display in the 'World City Gallery'.

The model as well as the series of photographs produced by Hunter is just one of many attempts by London's squatters to record their own actions. This is a community that has, over the past few decades, devoted significant energy to *archiving* their own practices and representations and to documenting the spaces they created and the identities they performed, often in the face of their imminent destruction. Memory, as we're often told, is productive. It produces archives, bodies of writing, ways of being and talking. For London's squatting community, the makeshift archives they produced were conscious acts of remembrance rooted in wider struggles over the city's past, present and future.

London is a city that has been continuously made and remade through struggles over space, whether as buildings, commons or communities.[8] Squatters have occupied an important if overlooked place within these conflicts, especially as 'squatters' rights' have, until recently, encouraged Londoners to house themselves.[9] As the organisers of a 2013 exhibition, *Made Possible by Squatting*, concluded, 'historically, squatting an empty building has been a way to create a temporary home. The occupation of an empty building may last days, weeks or years, but once evicted, buildings are eventually demolished or redeveloped along with the lives that were lived inside them.'[10] While some of London's squatted spaces have endured and survived, many simply vanished without a trace. For many squatters, holding on to the fragments and remainders of these spaces, not to mention the actions which animated them, matters.

The desire to assemble such an archive has always been loaded with 'emotional urgency and need'.[11] It is, on the one hand, shaped by a conviction that ongoing forms of squatting must necessarily emerge from a historically grounded understanding of their own past. On the other hand, it is driven by a commitment to capturing something of the experience of being part of a movement.[12] These are archives that provide us with important clues into what it meant (and means) to be a squatter in London.

They point to the often precarious forms of survival sought by some of London's most desperate residents. And yet, they also show that the squat was a place of collective *world-making*: a place to express anger and solidarity, to explore new identities and different intimacies, to experience and share new feelings, and to defy authority and live autonomously. It is perhaps no surprise that the history of squatting in London has always been characterised by its sheer diversity, attracting students, apprentices, runaways, workers, drop-outs, anarchists, punks, gay and lesbian activists, queer and trans groups, black nationalists, migrants, refugees and environmentalists.

With the exception of *Squatting: The Real Story*, an edited collection first published in 1980, the complex and ever-changing histories of squatting in London and elsewhere have, however, received little sustained attention. A whole host of practices and subcultures and the different spaces (art spaces, bookshops, crèches, free schools, protest camps) they created and supported have been largely neglected. These are histories that demand to be written.[13]

In the case of London these are, in turn, histories that date back to the late 1960s, though there origins are much older. As the activist and former squatter, Ron Bailey, reflected at the time, 'the current squatters movement was born in 1968 but, like all new-born organisms, the seed had been sown long before'.[14] According to Bailey, after the First World War a sharp rise in unemployment prompted many men to seize empty municipal property with a view to setting up relief organisations within local neighbourhoods. Rent and rate strikes were also common, especially in the East End.

A number of historians have shown that the interwar years were also marked by a significant rise in self-build housing on marginal plotlands near London, most notably in Essex, on small patches of land that were no longer used for agriculture (known locally as 'three-horse land') as well as reclaimed coastal sites including Jaywick Sands and Canvey Island. Colin Ward reminds us that 'plotlanders' were not squatters in any strict sense. Most had, in fact, paid for their sites which were slowly and incrementally transformed from makeshift army huts, chalets and sheds into more permanent forms of housing. The 1947 Town and Country Planning Act put an end, however, to this kind of 'self-help house-building'.[15]

It was with the end of the Second World War, that squatting re-emerged on an unprecedented scale.[16] These were campaigns that began in 1945 as a direct action movement against rising homelessness and the lack of social housing for veterans and their families. The returning soldiers responded by seizing empty properties. In Brighton, a group of veterans (known as the 'Vigilantes') occupied three empty homes in which the families of servicemen were installed.[17] Other properties across the country were also squatted, many of which were located in south coast resorts and had been left empty to profit from high holiday rents during the short summer season. The movement soon expanded to the mass takeover of service camps and, by October 1946, there were 39,535 people squatting in 1,038 camps in England and Wales. There were a further 4,000 squatters in Scotland.[18]

The government clamped down on the campaign, focusing in particular on squatters in London who had begun to occupy a number of high-profile buildings including a series of luxury flats in Duchess of Bedford House in Kensington. What became known as the 'Great Sunday Squat' was organised by members of the Communist Party who were successful in moving over one hundred families on 8 September 1946 with the help of the Women's Voluntary Service, as well as police officers who carried luggage for the squatters. So many people turned up hoping to be housed that Communist stewards were forced to scour the neighbourhood for additional housing. Eight other empty buildings were found and taken over. Other would-be occupiers were moved to a building in Marylebone. A further two buildings were squatted the next day in Pimlico and St John's Wood.[19]

The squatters' own case histories provide a glimpse into the kind of housing insecurity they and many others faced:

'Husband, wife, 5 children ...
2 Rooms, one very small used as kitchen. All slept in one room. Shared lav. In bad repair.'
'Husband, wife, 2 children under 14, baby expected.
Room damp infested. Officially overcrowded.'
'Husband, wife, 4 children ...
Had two rooms, but one burnt out so living in one room. Beetles, damp and rot.'
'Widow, 3 girls ... Three rooms basement and ground floor. Running with water and ceiling falling down. Slugs and beetles all over floor, climbing on tables and shelves. Rats.'[20]

While the actions of the squatters were generally well received in the press, and even celebrated in some quarters as an expression of English patriotism, the government took a firm stance.[21] Possession orders were served on the leaders of the movement. The Cabinet also instructed the Home Office to draft a new law that would make squatting a criminal offence. At the same time, a more heavy-handed approach was adopted by the authorities. Guards were placed on empty buildings across London. Some houses were blockaded by the police. Food and other supplies including bedding were prevented from reaching them, though in the case of the squatters in St John's Wood, an elaborate pulley system to deliver supplies from a neighbouring house was devised.[22]

In the face of intense pressure, the occupations in London quickly crumbled. The Communist Party backed down despite plans for a new wave of occupations. The government seized the opportunity, issuing a statement promising immunity from prosecution to any squatter who was willing to leave voluntarily.[23] Efforts were also made to secure temporary accommodation for those who would otherwise be homeless. The plans for new criminal legislation were quickly scrapped. While there was some resistance, the squatters reluctantly caved in. The occupants of Duchess of Bedford House left on 20 September accompanied by a small marching band. They were moved to an Old Ladies Home in Hampstead along with other squatters from across the city.[24]

The squatted service camps were equally successful. Many were handed over to their occupants, though over time they were incorporated into the wider public housing system and used by social services to house homeless families well into the 1950s. As a series of reports produced by Mass Observation in the late 1940s and early 1950s show, the majority of the camp 'squatters' were not politically motivated or committed to the overthrow of private property. They were driven by a more immediate need to secure housing. This was, as one commentator later opined, 'mass action by ordinary people' who turned to squatting as the only possible way to try and get a decent home.[25] As the conditions in the camps worsened over time, many of their occupants simply left.[26]

The 1945–6 campaign served as an important if often forgotten point of reference for the next wave of squatting which emerged in London and elsewhere in the UK in the late 1960s. The main impetus for the so-called 'rebirth' of the squatting movement came from activists linked with the Committee of 100, a nuclear disarmament group, and the Vietnam Solidarity Campaign. Others belonged to a series of equally small groups such as the London Anarchists, the East London Libertarian Group, Solidarity and Socialist Action.[27] Many were also involved in a series of direct action struggles that targeted the poor living conditions faced by many working-class families living in temporary accommodation or Greater London Council (GLC) slums in and around London. Local authorities had a statutory duty to house families, though they were often dispersed or put into hostels where the conditions were usually poor.[28] It was against this backdrop, moreover, that Ken Loach's *Cathy Come Home*, a film documenting the experience of homelessness in the UK, was first televised, sparking widespread anger and concern. Both Crisis and Shelter, national charities dedicated to the fight against homelessness, were also set up in the wake of the film.[29]

While Crisis and Shelter worked closely with local authorities, others advocated a more militant self-help approach. The London Squatters Campaign was, in this way, formed on 18 November 1968 during a meeting hosted by Ron Bailey. The aim of the campaign was to rehouse families from hostels or slums by 'means of squatting'. As Bailey added:

> We hoped that our action would spark off a squatting campaign on a mass scale, and that homeless people and slum dwellers would be inspired to squat in large numbers by small but successful actions ... We saw our campaign as having a radicalising effect on existing movements in the housing field – tenants associations, action committees, community project groups, etc. If these could be radicalised and linked together then we would really have achieved something.[30]

On 1 December 1968, activists from the campaign linked up with a small group of homeless families to occupy an empty block of luxury flats on Wanstead High Street that had been vacant for over four years. A second occupation of an empty vicarage in Leyton followed on Christmas Day. While the occupations were largely symbolic in nature, the campaign escalated in the new year as its organisers began to install homeless families into a series of properties in the London Borough of Redbridge. Redbridge Council had been planning a major redevelopment scheme in Ilford, though it had not been approved by the Ministry of Housing. The council nevertheless chose to leave a number of houses in the neighbourhood to rot (some for over ten years), though they remained in good condition.[31]

Beginning in February 1969 and over the course of the next six months, a total of seventeen houses were squatted by thirteen separate families, one of whom had been homeless for over twelve years.[32] The council responded by taking the squatters to court. In one particular case, they applied to the Barking Magistrates Court for restitution of a property under the 1429 Forcible Entry Act. A breach of the act would have given the council the opportunity to apply to the local magistrates to clear the premises, arrest the occupiers and hand the property back to them.

As it happened, Ron Bailey was sitting in the public gallery as the council barrister argued that the squatters were 'forcibly detaining' the premises. The magistrates insisted that they view the premises to see for themselves whether this was indeed the case. Legally, it was within the right of the squatters to refuse to grant the owner access to the property. They were obliged, however, to provide access to the magistrates. Bailey later recalled how he had to dash from the courthouse to the property in question (a house on Cleveland Drive) in order to warn the occupants that the magistrates were on their way and that they were to be let in when they knocked on the door. A couple of minutes later, the magistrates arrived and were shown in.

A few days later, they ruled in favour of the squatters. They saw no reason to hand back the premises to the council, who sought an Order of Mandamus from the High Court. The case was ultimately adjourned *sine die*, with Lord Justice Salmon referencing an old case heard during the reign of George III in his speech. 'The poorest man,' he noted, 'may, in his cottage, beat defiance to all the forces of the Crown. The storm may enter, the rain may enter, but the King of England may not enter. All his forces dare not cross the threshold of a ruined tenement.'[33]

The Redbridge squatters were 'in possession' and the High Court therefore insisted that a court order was needed to evict the occupiers.[34] The council was successful in obtaining a series of named possession orders, which prompted the squatters to adopt a new tactic. The occupants simply swapped houses so that the people named on the possession order where no longer resident at the property to which the order was applied. The council was forced to start again.[35]

Frustrated by the squatters' success, the council resorted to more destructive measures. A 'scorched earth' policy was rolled out as council workmen were employed to gut dozens of houses in the borough. Floorboards were removed, sinks and toilets smashed, electrical fittings and wiring ripped out. They also turned to other forms of violence. A firm of private bailiffs were hired and carried out a series of illegal evictions in April 1969. A number of squatters were beaten up by the bailiffs, many of whom were sporting National Front badges.[36] As one squatter recalled in an affidavit describing their eviction, 'I was never served with any court order ordering me to hand over possession of the property to the Council or to anybody else. I firmly believe that there was never any legal steps taken to make us quit the premises.'[37]

The April 1969 evictions were a major blow to the Redbridge squatters, who regrouped and began a new series of occupations in June. They also made preparations in anticipation that the council would act quickly to clear them out. When the bailiffs returned to (illegally) evict the squatters, they were rebuffed and forced to strike a retreat. By this point, the struggles in Redbridge had reached the national press and a second unsuccessful attempt to evict the squatters on 25 June was featured in all the evening papers. Pictures of helmeted bailiffs attacking a house with bottles and bricks were greeted with widespread condemnation as public sympathy for the squatters grew. The squatters were interviewed by journalists from all over the world including *Izvestia* and Moscow Radio.[38]

The media spotlight and negative publicity forced the council to back down and negotiate with the squatters. In July 1969, a formal agreement was reached, though some of the squatters were reluctant to vacate houses they had occupied and defended.

They denounced the agreement as tantamount to 'surrender'.[39] In the end, however, they voted two to one to accept the agreement. As a result, some of the squatters were immediately rehoused in permanent council accommodation, though it was only after a lengthy review that a number of empty properties were licensed on a short-life basis to homeless families in the borough.[40] Several properties were handed over to squatters on similar terms in 1972.

The success of the London Squatters' Campaign triggered a rapid expansion in what became a mass movement of sorts. A number of short-lived campaigns came into being in Notting Hill, Harringay, Wandsworth, Fulham, Greenwich and Lewisham. While the squatters in Fulham adopted a defensive approach which ultimately contributed to their eviction, their counterparts in Lewisham, the South East London Squatters, began negotiations with the local council in order to secure empty properties on short-term licences.[41]

The negotiations lasted months as the Labour minority on the council attempted to block a deal with the squatters. An arrangement was nevertheless reached in December 1969. According to the deal, only families on the council waiting list were to be housed as licensees. They were required, on the one hand, to leave a property when requested and there was no guarantee that they could be rehoused. The same families, on the other had, had their points 'frozen' on the waiting list for a council house so that they would continue to be assessed on the basis of their pre-squatting points. It was, in this context, that the Lewisham Family Squatting Association was established. By early 1970, it was responsible for over eighty houses. Ron Bailey, one of the founding members of the London Squatters' Campaign, was hired to help run an association that came to house over one hundred families at any given time over the next five years.[42]

Licensed squatting was adopted across the city as councils in Camden, Tower Hamlets, Greenwich and Lambeth reached agreements with local squatting groups. It is also in this context that the Family Squatting Advisory Service (FSAS) was set up with funding from Shelter. The main focus of the FSAS was to provide support to family squatting groups who were encouraged to organise and run their own groups within a wider grassroots network. The FSAS also provided support on the legal and practical aspects of squatting, and by the end of 1971, twelve separate London councils had reached an agreement with local squatting groups who represented more than 1,000 licensed squatters.[43]

And yet, the creation of licensed squatting was equally responsible for growing divisions between squatters, and raised important questions about what it meant to be a squatter and the extent to which squatting was still seen as a desperate if acceptable course of action. On the one side, were 'responsible' working-class families who squatted out of a desperate need for housing. On the other side, were growing numbers of young people – many homeless and sleeping rough in London's parks or in 'derrys' – who were in search of somewhere to live communally.[44] It was the occupation of an empty fifty-room mansion at 144 Piccadilly by members of the London Street Commune in September 1969 that brought these divisions and tensions into sharp relief. The LSC, as it was known, was led by Phil Cohen, a former member of King Mob, an offshoot of the British Situationist International. Under the slogan 'We are the Writing on your Walls', the group was responsible for a number of high-profile occupations in 1969, including 144 Piccadilly.[45]

Unlike the squatters in Redbridge, the 'communards' were widely criticised in the press as 'hippie thugs', 'scroungers' and 'parasites'. Even the London Squatters' Campaign were at pains to distance themselves from the occupiers of 144 Piccadilly who, in their eyes, were 'simply amusing themselves'. The campaign issued a statement where they noted that:

> Those of us who advocate and organise to secure the rights of the homeless and badly housed, are concerned to change and improve society – not to amuse ourselves. We have no intention of joining in the current anti-hippy chorus but we wish to stress the difference between the two types of operation.[46]

The illegal eviction of 144 Piccadilly – the police entered the premises without a possession order – was widely celebrated in the press. An editorial in *The Times* went so far as to call for the criminalisation of squatting and argued that 'if groups of hippies continue to roam from one unoccupied building to another, they could be prosecuted under the Vagrancy Acts'.[47]

The legacy of the events of September 1969 was wide ranging. As a number of commentators have argued, it provided the 'historical basis for later popular ... media images of squatters'. At stake here was a distinction between so-called 'deserving' and 'undeserving' squatters, between those who squatted out of immediate necessity and those who did so for cultural and political reasons. Out of these distinctions, a host of enduring media myths emerged which routinely portrayed squatters as 'hardened political militants who lived rent-free on social security handouts, using the homeless for their own ends'.[48]

A close analysis of the countless flyers, pamphlets and press releases produced by squatters and other activists during the 1970s yields a rather different picture. As Kesia Reeve has shown in a careful examination of over 430 documents produced by squatters between 1969 and 1980, of the 220 which clearly stated their objectives, all but twelve focused on addressing immediate housing needs (relieving homelessness, increasing supply of affordable housing, etc).[49]

These needs only intensified in the early 1970s as neighbourhood gentrification and property speculation served to deepen an existing housing crisis. A growing number of people were frozen out of home ownership and were unable to secure a council tenancy. Rent hikes in the private sector combined with widespread displacement and a growing number of vacant properties, many of which had been left empty by borough councils pending redevelopment schemes which had not yet commenced or had been postponed or abandoned.

If there were roughly 1,000 licensed squatters across London at the end of 1971, there were fewer unlicensed occupiers. In the years that followed, however, it was a sharp rise in the latter that characterised the rapid development of the squatting movement in London. The geographical concentration of empty council property provided a critical mass of homes that, in turn, provided an infrastructure ideally suited for organisation and mobilisation. The numbers of squatters quickly grew and, by 1974, the number of licensed and unlicensed squatters in London had risen to 3,000 and 7,000 respectively.[50]

Where possible, squatters targeted clusters of empty properties owned by local authorities. They were easier to hold – legally and politically – and doing so drew attention to the failings of the state in meeting their own stated obligations regarding the provision of affordable housing. A number of new groups sprang up that were, more often than not, rooted in neighbourhoods and grounded in struggles that were intensely local. This was reflected in the names they chose (the Islington Squatters, the Elgin Avenue Squatters in Maida Vale, the Finsbury Park squatters in Harringay, the Villa Road Squatters in Brixton, the Broadway Market Squatters Association in Hackney, etc.).[51] It was also reflected in the infrastructures and tactics adopted by the groups. Local meetings were held regularly in order to generate support within the local community. Many groups also produced their own flyers and newsletters which drew further attention to local campaigns around squatting as well as wider political struggles.[52] In some cases, squatters were successful in opening small offices that were used to share news and information, and provide support and assistance to people looking for a place to live.

At the same time, squatters began to move into privately owned properties in a series of high-profile actions. The most spectacular was the January 1974 occupation of Centre Point, a thirty-five-storey office block on Oxford Street that had been empty since its completion in 1963. There were other notable occupations during the same period. In Whitechapel, a block of nineteenth-century tenement houses on Myrdle Street and Parfett Street, was squatted in March 1972. The block was owned by Epracent, a small textile business, which was running the tenements down as the area had been marked for clearance by Tower Hamlets Council. The squatters were successfully evicted from a number of houses on Myrdle Street in February 1973 only to reoccupy a number of properties on neighbouring Parfett Street.[53] The houses were once again cleared. Each property was boarded up and a large Alsatian dog was led into each house. In response, the squatters hired a group of dog handlers who removed the dogs and took them to Leman Street Police Station as 'strays'. They then moved back into the properties and were eventually able to secure licences from the council.[54]

In Camden, a series of similar occupations began in 1973 in response to the activities of the Stock Conversion and Investment Trust, who were buying property and evicting tenants as part of future office development plans. On Camden High Street they were successfully stopped by squatters who occupied an old antique shop at number 220. In Tolmers Square near Euston Station, over forty-nine houses owned by Camden Council and Stock Conversion were squatted between 1973 and 1979. Many of the houses had been abandoned for up to eight years and were in need of serious repair. A number were painstakingly restored. A studio and workshop were established as well as a bakery, a wholefood store, a community garden and The Gorilla, a militant left-wing bookstore.[55] While Stock Conversion eventually took out summonses against the squatters, the company backed down in the face of widespread opposition. It finally agreed to sell its stake in the area to Camden Council in 1975, who went ahead with a scaled-back redevelopment of the square that included an office block and 250 public housing units.[56]

There remains, for the most part, little real data on squatters during this period. A 1975 article by Nick Wates in *New Society* gives us, however, a glimpse into *who* actually squatted in Tolmers Square. These were not the layabouts or hardened revolutionaries of popular mythologising. Rather, they were a 'diverse range of people with differing social status, age, wealth and attitudes'. According to Wates, of the 186 squatters occupying the square in June 1975,

There were 40 students, 16 white-collar workers, 16 workers in service industries, 13 artists and musicians, twelve manual labourers, twelve skilled labourers, eleven children, ten professionals, eight teachers, eight 'housewives' [sic], 24 registered unemployed, including a number of people in unclassifiable community activities, and six unknown.[57]

Some squatters did come from decidedly upper-middle-class households. They were architectural graduates, trainee solicitors, medical students and teachers. Others were young people who arrived in search of a place to stay, including a pair of 'junkies' who had been trapped in the 'hostel circuit' and were looking for a home of their own. Most were young and in their twenties, though there was a group of older squatters. As Wates concluded, the square became a 'haven for all kinds of social misfits'.[58]

And yet, if these were 'misfits' in search of affordable housing, they all shared a desire to establish some form of alternative living. In the words of one of their counterparts in Brixton:

To me living in Villa Road means more than just squatting and living on social security; it means living amongst people who are trying to set up alternatives for themselves, and anyone else who can no longer accept what society offers or is doing to itself; alternatives, for instance housing and ways of living with people, education, community care, sex attitudes, work and technology.[59]

The few modest surveys conducted with London squatters in the 1970s stressed the importance of housing.[60] But they also pointed to a correlation between the search for 'suitable accommodation' and the 'need to live more communally'.[61] Squatting opened up, in this way, new possibilities for the cultivation of alternative political identities and subjectivities. To be a squatter unsurprisingly meant many different things to many different people.

In East London, a group of feminist activists that were linked to a nationwide grouping, Big Flame, were developing 'new models of working and living and organising' in the early 1970s. Drawing on the work of groups such as Lotta Continua in Italy and Solidarity in the UK, the East London Big Flame (ELBF) challenged traditional forms of leftist militancy which, in their eyes, did not meet the needs of women nor address the problems that local communities of colour routinely faced. They advocated a form of autonomous politics that placed particular emphasis on 'developing *experimental* ways of living and relating'.[62]

The ELBF was active in East London between 1973 and 1975 and was involved in a number of different struggles that extended far beyond the workplace and included squatting on their own behalf and to support homeless families in the occupation of empty houses and abandoned blocks of flats. Members of the ELBF were also part of the Mile End Collective who were living in a number of houses around Bow. Two of the houses were squatted and one was used for the establishment of a community playgroup. A food co-operative was set up by the ELBF on the Lincoln Estate in Bow, though this was forced to close due to constant police harassment.[63]

Other members lived in Tower Hamlets and played an important role in the Tower Hamlets Housing Action Group which brought squatters, tenants and other activists together to 'do something to stop the destruction of their part of London'.[64] The Group helped to support the fifty families squatting Sumner House, an empty block of flats, in the autumn of 1974. ELBF members were also linked to the Bengali Housing Action Group (BHAG), who were installing families in properties on the Stephen and Matilda Estate near Tower Bridge in the mid-1970s.[65]

The emergence of the feminist movement in the 1970s ultimately played a decisive role in the establishment of a number of women's centres across London including the South London's Women Centre on Radnor Terrace in Vauxhall, the Crossroads Women's Centre on Drummond Street near Euston and the Brixton Women's Centre on Railton Road.[66] These were spaces grounded in struggles around women's liberation and, as such, they provided a radical milieu where new forms of resistance against patriarchal power structures, endemic sexual violence and other forms of oppression were developed.

These were also struggles linked to the various histories of gay radical culture in 1970s London and the questioning of queer sexual identities that emerged during this period. The Gay Liberation Front (GLF) was, after all, set up in October 1970 in a meeting at the London School of Economics. The GLF drew inspiration from various liberationist groups in the United States and was committed to a social and sexual revolution that was predicated, in part, on experiments with alternative forms of communal living.[67]

While the first incarnation of the GLF dissolved in 1972, the spirit of the original organisation was carried forward by local groups in London and elsewhere who were inspired by earlier GLF communities in Brixton, Notting Hill and Bethnal Green. In Brixton, beginning in 1974, members of the South London GLF squatted a number of dilapidated back-to-back houses on Railton Road and Mayall Road which were home to over sixty men and were later converted into a housing co-operative.[68] They also set up the South London Gay Community Centre at 78 Railton Road, which opened in March 1974 and was evicted in April 1976. The squats were widely seen as a pragmatic, practical solution to the challenges and difficulties of living a straight 'separatist life'. At the same time, they also represented an 'experimental space where men with loosely shared politics, sexuality and investment in youth and counterculture came together'.[69]

The centre became, in its own right, a key site within the radical queer community in South London. It hosted a number of different groups and events and, until its closure in 1976, was part of an infrastructure of alternative community-based groups on Railton Road which included two women's centres, an Anarchist News Service, the Brixton Advice Centre and a food co-operative on nearby Shakespeare Road.[70]

The development of the queer squatting scene in Brixton was, as the historian Matt Cook reminds us, 'part – and partly representative – of a broader history of 1970s counterculture in London and beyond'. The Brixton squatters were, in many ways, successful in articulating 'an alternative vision of queer urban life' and they did so through a form of 'direct action' which afforded them a 'degree of self-determination within the city'.[71] And yet, these were alternative identifications and community formations that were part of an expansive history with its own exclusions and blind spots. These are stories that have tended to be colour-blind, overlooking the role assumed by communities of colour within London's squatting community.

It was, after all, on Railton Road in Brixton in 1972 that Olive Morris and Liz Turnbell, members of the British Black Panthers Movement, squatted an empty flat. The first successful squat of a private property in Lambeth was 121 Railton Road. Morris and Turnbell resisted a number of evictions over the course of the next few months though, in the face of growing police pressure, they eventually moved down the road and squatted a council property.[72] Once they had moved, a bookstore, Sabaar Bookshop, was opened at 121 Railton Road. It doubled as a meeting place and advice centre for local black activists. The flat above the bookstore was, in turn, occupied by a group of squatters linked to the Brixton and Croydon Collective. They were previously involved in a major squat on Evendale Road near Loughborough Junction and were part of Black Roof, an organisation that played an instrumental role in coordinating and defending black squatters living in Brixton and Clapham.[73]

The British Black Panthers dissolved in 1973. It reformed as a group of organisations including the Brixton Black Women's Group, which was set up by Olive Morris and other women to address specific issues faced by black women living in the UK. It operated out of a squat at 64 Railton Road before moving to Stockwell Green where it became the Black Women's Centre. The Race Today Collective was started in the same year and was based at 165–7 Railton Road (C.L.R. James later lived at the same address). It's membership included Darcus Howe, Farukh Dhondy, Leila Hassan, Gus John and Linton Kwesi Johnson. Dhondy, in particular, played an important role in the BHAG, who were squatting flats across East London.[74]

Looking through the lens of critical race and feminist theory, it can be argued that various struggles over squatting in London were, in some ways, intersectional.[75] Issues of race, class, gender and sexuality were all present and raised by different groups, though these entanglements were often ignored and the approaches that were adopted by activists across the city were largely non-inclusive. What is nevertheless clear is that the number of squatters in London had risen sharply by the mid-1970s. A survey in September 1975 estimated that there were 20,000 squatters in council properties alone. The figure excluded those living in GLC and private properties, and it was suggested by some commentators that the overall number of squatters in the city could be upwards of 50,000.

As the number of squatters across London grew, efforts were made to coordinate at a citywide level. The first edition of the *Squatters' Handbook* was produced in 1973 by a group of squatters in Islington. The same year, the All London Squatters (ALS) was founded with a view to defending the interests of unlicensed squatters. The ALS soon clashed with the FSAS over their approach to direct action and their willingness to negotiate with local authorities. Similar tensions within the FSAS led to the dissolution of the group and its reformation as the Advisory Service for Squatters (ASS) in July 1975. The ASS is still active and continues to support both licensed and unlicensed squatters. It offers legal and practical advice to squatters across London and is responsible for the publication of the *Squatters' Handbook* (now in its 14th edition). Other citywide efforts including the Squatters' Action Council and the London Squatters Union were largely unsuccessful in mobilising squatters.[76]

The disagreements and tensions that erupted between squatters in the mid-1970s pointed to enduring questions surrounding what it meant to squat. It also prompted a series of legal moves that reflected shifting attitudes to the nature of squatting. A new era of legal 'revanchism' was ushered in which challenged the limited protection afforded to squatters in the civil courts. In 1972, this was extended to criminal law as the Law Commission began to reconsider the statutes on trespass. The Commission published its preliminary findings in June 1974 and recommended the repeal of the Forcible Entry Acts and the criminalisation of all forms of trespass.[77]

In the wake of intense criticism, a watered-down Final Report was published in March 1976. The report formed the basis for the Criminal Law Act of 1977, which represented an 'extension of the criminal law in the area of trespass'. While new offences came into force and were punishable through prison sentences, neither squatting nor trespass was, as such, made illegal. The act made it easier, however, to evict squatters. A squatter who resisted a request to leave a property on behalf of a 'displaced residential occupier' or a 'protected intended occupier' could be arrested and evicted without a court order. Resisting court-appointed bailiffs was reclassified as a form of 'obstruction'.[78]

In the late 1970s, London squatters were thus under sustained attack, legally or otherwise. There were countless high-profile evictions (Cornwall Terrace in 1975, Hornsey Rise in 1976, St Agnes Place in 1977). And yet, many organised squatting groups were remarkably resilient and were successful in eking out concessions, including the Street Group who managed to save a number of houses on Villa Road in Brixton which became part of a housing co-operative scheme.[79]

Determined resistance by squatters prompted a volte face by the Conservative Administration running the GLC. In October 1977, they announced an amnesty to all squatters living in GLC properties provided that they registered within a month. Over 1,300 properties (out of 1,850) responded to the offer. Some were given tenancies, others licences.[80] The majority were eventually rehoused in other GLC properties. A number of squatting groups used the opportunity to set up housing co-operatives. Others, including a group living in a row of derelict GLC properties on Freston Road in West London, adopted a more imaginative approach. They declared independence from the UK and set up the 'Free Independent Republic of Frestonia'. They even went so far as to write to the United Nations and request the presence of UN peacekeepers to prevent their imminent eviction. The UN never replied, though the media publicity led to negotiations with the GLC and the site was eventually handed over to the Notting Hill Housing Trust.[81]

During 1977, over 5,000 squats across London were ultimately legalised as a result of the GLC amnesty and through arrangements made between squatters and local councils. Combined with the Criminal Law Act, organised squatting and the wider housing struggle within which it was embedded – a struggle for decent affordable housing *and* the right to live co-operatively and communally – declined or had, at the very least, been neutralised. Most local squatting groups had folded by the end of 1979, though the ASS limped on as government cuts began to bite and a new generation of squatters slowly emerged.[82]

The history of squatting in London in the 1980s has, in this context, received far less attention. The 'movement' of the 1970s was a mass housing movement. The various identities it produced and the radical social relations it prefigured were forged within a wide-ranging landscape of protest and resistance. Squatting in the 1980s and 1990s was, in contrast, characterised by the formation of dynamic albeit highly localised micro-communities and subcultures.[83] While electoral success brought the Left into power in a number of cities across the UK, councils were forced to adopt a defensive pragmatic stance in the face of cutbacks and pressures against social housing. By the mid-1980s, as one historian of the movement concluded, 'the Left had dumped squatting as both a political project and as a practical solution to aspects of the housing crisis'.[84]

There were of course efforts to recreate the kind of organised squatting that was successful in the 1970s, most notably perhaps around Bonnington Square in Vauxhall where a group of squatters occupied a number of empty properties in the early 1980s that had been acquired by the Inner London Education Authority.[85] The group formed a housing co-operative and were able to secure a lease for the properties, which were carefully restored. A community café and garden were also established.

At the same time, many of the organised squatting groups active during this period drew on an action repertoire that was increasingly indebted to the practices adopted by anarchists and autonomists in the UK and elsewhere. In Brixton, 121 Railton Road was reoccupied in 1979 by a group of Australian anarchists. Until its eviction in 1999, the 121 Centre served as a key meeting point for squatters across London. The Centre at various points included a café, a gig and rehearsal space, a bookshop, a printing room, meeting spaces and offices. A number of campaigns and groups were also based at the 121 Centre, including the radical women's magazine *Bad Attitude*, AnarQuist (an anarcho-queer group), the Brixton Squatters' Aid and the prisoner support group Anarchist Black Cross.

On the other side of South London, the anarcho-cum-experimental music group Bourbonese Qualk set up the Ambulance Station in an abandoned five-storey building on the Old Kent Road. After lengthy renovations, the top two floors of the squat were converted into artist studios. The squatters lived on the middle floor, while the first floor included a café and a series of meeting spaces for local anarchist groups and the Squatters Network of Walworth (SNOW). The ground floor encompassed a large performance space, a recording studio and a series of print workshops.[86]

While the Ambulance Station is largely remembered for its place within an underground alternative music scene hosting a number of soon-to-be-famous bands (The Jesus and Mary Chain, Pulp, Primal Screen, etc.), through the work of SNOW, it was also linked to a series of largely neglected efforts to build a mass squatting movement in South London. SNOW were active between 1983 and 1988 and played an important role linking squatters to council tenants while providing 'physical assistance with practical problems, and an opportunity to meet ... other squatters'.[87] They published a fortnightly squatters' magazine (*The Wire*), set up the Tenants and Squatters Campaign of Southwark and were responsible for housing over 3,000 squatters, many in empty council properties. There were active campaigns on a number of local estates (Rockingham, Kingslake, Pullens).[88]

On the Pullens Estate, a strong tenant and squatter alliance had been established which successfully resisted a series of evictions in June 1986. It was, in fact, on the same estate that an abandoned building on Crampton Street was squatted in 1988. The front of the building was converted into the Fareshares Food Co-operative. The rest of the building was occupied by a group of local anarchists who set up the 56a Infoshop. Modelled on similar spaces in Germany and Holland, the 56A was the first of its kind in the UK serving as a social centre, bookstore, radical archive and bike workshop.[89]

In North and East London, there were similar efforts to carve out autonomous spaces that provided, in turn, a context for the development of a range of youth identities and subcultures around casual drug use, punk and electronic music, environmentalism and queer politics. Throughout the 1980s and 1990s, there were large squatting communities in Hackney, Haringey and Stoke Newington. Many houses were only briefly squatted, other squats lasted for years. The majority of the houses were owned by the council and, in some cases, their occupiers were successful in securing short-term licences or tenancies. A number of squatted spaces were also set up to host gigs, parties and raves, though there remained a strong autonomist ethos among the squatters as was seen in the kind of militant tactics adopted by a group occupying the Stamford Hill Estate in Hackney. Over 500 police officers were deployed as 'Orgreve came to Hackney' in March 1988. The squatters responded by erecting a series of burning barricades. After three days of violent clashes with the police, they were finally evicted.[90]

By the early 1990s, the squatting scene in London was far more subcultural than it had been in the 1970s, 'disconnected', in the words of one commentator, 'from the waning levels of class struggle around labour, welfare and housing, though it was never entirely severed'.[91] At the same time, the emergence of a thriving free party scene in the late 1980s and early 1990s led, in particular, to a series of high-profile rural raves and the exodus of thousands of Londoners on to illegally squatted plots of land.[92] In the moral panic that ensued, the government passed the 1994 Criminal Justice and Public Order Act which provided a host of new powers to proscribe 'trespassory assemblies' and 'remove persons attending or preparing for a rave'.[93]

As part of the same act, the government also proposed a series of additional clauses on squatting. These changes were tantamount to further criminalisation and were challenged by a host of housing organisations and charities as well as a new group known as SQUASH (Squatters Action for Secure Homes). In the end, the government was forced to climb down and settle for less draconian measures (clauses 72–6 of the Criminal Justice Act).

The remnants of the squatting scene in London that survived into the late 1990s and early 2000s was no longer part of a wider housing movement in the city. If anything, it subsisted within a series of protest cultures that were receptive to a growing range of political identities. These were, moreover, cultures and identities that were increasingly embedded within an anti-globalisation movement that transformed many squats into convergence spaces hosting activists from around the world as part of anti-summit mobilisations, social forums and other international conferences. Other squats were set up as social centres that focused their activities 'around the material emergencies of daily life' (precarious work and housing) and their relationship to larger economic and ecological crises.[94] This includes a group of activists who occupied a disused market garden in the village of Sipson to protest against the construction of a third runway at Heathrow Airport. Over the past six years, Transition Heathrow has become a vital community space offering courses in food production, gardening and renewable energy.[95]

The last few years have also seen a wider revival of squatting in London in the wake of the global financial crisis that began in 2007. The austerity measures rolled out by the coalition government after 2010 led to a wave of occupations by students and other anti-austerity activists. The government responded in

2011 with the launch of a consultation on the criminalisation of squatting. SQUASH was reformed to challenge the proposed legislation which was ultimately fast-tracked as an amendment to the Legal Aid, Sentencing and Punishment of Offenders Act. The law came into force on 1 September 2012, and for the first time it became a criminal offence to squat a residential building in the UK.[96]

For many academics, charity workers and legal experts, the new law was anticipatory. In their eyes, it legislated against various *future* struggles for social justice and the use of 'occupation' as a direct action tactic.[97] Others argued that it would simply exacerbate a growing housing crisis in London.[98] Given the city's unique position as the epicentre of a financialised corporate capitalism, this is a crisis that has, if anything, intensified over the past five years reinforced by the rapid 'transformation of the city's real estate market into a hub for footloose global capital'.[99] In London, urban regeneration, state-led gentrification and welfare cutbacks have all combined to create a housing market characterised by its inequality and insecurity.[100]

And yet, for the young single mothers of the Focus E15 campaign who, in 2014, occupied a series of empty low-rise flats on the Carpenter Estate in Newham, or the feminist activists from the group Sisters Uncut who have been occupying an empty council home in Hackney to highlight the lack of support for survivors of domestic violence, squatting remains an urgent and necessary course of action.[101] In other words, the squatting of empty buildings in London has a long history, *but it also has a present and a future*. Whether it is the Focus E15 campaign or the 2015 occupations of the Sweets Way and Aylesbury estates, or the tactics adopted by Sisters Uncut, what it means to be a squatter in London today can be understood as a source of new political alliances, solidarities and identities.

It would be wrong therefore to reduce and essentialise squatting to the singular pursuit of housing, however important and necessary this has been for numerous Londoners. For many, the very choice to squat was also predicated on a refusal to accept the categories and structures imposed on them. But if these are actions that provide a glimpse into another version of a 'rebellious London', we should finally remind ourselves of the thousands of people who squatted in the city with little or no link to any wider housing struggle.[102] However invisible, these are stories that remain just as urgent even if they only appear fleetingly in court proceedings, charity reports and newspaper articles.[103] These are stories such as the one of Daniel Gauntlett who, having earlier been charged under new anti-squatting legislation, froze to death outside an empty bungalow in Aylesford outside London in 2013.[104] These are stories that are all too quickly forgotten, at a time when they need to be told more urgently than ever.

3

Building a Squatters' Movement: The Politics of Preservation and Provocation in Amsterdam and Copenhagen

The neighbours are our best barricades. (*Naboerne er vores bedste barrikader.*)

Popular Slogan, Nørrebro Residents Association
(housing activist group active in Copenhagen, 1973–80)

Squatting has always been a mode of confrontation. If you want to change something, you have to not only engage in confrontations but also provoke them.

Amsterdam squatter[1]

On 29 April 1980, a children's adventure and activity playground on the corner of Stengade and Slotsgade in the working-class district of Nørrebro in Copenhagen was demolished in a major police operation. The playground known as 'Byggeren' (slang for a 'place to build') was squatted in June 1973 by activists from the Nørrebro Beboeraktion (NB), a grassroots tenant association that had been formed a few months earlier to challenge the planned urban redevelopment of the neighbourhood.[2] Over 800 police officers were deployed to provide support to the work squad whose bulldozers crashed into the makeshift structures erected on the site. A number of activists had, however, climbed on top of the structures to protest their destruction. They fell to the ground as the roofs caved in and were forced to scramble away to avoid being run over by the bulldozers.[3]

Local residents and activists responded to the brutal tactics adopted by the police by erecting a series of barricades in the streets. A city bus was commandeered and placed sideways across an intersection to block traffic, its tyres deflated. Containers from a number of building sites were also used, with banners draped across them reading 'Police out of Nørrebro – Byggeren will never surrender' (*'politet ud af Nørrebro – Byggeren overgiver sig aldrig'*). In the street fighting that ensued, the police were driven out of the neighbourhood.[4] The playground was carefully rebuilt during the night, only for it to be destroyed again a few days later in another major police operation. As one activist recalled:

> We were beaten up by the police; they followed us up the stairways and inside the flats; they drove down the streets on their motorcycles randomly beating up people with their clubs. A legally assembled protest demonstration was violently smashed – people were held isolated for weeks in prison … It was civil war in Nørrebro.[5]

What became known as the 'Battle of Byggeren' ('*Slaget om Byggere*') led to a series of violent confrontations with the police over the next two weeks. A number of protesters and officers were injured. Several arrests were made.[6]

At the same time as the Copenhagen police were busy demolishing a playground, a few hundred miles away in Amsterdam a group of squatters were making the final preparations for a day of action to mark the coronation of Queen Beatrice. The coronation was, by law, required to take place in Amsterdam. While authorities were planning a day of national celebration, they were worried about the threat of disruption from the city's growing and increasingly radical squatters' movement. It was, after all, only a month earlier that tanks had rolled on to the streets of the city as part of an operation to evict a squat on the Vondelstraat.[7]

For their part, the squatters' movement declared April to be a month of action under the slogan 'no housing, no coronation' ('*Geen woning, geen kroning*'). What this meant in practical terms was twofold. The squatters planned, on the one hand, to use the campaign to draw further attention to an ongoing housing crisis in Amsterdam. On the other hand, they saw the coronation as an opportunity to 'crack' and squat as many houses across the city as possible.

Some squatters, however, were unsatisfied with the tactics adopted by the wider movement and advocated a more aggressive and confrontational approach. A group calling itself the Autonomen (Autonomists) began circulating (anonymously) a flyer across the city advocating a 'day of action' (*'aktiedag'*) on 30 April 1980. The flyer itself included pictures of Beatrice superimposed on bombs, a reference perhaps to the smoke bombs which disrupted her wedding in 1966. A second poster appeared a few weeks later calling for a demonstration 'with effects'.

Most squatters were at pains to distance themselves from the proposed demonstration, which nevertheless went ahead despite police efforts to lock down the city. It sparked a series of violent riots that drew in a large crowd, many of whom were not squatters. The 'Coronation Riots' lasted well into the night and were some of the worst that Amsterdam had ever seen, prompting widespread public condemnation. Over forty arrests were made, none of whom were connected to the squatters' movement in the city. Thirteen were later convicted.[8]

The 'Battle of Byggeren' and the 'Coronation Riots' are events that have come to occupy an important place within the history of squatting in Copenhagen and Amsterdam respectively. Social historians often remind us that riots are insurrectionary moments of crisis.[9] They throw into sharp relief the breakdown of wider economic, social and political structures. They also tell us something about their participants and the various populations and movements from which they emerge. 'To act,' as one leading scholar of protest has recently concluded, 'is not just to do something, it is *to be* something.'[10]

To 'be' a squatter in Copenhagen or Amsterdam in April 1980 increasingly meant that one was also part of a wider social movement with all its achievements, goals and routines as well as its disappointments, disagreements and losses. For squatters, events such as the 'Battle of Byggeren' and the 'Coronation Riots' helped both to shape and to question the activist identities that they collectively shared. At the same time, these were events that did not work on the basis of any single vision of social change.[11] To be in a movement was to be part of a complex process that challenged how a city could be imagined, lived and ordered differently. The squats set up by activists in Copenhagen and Amsterdam were more than spaces simply to live. They were sites of radical possibility and promise as well as sources of intense despair and disappointment. These were, finally, spaces whose histories have also helped us to understand how an urban social movement comes into being, develops, and later falters and declines.[12]

Social movements are usually seen as a form of 'contentious politics' characterised by sustained campaigns of 'claim-making' that, in turn, depend on an array of performances and practices. These are often claims to the rightful assertion of specific identities and the exercise of alternative social and political programmes.[13] In the case of squatting, the story in Copenhagen and Amsterdam begins in the 1960s as young people across the United States and Europe started to move in and occupy classrooms, university departments, parks, factories and abandoned houses in order to create free spaces for alternative living but also, in many cases, to meet immediate needs around housing.[14] The first occupation of a house in Copenhagen began on 24 February 1963, and was undertaken by a small radical anti-imperialist and socialist organisation known as Gruppe 61, who were active in the Danish campaign for nuclear disarmament.[15]

A couple of years later, a row of condemned seventeenth-century houses near Christianshavns Square were occupied by a group of young people. The squatters were successful in negotiating an agreement with the owner of the houses. They were allowed to occupy the houses, forming an autonomous community that numbered between 100 and 150 people. The community was known as the Republic of Sofiegården after the street on which it was located. The houses were finally cleared in 1969 and 1970 by the police. Some of the former residents became involved in the development of student housing, though many turned to the squatting of abandoned flats and buildings in Copenhagen.[16] The city's first squatter movement (*Slumstoermerbevægelesen*) was, in this way, born. Building on a combination of radical youth subcultures and DIY practices, the early wave of squatters in Copenhagen and elsewhere in Denmark were known as slumstormers (*Slumstormere*) and included students, activists, runaways and former drug offenders. They occupied abandoned houses and set up a series of utopian experiments and hippie-inspired communities (Hudegården, Jægergården, Stengården, Fredensgården, Tømrergården, etc).[17] There were admittedly other squatters who, in this context, were active as early as 1966 and were based in the old working-class neighbourhood of Nørrebro studying as apprentices at the local bricklaying college. By the end of the decade they were widely seen as part of a citywide movement which was starting to find its feet.[18]

In the decades that followed, social movement historians have detected at least three separate if connected squatter movements in Copenhagen. The first generation of squatters were largely based in the inner city. Some were closely connected to the countercultural experimentation that was emerging during this period. Others were more firmly rooted in local neighbourhoods and were active in establishing tenant associations and other community initiatives. The second wave of squatting began in the early 1980s. It encompassed the BZ-movement (BZ is the phonetic shorthand of the Danish word for squatting) and drew on activists who adopted a more confrontational anti-capitalist ethos. As the BZ-movement dissolved in the 1990s, a third autonomous scene emerged which was less cohesive and wired into a wider transnational landscape of protest.[19]

There is much to support this periodisation, though the evolution of the squatter movement in Copenhagen in the late 1960s and early 1970s was ultimately characterised by the emergence of two different albeit connected squatting scenes with their own repertoire of practices, tactics and strategies. On the one side, was a faction of young activists who were involved in the establishment of an alternative self-organised community that became known as Fristaden Christiania (Freetown Christania). On the other side, was a group that adopted a grassroots approach to neighbourhood organising. They did so to challenge the redevelopment of Copenhagen, the lack of affordable housing and the displacement of its working-class residents from the city centre. The most successful of these organisations was Nørrebro Beboeraktion, which was active between 1973 and 1980.

The establishment of Christiania admittedly represents one of the key founding mythologies in the long history of squatting in Copenhagen. In early September 1971, local residents based in Christianshavn tore down part of the fence surrounding the recently abandoned Bådsmandsstræde Barracks, a former military base in Christianshavn that was located alongside parts of Copenhagen's seventeenth-century defensive ramparts. They set up a small playground for their children. Three weeks later, on 26 September 1971, a group of activists including Jacob Ludvigsen, founder of the alternative newspaper, *Hovedbladet*, broke into the base and began to explore the over eighty-five acres of barracks, workshops and halls. They documented their 'adventures' and, a few days later, Ludvigsen published a story in the *Hovedbladet* inviting people to come and explore the 'forbidden city' ('*forbudte by*'). 'Here was the framework,' Ludvigsen proclaimed, 'for an alternative city (*alternative by*) that could be produced,' he continued, 'through a range of shared experiments (*samværseksperimenter*).'[20] A call was made for 'settlers' to 'emigrate with bus number 8'. The area was soon swamped by young people who quickly established themselves in the barracks.[21]

The Danish Ministry of Defence was caught by surprise and did little to deter the occupiers. Local authorities were similarly reticent to intervene. A November 1971 meeting on Christiania between representatives from various ministries, the Copenhagen Municipality and the Copenhagen Police concluded that it was not 'practically possible' to evict the squatters and that it was necessary to reach a 'normalisation of the relationship between the inhabitants and the authorities'.[22]

At the same time, the squatters living in Christiania released a handwritten manifesto which set out their own vision:

> To create a self-governing society (*selvstyrende samfund*) whereby each and every individual holds themselves responsible for the well-being of the entire community. This society is to be economically self-sustaining and its common aspiration is to be steadfast in the conviction that psychological and physical destitution can be averted.[23]

By early 1972, there were over 300 squatters living in Christiania. The number soon rose to 500. A police eviction was ruled out once again by the authorities, who set up a contact group to negotiate with the squatters. On 31 May 1972, an initial agreement between the state and Christiania was signed. The following year, the government officially designated the site as a temporary 'social experiment'. It was allowed to continue until its future use was determined. For the inhabitants of Christiania, this became an experiment in alternative forms of decision-making, living and organising that was, in turn, supported by a thriving underground economy that included the widespread sale of drugs.[24]

In the end, as a Ministry of Justice report on the intelligence-gathering activities of the Danish Security and Intelligence Service (Politiets Efterretningstjeneste, or PET) has shown, the occupation of the Bådsmandsstræde Barracks in 1971 was simply the most spectacular action within a much wider and complex field of action that connected squatters to a range of different activist groups such as the Black Panthers Solidarity Committee and the Danish Vietnam Committee (De Danske Vietnamkomitéer). One September 1971 notice from a PET operative drew attention, in particular, to the formation of a new housing action group (Boligfronten) which soon launched a series of occupations, blockades and demonstrations across Copenhagen.[25]

One of the actions involved the occupation of an empty building in between Griffensgade and Stengade in the district of Nørrebro. The house became known as the Folkets Hus (People's House) and it was located within *den sorte firkant* (the black rectangle), which was a popular name for a run-down area within Nørrebro whose name comes from the factories that were established in the late nineteenth century belching black soot across the neighbourhood. The name also derives from the black lines that marked out a twenty-five-block area on the municipality's 1971 slum clearance plan. Housing in the predominantly working-class neighbourhood was in poor condition. Many properties had been empty for years in anticipation of their demolition. Local residents were, however, largely ignored in the drawing up and implementation of plans to redevelop the area.[26]

On 13 January 1973, the NB (also known as the Nørrebro Residents Association) was set up by a group of activists in the neighbourhood. Their aim was to 'improve the environment and living conditions of the current residents according to their own desires'.[27] The group had emerged from the squatter movement in Copenhagen though it also drew on a wider leftist milieu in the city. Unlike activists in Christiania, who were largely focused on internal subcultural practices, the NB concentrated their efforts on building links with local residents as part of a broad-based housing movement.

For the NB, 'claim-making' was predicated on the right of local Nørrebro residents to participate in and shape the redevelopment of their neighbourhood. The group and its supporters challenged plans for the demolition of housing, arguing that it could be preserved and modernised. They also insisted that displaced local residents should be rehoused in the neighbourhood and that efforts were made to improve the provision of community services.[28]

In practical terms they developed a number of tactics, adopting the slogan 'action leads to transformation' ('*handling gi'r forvandling*').[29] This encompassed a slum clearance patrol which went through the neighbourhood building by building reporting code violations. The NB also attempted to preserve and fireproof many of the district's older and often empty buildings. Block protection units were set up to prevent the removal of tenants and were, in many cases, successful.[30] A wide repertoire of protest techniques were also used, from organised parades and street theatre performances to the squatting of buildings and the occupation of open spaces. The group insisted on non-violent forms of resistance, arguing that it was crucial that they were able to build networks of trust and solidarity with their neighbours. They set up a training course for activists, and organised a number of social and cultural activities and spaces, including the establishment of the Byggeren playground which was part of the very first action undertaken by the NB in June 1973.[31]

The events which culminated in the eviction of Byggeren in 1980 were ultimately responsible for the dissolution of the group. There had already been an earlier split between members who valued concrete action and those who adopted a more theoretical approach.[32] The demolition of the playground and the riots that ensued proved, however, decisive. Many local residents felt that the NB had achieved all that it could and were wary of the growing number of young people who had joined the protests to save Byggeren and were willing to use violence as a form of protest.

The decline of the NB as a movement was followed, in many ways, by the emergence of a second squatter movement in Copenhagen in 1981. While it is tempting to link the decline of the former with the rise of the latter, the history of squatting in Copenhagen was never so linear. Few, if any, members of the NB took part in the BZ-movement. Some of the young people who had participated in the 'Battle of Byggeren' would later take part in the actions and squats of 1981, though they had little other connection to the tenant-based activism practised by the NB.

The development of what became known as the BZ-movement was, if anything, more closely connected to the Europe-wide wave of squatting that swept through Amsterdam, Zurich, Freiburg and Berlin between early 1980 and the spring of 1981, and which was, in turn, modelled on earlier forms of autonomist militancy that flowed out of Italy in the late 1970s. In Copenhagen, it was on 15 August 1981 that an '*Initivgruppen*' for the establishment of an autonomous self-organised youth centre in Nørrebro was set up. The group demanded the provision of housing for young people in the city. It counted over thirty members and included students from the Free Gymnasium School, members of various socialist organisations, punks, feminists from the Red Stocking movement and several youngsters from Christiania.[33]

The city was unwilling to negotiate and, in October 1981, a series of occupations were launched by the *Initivgruppen*. The empty Rutana bakery in Nørrebro was briefly squatted on 15 October in a symbolic action. On 24 October, a former rubber factory in the same neighbourhood, Schiønning og Arvé, was occupied. The authorities reacted swiftly and violently, using tear gas to clear the occupiers a few days later. Over ninety arrests were made.[34] The protests nevertheless continued and, a couple of weeks later, an old disused monastery in Vesterbro was squatted. The Abel Cathrinsgade squat lasted for over three months, but eventually dissolved in the face of internal disagreements and a lack of guidelines and rules.

While many left the new movement, others continued to explore the possibility of squatting. Two houses in Vesterbro including a former museum for musical instruments was squatted in March 1982. A number of new houses in Nørrebro were occupied in the months that followed. These houses (Allotria, Bazooka, Den Lille Fjer) formed the 'backbone of the early BZ-movement', and their occupants were successful in creating a network of autonomous spaces that included music venues, cafés, pubs and workshops.[35] Not all the squatters were young. A group of pensioners known as the 'grey panthers' were also active in two houses on Korsgade during the same period.[36]

Local authorities remained reluctant, however, to concede any ground to the squatters, though they realised that they had to do something. On 31 October 1982, the administration and running of the former Folkets Hus on Jagtvej 69 was handed over to a group of young people while the city retained ownership of the space. The Folkets Hus was originally built in 1897 and for many years was the headquarters of the Danish labour movement. Clara Zetkin, Vladimir Lenin and Rosa Luxemburg all visited the centre in its early years. It now became the Ungdomshuset or Youth House and soon established itself as a key social centre for the BZ-movement, the autonomous scene and a wide range of youth subcultures.[37]

While the Ungdomshuset thrived, a police crackdown led to the eviction of a number of squats a few months later. Over a thousand officers descended on the group of houses in Nørrebro. The occupants of the Allotria were able, however, to avoid the police, having escaped through a tunnel that they had dug under the street. The stunt was celebrated in the press and while the squatters were widely praised, the previously squatted buildings (including the Allotria) were all bulldozed by the authorities.[38]

The January 1983 evictions were a major blow to the BZ-movement, though it regrouped during the summer of 1983. A number of new houses were occupied, including an empty block at Ryesgade 58. Each floor in the house was turned into an independent collective responsible for the organisation and management of their own space.[39] Other squats sprang up across Copenhagen in the next couple of years including Kapaw in Østerbro, Bumzen in Nørrebro, Gyldenløvesgade in Indre By and the Sorte Hest in Vesterbro.[40]

The resilience and survival of the BZ-movement pointed to a movement that was successful in connecting struggles over housing to wider political and social issues. It is often argued, in this context, that social movements have two faces: a 'front stage' that interacts with the state, the media and a wider public and is the predominant context in which 'claim-making' performances take place; and a 'back stage' where the complex and often divisive internal negotiations and practices of a movement or 'scene' are performed.[41] A movement's evolution and decline is, more often than not, related to how these two 'faces' interact.

For BZ-activists in Copenhagen, the 'front stage' increasingly consisted of a wide repertoire of contentious actions. One study has shown that over the course of the movement's history between

1981 and 1994 there were over 538 separate actions, with 116 of these directly related to squatting. There were eighty-one incidents or actions involving the police, a further fifty-eight against members of the far right and forty-one related to environmental issues. Overall, 357 actions were rooted in local Danish affairs. The remainder were linked to a wider international context. The BZ-movement was, if anything, a broad-based movement that encompassed both an autonomous community of squatters and a group of activists committed to anti-imperialist and anti-racist struggles in Europe and elsewhere. There were strong links with left-wing radicals in Germany and the Netherlands in particular.[42]

The movement's 'back stage' was deeply rooted in the fight for 'autonomy' and the desire to create autonomous spaces in the city. This was a fight that still presumed a mass of young people who not only saw themselves as marginal to mainstream society, but had both the time and space to explore and develop distinctive collective arrangements. At stake here, was an existential search for a different identity and a collective form of living that took place primarily within squats and other 'scene' spaces including bars, concerts and social centres such as the Ungdomshuset. The pages of *Fingeren*, the most prominent magazine of the BZ-movement, tended to focus on and document the high-profile actions, evictions and occupations that constituted the movement's front stage. There was the occasional article – especially in *Ravage*, the follow-up magazine to *Fingeren* – where one caught a glimpse of some of the backstage disagreements, hierarchies and tensions that ran through many of the squats. In the face of intense public scrutiny and pressure, it is perhaps not surprising that the BZ-movement became fragmented and politically disoriented in the end because, as many activists later conceded, this was largely a product of internal tensions and struggles.[43]

For the same activists, it was the protracted negotiations and eventual eviction of Ryesgade 58 in 1986 that came to represent one of the decisive moments in the history of their movement.

Discussions between the squatters and the owners of the house continued throughout 1984 and 1985. They eventually came to an agreement in 1986 which would have given the residents full control of the house as an official 'social experiment'. However, the city council vetoed the deal and insisted that the illegal occupants of the house were evicted. The owners complied and the squatters had until 14 September 1986 to leave. On the day of the planned eviction, a major demonstration culminated in the erection of a series of barricades along the Ryesgade that stretched over a number of city blocks. The police attempted to storm the barricades but were easily repelled by the squatters, who had organised themselves into a number of units that assumed different defensive roles.

Over the next few days, the squatters were able to hold their position on the Ryesgade despite a series of increasingly violent battles with the police. As the prospect of an armed operation loomed the squatters made the decision to leave, having resisted the police for over nine days. On 23 September they called a press conference. Reporters arrived only to find that the squatters had all vanished and had managed to elude the authorities. A message was left which read: 'We have left our house because we can not sit and wait on a solution ... We will not be pawns in their game. Nor will we be slowly smothered in red tape. Our struggle continues and we will decide when we fight (*Vores kamp fortsaetter, og vi bestemmer selv, hvornår vi vil slås*)'.[44]

The BZ-movement had suffered a major setback, though for many it had emerged stronger from the confrontation on the Ryesgade, having gained new supporters and considerable public attention. In the years that followed, the remaining squatted houses continued to act as bases for a wide repertoire of actions. It was only with their clearance in 1990 in a series of violent police raids that the movement began to finally fray and dissolve. With the exception of the Ungdomshuset, the BZ-movement had lost all of its main meeting places. Attempts were made to resquat the houses, though they proved futile in the face of a police force that was far better equipped and organised.[45]

The new autonomous 'scene' that emerged in the aftermath of the BZ-movement lacked the scale, militancy or cohesion of its predecessors despite efforts to open up new spaces in the early 1990s. Squatting and other forms of 'occupation' were largely eschewed as activists focused on the building of alliances and networks with other radical groups and organisations in Copenhagen and beyond. The alter-globalisation movement that was emerging at the time placed far less emphasis on housing, finding inspiration in a different set of political priorities.

One constant throughout the period, however, was Christiania which had, over the years, survived a number of challenges (from an increasingly violent drug scene to police intimidation) and persistent state interference. In 1989, a 'Christiania Act' was passed in the Danish parliament. The act legalised the squat while making it possible for the inhabitants of Christiania collectively to use the area. This was reversed in 2004, as a right-wing coalition government imposed a series of significant changes on the earlier 1989 law. The changes called for a process of 'normalisation' which, in turn, conferred individual ownership on all Christiania property.[46] The inhabitants of Christiania took the government to court. They lost the case but were able to secure a compromise according to which they were able to purchase the whole community at a below-market rate while maintaining their own system of communal land ownership and a high degree of political autonomy.[47]

The fortunes of the Ungdomshuset proved rather different. During the 1990s, the house represented one of the last vestiges of the earlier BZ-movement and remained synonymous with Copenhagen's 'radical political and cultural youth milieus'.[48] The centre attracted a new generation of activists who lacked the experience of their earlier counterparts, and the house was hit by a fire in 1996. The council used the fire as an opportunity to close down the centre, though its occupants were successful in repairing the damages and meeting the necessary fire safety standards. The city nevertheless sold the building in 2000 to a newly established limited company who quickly sold it on to an evangelical Christian sect (Faderhuset) who served notice on the occupants of the Ungdomshuset.

Despite efforts to save the house, it was eventually cleared on 1 March 2007 in an operation organised and carried out by a Danish anti-terrorist unit. The house was demolished five days later after days of rioting. The destruction of the Ungdomshuset only served to trigger a new wave of demonstrations, actions and occupations. On 31 March, the supporters of the youth house joined forces with the residents of Christiania on a march through Copenhagen under the banner 'Free spaces for everyone'. Growing public sympathy and anger at the violent methods used by the police forced the city council into negotiations with the protesters. In June 2008, a municipal building was given to the activists as compensation for the destruction of the Ungdomshuset.[49]

If the struggle to save the Ungdomshuset revitalised the radical scene in Copenhagen, it also spawned a series of solidarity actions across Europe and North American, including a march in Amsterdam whose own history of squatting has, in many ways mirrored the struggles that took place in Copenhagen. This is a history, after all, whose traditional provenance can be traced back to the 1960s and was itself a source of widespread mythologising. At the same time, it is a history that depended on a range of actions, ideas and practices that pointed, if anything, to a diverse and complex set of movements that ultimately exceeded the narratives that have usually been assigned to them.

As in the case of Copenhagen, a longer view of the history of squatting in Amsterdam yields a story rooted in the search for affordable housing in a context marked by its scarcity. For most historians of squatting in Amsterdam, the roots of the movement(s) that would emerge in the 1970s and 1980s can be traced back to the mid-1960s.[50] There were, admittedly, earlier efforts to squat in the 1930s as many workers lost their homes during the global economic depression. Tenant associations were set up to help evicted families move into a growing number of empty apartments; often the ones that they had been forced to leave.

Legally, they simply had to move their belongings back into the property in order to force the landlord to negotiate with them. Most of the tenants, however, did not see themselves as squatters. Squatting was simply, in their eyes, a means to an end – a tactic – rather than a movement in its own right.[51]

In the post-war period it was not uncommon to find families squatting empty properties that had been overlooked by Amsterdam's various housing corporations. Most of these actions were conspicuously clandestine and hidden from public view. The most commonly used term for squatting at the time was unsurprisingly *clandestien bezetten* (to occupy secretly).[52] Squatting was largely invisible and its success was contingent on avoiding detection. There were a few cases where the phenomenon of young people occupying empty spaces illegally featured in the media. This included a 1964 story in the student newspaper, *Propria Cures*, in which an appeal was launched to find people to live in a series of buildings on the Kattenburg east of the city's Central Station which had already been squatted. The houses were slated for demolition and their occupiers were evicted within a few months, though their actions briefly occupied the media spotlight.[53]

It was only in the late 1960s that the act of squatting in Amsterdam (and for that matter elsewhere in the Netherlands) became the basis for a movement in which more and more people saw them as squatters and saw their actions – occupying a building, repairing it and making it liveable, and defending it from the owner or the police – as a key part of their own identity. To squat, in other words, may have begun, for many people, as a practical solution to their own immediate housing needs. It now pointed to the possibilities for creating a more just and sustainable city as part of a wider collective endeavour.[54]

There were, of course, numerous plausible starting points to the history of the squatter movement in Amsterdam. Most former squatters insisted that it only began with the Vondelstraat evictions in 1980. Others, however, have suggested a more complex and uneven series of events. This is a history, they argued, that can, in fact, can be divided into four discrete periods with their own movement goals, practices and repertoires. The first was closely connected to the actions of the Provos, a radical artist collective that was active in the late 1960s and was responsible for the establishment of a number of groups that publicly squatted houses. The second emerged as a part of a series of protests in the mid-1970s, against the destruction of the Nieuwmarktbuurt in the centre of Amsterdam and the forced displacement of its working-class residents. This was followed by the widely mythologised movement of the late 1970s and early 1980s and, in its dissolution, a more fractured squatting scene that encompassed a number of different cultural, social and political aims. This was not, in the end, a movement or a series of successive movements that could be easily subsumed under a single strongly vectored narrative, despite the efforts made by many of its protagonists to do so. It was instead a collection of actions that, taken together, pointed to a different understanding of Amsterdam as a space of political possibility.[55]

The Provos (a shorthand for 'to provoke') first emerged in the mid-1960s as an anarcho-Situationist youth movement that challenged the stale consumerism and baleful authoritarianism that, they believed, characterised Dutch society. They combined artistic happenings with political agitprop, and their 'performances' attracted hundreds of participants and supporters. While their actions were often disruptive, as in the case of the smoke bombs they launched at the wedding of Princess Beatrice in 1966, they also came up with creative plans for reimagining the city and the collective life of its inhabitants.[56] The 'white plans', as they were known, focused on issues such as the free provision of bicycles, though they also highlighted a growing crisis in housing. The group's 'white houses plan' ('*witte huizen plan*') proposed that the doors of empty properties in the city should be painted white in order to draw attention to the effects of real estate speculation in the city, while lists of the properties were to be made available to the public and to tourists who visited Amsterdam.[57]

While the actions of the Provos were dismissed as a series of pranks, they succeeded in bringing the question of housing into a wider public sphere. The group dissolved in 1967. They donated their 'archive' to the University of Amsterdam and the funds that they acquired were used to help support a number of alternative political causes including the Woningsburo de Kraker (WdK or the Squatter Housing Agency), one of three separate groups that began to squat houses publicly in the late 1960s as a way of dramatising the lack of social housing for young people in Amsterdam.[58]

The WdK adopted a more hands-on approach than its predecessor, advising people how to squat and transform an empty house into a home. To do so, they created a network of activists in Amsterdam who were willing to help provide assistance and the appropriate technical skills and DIY know-how. For the WdK, squatting was no longer seen as a hidden activity but a public act of occupation that demanded a new and more accessible nomenclature. They began to use a popular slang term. To squat a building was to now 'crack it' ('*kraken*') while squatters themselves were increasingly referred to as *kraker*.[59] The new terms conjured images of the initial opening or crack of a door as one entered a building and was pulled into another different space. Cracking a house demanded, in this way, the crossing of a threshold – a form of transgression – that quickly entered into the movement's folkloric self-identity.[60]

Over the course of 1969, the WdK undertook a series of high-profile occupations with varying degrees of success. As public spectacles, they were able to expose a systemic undersupply of affordable housing for young people. They, in turn, drew attention to the possibilities that practical self-determined solutions could bring to the meeting of basic housing needs. As a growing number of people sought out the WdK for advice, they decided to publish a *Guide For Squatters* (*Handleiding voor krakers*) which appeared in May 1969.[61]

Under the slogan 'Do it yourself! Take the solution of the housing problem into your own hands' ('*Doe het zelf! Neem de oplossing van het woningprobleem in eigen hand*'), the fourteen-page guide provided detailed if rudimentary instructions into how to crack and repair a house (breaking and reinstalling locks, fixing toilets, installing plumbing, repairing roofs and floors, etc.) and all the legal ins and outs that a squatter needed to know. As the book's cover, with its crossed sledgehammer and crowbar made clear, at stake was an 'ethos of political empowerment through direct, productive action' and the 'reskilling' of its readers (and users) as a means towards these ends.[62]

The handbook counterposed technical instructions with detailed information on planning and housing policy in Amsterdam. It was, after all, printed in a shop in Amsterdam's Nieuwmarkt, a neighbourhood in the centre of the city that had been earmarked for a major redevelopment scheme as early as the 1950s. The scheme called for the demolition of much of the neighbourhood's built fabric and the imposition of a major transit corridor lined with high-rise housing and offices. The shop became a key meeting place where growing resistance to the plan was organised. A number of different groups were involved, from preservation-minded residents to local business owners to autonomist Marxists. Some of the more radical elements eventually came together to form the Actiegroep Nieuwmarkt (Nieuwmarkt Action Group) and began squatting empty properties in the neighbourhood as part of an effort to disrupt the city's reconstruction plans.[63]

There were other developments within a wider squatting 'scene'. A number of alternative youth welfare organisations in Amsterdam had come together to set up their own *Kraak-pandendienst* (squatted houses services) to provide support to young people squatting houses. At the same time, a group of former Provos launched a political movement known as the Kabouter (gnomes) whose policy was to squat houses as part of what they laconically called the Oranje Vrijstaat (Orange Freestate). In 1970, the Kabouter combined with Aktie '70, itself a merger of three squatting groups including the WdK, to launch a national day of squatting on 5 May 1970, the twenty-fifth anniversary of the liberation of the Netherlands at the end of the Second World War. A number of buildings were squatted in cities across the country.[64] Most of the squatters were ultimately evicted, though some were successful in securing concessions from the local authorities. A month later, the Kabouter party won over 11 per cent of the vote in city council elections in Amsterdam. The party quickly dissolved, however, in the face of infighting.[65]

If the first major wave of squatting waned with the collapse of the Kabouter party, a 1971 ruling by the Dutch Court of Appeals provided the impetus for the emergence of a new movement. The court ruled that squatters possessed the same rights as tenants and homeowners to domestic peace should they establish residence in a building that had been unoccupied for over a year. Only a court order could legally evict the squatters.[66]

The new legal context prompted a renewed interest in squatting as both a tactic to secure housing and as part of a shared movement to occupy flats and buildings. The actions taken by Surinamese migrants in the district of Bijlmer have, in this context, been largely ignored.[67] New housing estates in the neighbourhood were being squatted in the early 1970s as a response to high rents, overcrowding in guesthouses and racist discrimination within the housing market. In 1974 alone, over one hundred homes were occupied by families with the assistance of the Surinamese Aktiekomité (Surinamese Action Committee) and the Werkgroep Huisvesting Surinamers en Antillianen (Surinamese and Antillean Housing Working Group).[68] The Surinamese squatters secured a number of demands, having adopted a range of tactics including demonstrations, rent strikes, occupations, photo exhibitions and workshops and, while their actions have been traditionally side-lined within the squatter movement, there were clear connections between them and the wider 'scene', especially as events around the Nieuwmarkt began to unfold.[69]

Organised squatting had continued during the early 1970s in the Nieuwmarktbuurt, where local residents and activists were resisting the planned demolition of an eighteenth-century Jewish neighbourhood that had languished since its residents had been deported and killed during the Second World War. The plans included the construction of a subway line through the neighbourhood, the demolition of all the buildings that stood in its path and the displacement of the neighbourhood's predominantly working-class residents who were to be resettled on the city's periphery. However, many neighbourhood residents refused to leave, and linked up with other housing activists including squatters connected to the Actiegroep Nieuwmarkt. Despite widespread disagreements and tensions between local residents and the squatters, a large number of buildings were occupied to protest the development. Hundreds if not thousands of squatters moved in under the banner '*wij blijven hier wonen*' ('we are staying here to live').[70]

Construction plans soon stalled. It afforded the squatters the necessary time and space to assemble a radical infrastructure within the neighbourhood and experiment with new forms of communal living. As one historian has recently concluded, 'squatting had become a means for creating a better world, for building alternative institutions within society ... This was no longer just about the metro; it was now about [the squatters'] homes and their community.'[71] The campaign to save the Nieuwmarkt transformed the efforts undertaken by squatters in Amsterdam into a broad-based movement. *Kraakspereekuren* (KSU, or squatting information hours) were established across the city. They provided valuable assistance to would-be squatters and helped to support the maintenance of occupied houses. In the Nieuwmarkt, a telephone network was set up using wires shot across the rooftops with a bow-and-arrow. The squatters established a phone tree system to summon supporters when needed.[72]

Construction on the metro finally began in 1974, and the squatters were evicted in March 1975 by the city in a major police operation despite the defensive barricades and rooftop bridges that had been erected by the protesters. The buildings

were demolished, their residents displaced. The campaign nevertheless succeeded in forcing the city to scale back its plans for
the redevelopment of the Nieuwmarkt. The proposed motorway
was cancelled and the number of metro stations reduced.[73]

The significance of the squatter movement that emerged around
the struggles in the Nieuwmarktbuurt cannot be underestimated.
Squatting was no longer seen as a symbolic act of protest. It was
a large movement in its own right with a claim-making repertoire and a growing number of supporters across Amsterdam
who saw their actions as part of a struggle to create an alternative infrastructure and a different sense of shared city living.

The so-called 'golden age' of squatting in Amsterdam that
emerged in its wake in the late 1970s has been the subject of
considerable historical attention, not to mention mythologising as *the* squatter movement synonymous with the history of
radical housing politics in the city. Not unlike its counterparts in
Copenhagen and elsewhere in Northern Europe, much of this has
hinged on a heroic 'front stage' retelling of the militant actions
and practices adopted by squatters in defence of their houses.[74]

This is a story that traditionally began with the brutal eviction of the Kinker squat in Amsterdam-West on the corner of
the Nicolaas Beetstraat and Jacob van Lennepstraat in 1978.
The indiscriminate use of violence by the Mobiele Eenheid (Riot
Police) against a group of squatters who were blocking the building prompted many squatters to push for a more confrontational
and militant defence of their movement.[75] This was a position
advocated, in particular, by a group of 'political' squatters based
in the Staatsliedenbuurt district.

This new defiance was put to the test on 26 October 1979,
when the Groote Keijser, a series of six squatted offices on the
Keijsersgracht, received their eviction notice. Up to that point,
the complex had a reputation as a party squat and most of the
residents complied with the notice. Ten, however, refused to
leave and barricaded themselves into the complex. They were
soon joined by their militant Staatsliedenbuurt 'comrades' who
set about refunctioning the squat as a defensive space. New

reinforced barricades were installed, while the occupants stock-piled paint bombs and Molotov cocktails in anticipation of their planned eviction. Training classes in physical fitness and self-defence were held. The squatters also began to broadcast from a pirate radio station in the basement of the house (known as Vrije Keijser or Free Keijser).[76]

The eviction never materialised as the mayor of Amsterdam, Wim Polak, decided that it was too dangerous to do so. In January 1980, the city bought the building and turned it into a housing complex for young people. The measures adopted to defend the Groote Keijser were nevertheless seen as a success and helped to strengthen the movement's increasingly strident militancy.

Within a month, the clash that everyone had been expecting finally arrived when a group of squatters reoccupied a previously evicted house on the Vondelstraat. Barricades were quickly assembled and the police were pushed back when they attempted to clear the house. A standoff ensued, and when negotiations between the squatters and the city council broke off, the authorities sent in the police once again.

The operation began in the early morning of 3 March 1980, as riot officers moved in on the squatters supported by eighteen units from the Dutch military police. Helicopters flew over the house dropping flyers warning the squatters to 'stay in the house' and that the police may be forced to use their firearms. A number of tanks were also brought in to demolish the barricades. The squatters' defences were finally cleared, though the property was left as it was.[77] In the aftermath, riots broke out across Amsterdam and the council had to backtrack. The squatters' initial demands were met and they were allowed to occupy the building.[78]

The events on the Vondelstraat, and the Coronation Riots that followed in April 1980, were key events in establishing the movement's self-identity as a radical housing movement. 'It forged a strong collective identity among the squatters,' as one historian later concluded, 'knitting diverse groups into a unified, coherent subject.'[79] By the end of 1981, the number of squatters in Amsterdam had risen to over 9,000. The movement's 'front stage' seemingly flourished as numerous new squats were set up, producing a radical infrastructure that also included cafés, bars, infoshops, bookstores, cinemas, bicycle repairs shops, clinics and gallery spaces. There were fifteen newspapers, several printing presses and the Vrije Keyser radio station. As was the case in Copenhagen and many other cities at the time, squatters were closely associated with a number of radical political movements (anti-Apartheid, anti-nuclear energy, anti-fascism, etc.).[80]

And yet, the movement's emphasis on militancy and violence led, just as quickly, to its decline and unravelling, especially after the eviction of the Lucky Luijk squat in 1982 in which an empty city tram was set on fire by a group of squatters. 'Old-style squatting was dead,' recalled one former activist, 'and its place was something I couldn't support.'[81] The 1985 death of Hans Kok, a twenty-three-year-old squatter, in police custody only served to further rattle a movement that had increasingly retreated into the Staatsliedenbuurt and had began to question what and for whom it was for.[82]

Tensions between the Staatsliedenbuurt 'political' faction – later known as the PVK (Politieke Vleugal van de Kraakbeweging or the Political Wing of the Squatters' Movement) and other less confrontational 'cultural' squatters from across the city also began to take its toll on the 'back stage' of the movement.[83] A civil war soon broke between the PVK and the wider scene. In at least one case, a squatter was kidnapped by the PVK and threatened with torture. Fights were commonplace and when the leader of the PVK faction was hospitalised in 1988, support for the group fell apart as did the wider movement on which it staked its increasingly romanticised identity.

There were, of course, other factors that contributed to the decline of the squatter 'movement' in Amsterdam in the 1980s. In many respects, squatters in Amsterdam were remarkably successful in propagating an alternative view of the city that led, in the end, to the construction of social housing, the preservation of existing stock and the democratisation of the planning process.[84] Housing was decommodified as thousands of houses were purchased by the state and placed under the control of local municipalities and housing associations. New rent controls were also implemented through a points system (*puntensysteem*) that was based on a property's use value.[85]

By the early 1990s, these developments were once again under threat as the city began to adopt a range of austerity measures that led to cutbacks in the provision of social housing and the dismantling of the system of subsidies and regulation that had only been established a few years later. The first sustained signs of gentrification also appeared during this period as part of a state-sponsored process of private reinvestment in Amsterdam's inner city, neighbourhoods paradoxically preserved by the actions of squatters.[86] New temporary tenure types such as anti-squat (*anti-kraak*) guardians grew rapidly as well. Such live-in guardians 'protected' properties – often spaces otherwise considered unsuitable for rent – on a temporary basis for a licence fee. Guardians lacked the legal rights that tenants possessed while acting as *de facto* caretakers, cleaners and security guards without ever being paid.[87]

Despite these tendencies, not to mention the hagiographic efforts of many squatters, their 'movement' did not end, so to speak, in the 1980s even if that was the view held by many of its protagonists. Geert Lovink and Jojo van der Spek, writers for the squatter magazine *Bluf!*, wrote in 1986 about the pressing need to distinguish between movement and what they referred to as *the* movement. The latter, in their eyes, was represented by the violent confrontations at the Groote Keijser and the Vondelstraat and the various failures that followed in their wake. In contrast, they elevated a sense of movement over the movement. Movement is movements, they argued, a process that encompassed the various different oppositional practices and subcultures that were, in some way, connected to squatting and the development of the extra-parliamentary left in the Netherlands from the mid-1980s onwards.[88]

Squatting in Amsterdam thus continued uninterrupted until its eventual criminalisation in 2010 (the law had been tightened in 1987 and 1993 respectively), though it now derived its animus less from the claim-making practices of a tightly bound group of militant activists than from a wide range of cultural, social and political motivations.[89] The historian Eric Duivenvoorden estimates that between 1964 and 1999 up to 70,000 people squatted in Amsterdam. More recent estimates are harder to come by. Some squatted out of a commitment to a movement, others did so to create an alternative form of city living. Some turned to squatting for fun. Many had to in order to meet basic housing needs. There were artist squats, vegan squats, feminist squats and punk squats. Some of these spaces still survive, though in most cases they have now been legalised.[90]

In the end, whether it be in Amsterdam, Copenhagen or a number of other major European cities, it was in the 1960s and 1970s that groups of young people began to squat houses in groups. They often saw their actions as part of a wider movement that, on the one hand, challenged housing inequality while creating, on the other hand, new forms of social organisation. As a movement, squatters adopted a range of practices, tactics and values that played a central role in the identities they assumed and the infrastructures they built. In the case of Copenhagen and Amsterdam, these were (and are) histories that have undoubtedly shaped the recent development of both cities. But these were also histories with their own biases, blind spots and exclusions that often told us more about what their participants believed and who they wanted to be rather than what they actually accomplished. In order to think of squatting as a radical urban social movement, we must return – for better or for worse – to what squatters actually *did*: the terms and tactics they deployed, and the ideas and spaces they created.

4

'The Struggle Over Housing Continues': Urban Squatting and Violent Confrontation in Frankfurt and Hamburg

Macht kaputt, was euch kaputt macht! (Destroy what destroys you!)

Ton Steine Scherben[1]

The stones that hit your head are from the house you pulled down.

Cover of *Wir Wollen Alles*[2]

At exactly 3:47 in the early morning of 23 May 1973, a newly formed police commando unit stormed into a 130-year-old apartment block on Ekhofstraße in the Hamburg neighbourhood of Hohenfelde. The building had been occupied since April by a group of over seventy squatters who were protesting against the plans of a local housing association to demolish a number of apartments in the neighbourhood and replace them with large nineteen-storey flats that included over 450 luxury units.

The long-term residents of the neighbourhood had been 'decanted' to other suburbs of the city, and many buildings remained empty or had been rented out to students on short-term contracts. Remaining residents formed a tenants initiative (Mieterinitiative Hohenfelde) to lobby against the actions of Bewobau, a subsidiary of the national housing organisation Neue Heimat. In the residents' eyes, neighbourhood 'regeneration' merely served as a pretext for higher rents, property speculation and widespread demolition. Not only, as they pointed out, did Bewobau organise 'thugs' to vandalise empty buildings and make them uninhabitable, in at least one case residents were threatened with large fines (1,000 DM) for every day that they remained beyond their scheduled eviction.[3]

Despite a year-long campaign, the tenants' initiative was met with official intransigence. Petitions, letters and flyers made little impression. In response, a group of activists including students, apprentices and workers decided to take matters into their own hands, and on 19 April 1973 an empty house at Ekhofstraße 39 was squatted. The occupants proclaimed that they wished to live in the house and that there was space for others to join them, including migrant workers and their families as well as runaways and local unemployed youth. The squatters envisaged the formation of an autonomous self-determined youth centre and an office that would provide medical assistance and legal aid.[4] As one squatter later recalled, the occupation brought together activists from a wide range of political backgrounds and groupings, from traditional Trotskyites to autonomist Marxists. There were runaways as well as youth associated with the local 'Rocker' scene. Others were connected to the anti-psychiatry movement, and the Heidelberg Socialist Patients' Collective was a major point of reference. Many, in turn, had links to other militant groups, including the Rote Armee Faktion (Red Army Faction or RAF).[5]

In the beginning, the squatters received considerable support and solidarity from the local residents. Meetings were organised to coordinate activities in the neighbourhood while a youth centre and office was established. At the same time, however, the occupation was widely demonised in the local press. The tabloid Springer Press unsurprisingly took the lead in the vilification as the squatters were impugned as 'masked men', 'gangsters', 'terrorists', 'criminals', 'violent offenders' and 'armed vigilantes'. When, in response, the occupants of the house challenged what they saw as a gross misrepresentation of their actions, demands and desires, they also drew attention to the almost constant harassment that they faced from the police. Residents, sympathisers and visitors alike were repeatedly stopped and searched as they entered and left the squat. Many were taken to the local police station where they were forced to leave their fingerprints.[6] The squatters responded, in turn, with 'organised militancy'. As violent confrontations with the authorities escalated, existing alliances and solidarities with the wider community began to crumble in the face of a near permanent police presence.[7]

It is against this backdrop that the police began their plans to evict the squatters. In the early hours of 23 May 1973, the area surrounding the house was sealed off by over 600 police officers. A then newly formed commando unit entered into the squat. The Mobiles Einsatzkommando (MEK) was set up in Hamburg in the wake of the 1972 attack at the Munich Olympics, and this was to be their first official operation. The commandos, equipped with machine guns, entered the squat firing indiscriminately according to a number of witnesses. This was later described in a slick promotional video produced by the police as 'three warning shots'.[8] The same video lauded the professionalism of the operation which lasted only eight minutes despite 'heavy resistance' from the squatters. The Hamburg Senator for the Department of the Interior, Heinz Ruhnau, described the efforts of the commandos as a 'testament to the courage, high level of training and leadership'. The Springer Press, in turn, celebrated the successful operation describing the 'storming of the house of *polit-rockers*' as a 'lightening action (*Blitzaktion*)'.

The squatters painted a rather different picture, however. In their eyes, the eviction was yet another example of the 'usual police brutality'. They described how the police only gained entry with the aid of an undercover informant. As they stormed the building, the occupants were viciously attacked. Those who did not immediately respond to the police were kicked and beaten before being handcuffed and transported to the local police station. At least two of the squatters were injured when the police commandos opened fire.[9]

In the end, more than seventy squatters were arrested; thirty-three were charged under article §129 of the German Criminal Code for their alleged 'membership in or support of a criminal organisation'. This was the first time that this section of the code was used under such circumstances. The majority were soon released, though four remained in custody and were later convicted. They eventually received sentences ranging between one year and fifteen months despite having already spent the better part of a year in detention.[10]

The brutal clampdown on the Ekhofstraße squatters represented a watershed moment in the history of housing activism in Hamburg. The activist and historian Karl Heinz Roth described it as a 'traumatic experience' that precipitated the immediate collapse of the struggle against urban renewal in Hohenfelde, and a wider crisis among various leftist groups in Hamburg. It also prompted many activists to go underground in search of other more militant organisations. As Karl-Heinz Dellwo, a former occupant of the Ekhofstraße squat recently pointed out, '[the house] was the last large militant occupation in the 1970s in West Germany'. Ten of the squatters later joined the RAF including Dellwo, Christa Eckes, Berhard Rößner and Stefan Wisniewski. Another three became members of another militant group, the June 2nd Movement.[11]

Militancy and violent resistance played a central role in shaping the early history of squatting in West Germany; a history of protest and resistance that quickly evolved into an intense struggle over urban space and the right to housing. What became known in the early 1970s as the *Häuserkampf* (housing war) was, for many activists, an undeniably violent experience. On the one hand, it anatomised the structural violence of late capitalism and its relationship to processes of uneven urban transformation.[12] On the other hand, the violence generated by such processes of abstraction – in this case recurring cycles of creative destruction and accumulation by dispossession – were acutely *felt* by many ordinary Germans. These were experiences that generated feelings of widespread anonymity and anxiety, but were equally marked by the elementary brutalities that accompanied forced eviction and expulsion.[13] If this prompted many West German squatters actively to return violence or pay it back in kind through a form of *counter-violence*, it also encouraged a wider appreciation of the political challenges and possibilities posed by the problem of violence in each of its forms.[14]

The *Häuserkampf* in West Germany found its most prominent expression in Hamburg and Frankfurt in the early 1970s,
only to be revived in Hamburg once again during the mid-1980s.
While West Berlin has always occupied a privileged place in the
imagination of German activists, the history of squatting in West
Germany encompassed a far more expansive geography of opposition, resistance and autonomy. Both Hamburg and Frankfurt
were governed by the left-leaning Social Democrats who, in each
case, attempted to balance a progressive reform-oriented agenda
with an ambitious programme of urban redevelopment. Both
cities also remained central to the ongoing development of the
anti-authoritarian Left in West Germany, especially in the wake
of the student movement which had all but collapsed by the end
of the 1960s.[15]

The transformation of the New Left after the 'crisis year' of
1968 ushered in a political landscape that was marked, in particular, by a 'new focus on workers in general and young workers in
particular'.[16] A wide range of political groupings emerged including Marxist-Leninist and/or Maoist cadre parties, the so-called
K-Gruppen. These parties were accompanied by the emergence
of 'rank-and-file groups' (*'Basisgruppen'*) as many young students sought to forge new political solidarities and mobilise
working-class youth.[17] While the *K-Gruppen* were largely
modelled on orthodox Marxist-Leninist lines, other groups
favoured an 'undogmatic' approach to political action. The
'Spontis' as they were known, advocated an anti-authoritarian
form of politics that privileged spontaneity and contingency and
they drew inspiration, in this context, from their counterparts in
France and especially Italy.[18] The Spontis formed loosely organised collectives that often worked in volatile communities within
schools, local neighbourhoods and the workplace. Sponti activists played a crucial role in the formation of 'Factory Project
Groups' (*'Betriebsprojektgruppen'*) that attempted to organise
with and support immigrant guest workers, many of whom were
Italian.[19] These groups scored some notable local successes, such
as the October 1971 action at the Opel factory in Rüsselheim

and the August 1973 strike at the Ford factory in Cologne.[20] The Spontis and other anti-authoritarian activists sought to translate these minor victories into other campaigns, including the struggle for housing as it opened up new possibilities of mobilisation that were hitherto impossible within the factory.

The first space to be squatted was unexpectedly in the West German city of Cologne where, in 1970, a group of protesters occupied a block on Roßstraße in the working-class district of Ehrenfeld.[21] The 'Social-Pedagogical Special Measures Cologne' ('*Sozialpädagogische Sondermassnahmen Köln*', or SSK) was established as an alternative autonomous youth centre that fought neighbourhood gentrification while working with local juveniles from youth homes and patients from psychiatric clinics. Forced to close almost immediately, it prompted a group of youth and their social workers to occupy the block on Roßstraße.

The turn to occupation was, in many respects, a direct product of the dissolution of the German SDS (Socialist German Student League) in the autumn of 1969. In its wake, new alliances developed between students, apprentices and other young workers as activists redirected their attention to the neighbourhood and concrete local struggles from youth politics to migrant housing, homelessness to urban regeneration.[22] The right to *occupy* space became, in this context, a key tactic of protest as both a means to achieve specific goals and as the expression of a wider desire to reclaim the city for alternative political ends.

Despite local support the activists were soon evicted, though a new occupation was initiated in an empty villa in Cologne-Marienburg a few months later. As the new occupants proclaimed, 'we believe that the current situation, which is well-known, is unacceptable. In Cologne, there are over 1,700 people stuck vegetating in homeless shelters including 1,000 youth who have no home and are increasingly criminalised by the circumstances in which they are forced to live.'[23]

The spaces established by the SSK quickly became an important destination for young people fleeing the repressive institutionalisation of youth homes. In Cologne, the SSK was briefly recognised by the local administration. The relationship, however, soured and it was only in an independent capacity that the SSK was able to draw attention to the poor conditions that plagued many local psychiatric institutions and youth homes.[24] At stake here, from a broader perspective, were a series of struggles over the politics of institutionalisation that were, at the same time, part of a wider historical current of movements.[25] A whole host of institutions (prisons, clinics, youth homes, asylums, etc.) were singled out and the struggles around these spaces, as one historian concluded, represented 'one of the signature motifs of the radicalism of the early 1970s'. For many young people, this was not simply a struggle over the right to create and manage their own youth centres but a bigger (and often violent) battle to save, transform and hold 'living space' in the face of urban regeneration and against the predations of speculators, developers and urban planners.[26]

By 1972, the campaign for self-administered youth centres counted over 500 groups across West Germany. The number rose to 2,200 in 1975.[27] There were important centres in a number of cities. If these centres highlighted a desire for reimagining the city as a source of radical possibility, the turn to occupation and squatting was also increasingly shaped by a need for basic affordable housing and infrastructure. The widespread squatting of houses in Berlin, Frankfurt, Cologne and Hamburg in the early 1970s was adopted by a number of leftist groups and, in Frankfurt and Hamburg in particular, it developed into a broad struggle over the right to housing and to a different vision of shared city life.

This was a vision that ran counter to the prevailing focus in many West German cities that had turned in the 1960s to urban renewal programmes promising regeneration, development and growth. Often these plans – in Berlin, Frankfurt, Hamburg and elsewhere – came under sharp criticism from planners, architects and grassroots neighbourhood organisations who argued that 'renewal' merely served as a pretext for higher rents, displacement and widespread demolition. Many inner-city residents were simply 'decanted' to newly built satellite towns on the outskirts of cities and housed in anonymous 'concrete silos' ('*Betonsilos*'). Local urban renewal agents favoured, in turn, the demolition of older housing as they were able to apply for major federal subsidies and tax exemptions to support new-build developments. In the case of owners, there was little incentive to undertake even the most basic of renovations when they could simply 'wait' for renewal plans to be implemented.

While architect-led groups such as Aktion 507 were already agitating in Berlin as early as 1968, it was in Frankfurt perhaps more than anywhere else where widespread speculation served as a catalyst for a new housing movement.[28] The movement's main focus was the city's Westend whose proximity to a new financial district made it an ideal target for developers. By the end of the 1960s, speculators had already purchased many of the neighbourhood's old *Gründerzeit* villas. Evictions and demolitions were commonplace as rents soared and thousands of long-time residents moved out.[29] Many remaining homes were left empty and those that were occupied were run down and left in need of serious repair. Landlords increasingly turned to migrant families who were crowded into homes in poor condition. In some cases, up to twenty people were living in a single room without any heat and little running water.[30]

At the same time, investors pressured the local Social Democratic Party of Germany (SPD) administration to extend commercial development into the Westend. They did not, however, come up with an official plan but rather an informal (and illegal) model – a blueprint of creative destruction – that focused on high-rise office development along five axes that cut through the Westend along traditional residential roads: Mainzer Landstraße, Kettenhofweg, Bockenheimer Landstraße, Oberlindau and Reuterweg. Developers quickly bought up land along these axes, receiving upwards of a billion marks in loans from seven banks including the Hessische Landesbank which had strong connections to the SPD in Frankfurt and the state of Hessen.[31]

In 1969, local residents formed a citizens' initiative, the Aktionsgemeinschaft Westend e.V (AGW). The AGW organised demonstrations and began a campaign for the 'preservation of a mixed functional, architectural and social structure in Frankfurt-Westend'.[32] They also called for a halt to the expulsion of residents and a commitment to retaining, where possible, the neighbourhood's older housing stock. However, little progress was made and student groups active in the area soon turned to a more radical repertoire of contention.

In the early hours of the morning of 19 September 1970, they linked up with a group of homeless families, migrant workers and apprentices to occupy an empty house at Eppsteiner Straße 47 in the Westend. 'Houses,' they proclaimed, 'belong to whoever is living in them' (*'Die Wohnungen gehören denen, die darin wohnen'*). The squatters distributed flyers around the Westend highlighting the reasons behind their action, and the occupation soon became a major flashpoint in wider debates about housing in the city.[33]

The squatting of other houses at Liebigstraße 20 and Cornelius Straße 24 followed a month later. The initial local response to the occupations was positive. They were generally viewed in the press and by many politicians as a legitimate means through which to protest and challenge the abysmal conditions of housing in the city.[34] Many of the squatters were linked to so-called rank-and-file activists groups (*Basisgruppen*) that emerged as the student movement faltered in the late 1960s. As new solidarities were formed with apprentices, workers and migrants, it is perhaps not surprising that the number of squats in the Westend rose and, within a few months, included houses on Bockheimer Landstraße (94/96 and 111/113), Niedenau (46, 51, 57, 50), Freiherr-von-Stein-Straße (18), Heidestraße (11/13), Schubertstraße (27) and Siesmayerstraße (3 and 6).[35]

The mood quickly changed in Frankfurt, as the rising number of occupations became part of a wider national movement against housing speculation, rent hikes and unfettered urban redevelopment. Many of the occupiers found common cause with an

anti-authoritarian Sponti scene that promised a further politi-
cisation of everyday life and a commitment to autonomy and
self-management. While groups such as Revolutionärer Kampf
(Revolutionary Struggle) in Frankfurt, Arbeiterkampf (Workers'
Struggle) in Cologne and Proletarische Front (Proletarian Front)
in Hamburg and Bremen were active in workplace struggles
across West Germany, organising around housing, living conditions, rent strikes and squatting offered new ways of scaling
up their actions. In an article in the journal *Wir Wollen Alles*,
members of the group Proletarische Front, argued that:

> To squat means to destroy the capitalist plot for our neigh-
> borhoods. It means to refuse rent and the capitalist shoe box
> structure. It means to build communes and community centers. It
> means to recognise the social potential of each neighborhood. It
> means to overcome helplessness. In squatting and in rent strikes
> we can find the pivotal point for the fight against capital outside
> the factories.[36]

By the autumn of 1971, a year after the first occupation, the
local administration was pushing for a ban on any new squats.
This position was reinforced, in the eyes of authorities, by the
violent events surrounding the eviction of squatters from a house
at Grüneburgweg 113 on 29 September 1971. As squatters and
their supporters formed a human chain around the house, bottles
were thrown at the police, who retaliated with a baton charge.
This was followed by some of the worst street fighting Frankfurt
had seen since 1968, resulting in over forty-two injuries.

In the aftermath of the eviction, the Action Committee for the
squatters warned of a 'less considerate' approach in the future,
while the police criticised the disproportionately violent tactics
adopted, in their view, by the squatters.[37] As a consequence,
city officials adopted a more conciliatory tone as elections
loomed in 1972. A new directive against the 'misuse' of property
(*Verbot der Zweckentfremdung von Wohnraum*) was published
in July 1972, while attempts were made to negotiate with the
squatters.[38]

While some squatters, many of whom were students, were willing to sign 'transitional use' contracts for the right to occupy buildings slated for demolition, others embraced the Sponti scene and looked to squatting as a more permanent form of political action. 'We will continue to occupy buildings,' the squatters insisted, '[and] declare war on a capitalist system that allows empty houses to remain empty' (*um dem kapitalischen System den Kampf anzusagen, dass es ermöglicht, dass leere Häuser leerstehen*).[39]

As the protests and occupations escalated, new tactics were also adopted by members of Revolutionärer Kampf working in solidarity with migrants involved in the wider housing movement. They turned to rent strikes, a tactic they borrowed from Italy and radical groups such as Lotta Continua and Unione Inquilini who had become active in Frankfurt at the time. The rent strikes were ultimately unsuccessful as the various activist groupings in Frankfurt were unable to deal with the rising number of court cases, which reached 150 by 1973. Only five cases were successful, amid growing tension between local activists and the wider migrant community.[40] As one commentator later argued, the paternalistic treatment of migrant activists only exacerbated the growing splits within the housing movement in Frankfurt.[41]

These were splits that also centred on the enduring question of violence and militancy. For many activists in the anti-authoritarian scene, the legitimacy of 'counter-violence' in the face of statist repression and police brutality was already well-established. As early as 1968, the West German journal *konkret* published a piece entitled 'Violence' (*'Gewalt'*) by a collective that included Rudi Dutschke, Bahman Nirumand, Hans Magnus Enzensberger and Peter Schneider. The collective not only argued that defensive violence may be necessary, but that such resistance must be grounded within transnational struggles against the 'permanent violence' of capitalism and the disagreeable materialities of colonialism.[42] While the collective's appeal to the legitimacy of 'counter-violence' was shaped by wider protest geographies, it was also a response to more immediate circumstances. As the historian Timothy Brown has argued, the tabloid press in West Germany 'may have blamed violence on demonstrators, but there is ample documentary evidence that, for a surprisingly long time, it was students who were overwhelmingly on the receiving end of violence'. 'It is clear,' according to Brown, 'that the left's attempt to come to grips with the prospect of violence ... was one it was forced into by the nature of the state's response to protest.'[43]

The response inevitably escalated into 'counter-violence' as imagined by Dutschke, Nirumand and the rest of the Berlin *Redaktionskollektive*. For some, the use of violence became an end in and of itself, as was the case with the RAF and other militant groups. There was never a direct line of continuity, however, as some have suggested, between these groups and the wider anti-authoritarian scene.[44] The RAF did not enjoy anything approaching universal support on the Left. Its actions were widely criticised and were increasingly viewed by many as part of a deeply personal and indeed 'private war against the government'.[45] The question of revolutionary violence and resistance nevertheless remained a subject of fierce debate shaped by ongoing struggles over the right to imagine and establish alternative political and social spaces. After all, as the German anarcho-pacifist magazine, *Graswurzelrevolution*, concluded in 1973:

> The society in which we live is defined through its violence, which can be felt daily in various new ways: whether in school or at university, through ideological indoctrination and the drive to succeed, whether it is at work ... whether it is in free time, through the general increase in consumer prices and the absence of social institutions (kindergartens, playgrounds, schools, health centres, etc.) or through the destruction of the environment.[46]

It is ultimately in this context that the early squatting scene in Frankfurt and Hamburg and elsewhere in West Germany must be seen. In Frankfurt, the first wave of occupations and rent strikes drew attention to the various forms of violence – both objective and subjective – that characterised the city's housing market. The Frankfurt branch of Unione Inquilini documented a long list of 'violent' methods adopted by the city's landlords, from rent hikes and forced evictions to other illegal forms of bullying and mobbing that included turning off the water, walling up windows and doorways, disconnecting phone lines, vandalising properties and repeatedly abusing and threatening tenants.[47] It is perhaps not surprising, therefore, that for many militant squatters the very nature of their struggle had shifted to the defence of buildings that they had already occupied. This included, most notably, a house at Kettenhofweg 51. The house was first squatted in February 1972, and by March of the following year it was threatened with imminent eviction.

As the putative date of their eviction approached, the Kettenhofweg squatters and their supporters in the Frankfurt *Häuserrat* – a council organised by the squatters – came to the conclusion that a letter-writing campaign and countless press conferences had done little to raise public consciousness or stall plans for the redevelopment of the Westend. In response, they staged a 'go-in' on 19 March 1973, at a meeting of Frankfurt's Building Committee chaired by the city's mayor Rudi Arndt.[48] The squatters broke into the meeting to demonstrate that they were 'not prepared to accept any decision made over the heads of those affected and in the interests of capital and speculators'.[49] A statement was read out by the squatters. 'Let us be under no illusions', they proclaimed. 'What takes place here and in this committee is about nothing more than a clarification of how capital's interests are distributed ... We came here to show that the days are gone where you could freely do what you wanted serving the interests of finance while leaving others disenfranchised.'[50] As the squatters wrapped up their impromptu statement, scuffles broke out. According to the local press, a series of paintings were defaced while a plate with four dinner rolls was reported missing.[51]

In the days that followed, the campaign of criminalisation in the press only intensified. The Kettenhof squatters adopted, in turn, a range of interdictory measures to help secure the house and protect its occupants from any attempt to evict them. As a pamphlet produced by the *Häuserrat* argued: 'the struggle against the destruction of living space, against profit and exploitation in basic life circumstances cannot be carried out at the level of critical theory, but *only* at the level of a revolutionary strategy'. These assertions may seem bold and startling, but they reflected a form of direct political action that increasingly sought to translate an understanding of 'revolutionary theory' into a tangible 'sensory experience'.[52] 'Translation', in the case of the Kettenhofweg 51, depended on a series of basic defence tactics that were adopted by the residents. Following instructions set out in the *Handbook for Squatters* (*Handbuch für Hausbesetzer*), the residents constructed a series of makeshift wooden barricades that pinned all the house's doors shut from behind. Windows were boarded up and other defensive tactics were adopted, including elaborate barbed wire structures known as 'Spanish riders'. Additional obstacles were placed in the house's stairwell and a scrapped car was left in front of the house blocking access to the entrance.[53] At the same time, mobile self-defence units known as *Putzgruppe* were set up by the activists to help protect squats from police intimidation and eviction. They included future German foreign minister and vice chancellor, Joschka Fischer, who was captured in a famous photograph clubbing a police officer during one such confrontation in March 1973.[54]

The Kettenhof squatters were also successful in resisting an attempt by city officials and the police to evict them on 28 March 1973. A court-appointed bailiff appeared in the morning as the squatters readied their defences. The bailiff was unable, however, to gain entry and for over an hour the squatters waited for the police to arrive. Around 11:00 am, a spontaneous demonstration began while a group of squatters remained in the house. Hundreds of activists wound their way through the city's main streets only to be confronted by the police as they entered the Zeil, Frankfurt's main shopping street.

In the fighting that ensued, the police resorted to the use of tear gas and water cannons. Protesters were chased into shops and brutally attacked. Barricades were hastily erected across Kettenhofweg as the protesters engaged officers in a series of hit and run attacks across the city's Westend. The police responded by lashing out indiscriminately. A number of bystanders were assaulted and, at one point, a pistol was drawn and a shot was fired, though this was later redacted from official reports. One eyewitness described how he was set upon by a group of police officers who beat him senseless even though he offered no resistance. He was arrested and taken to a local police station where he asked for a doctor and a lawyer. One officer responded by saying that 'they will come but only after we're finished with you, you scum'. Another witness, a city doctor, described how a well-known press photographer had her hand broken by the police as she attempted to take photographs documenting police operations. The offending officer disappeared before the doctor could take down his badge number. In the end, a number of protesters, bystanders and police officers were injured and dozens of arrests were made on what became known as 'bloody Wednesday'. Kettenhofweg 51 had not, however, been cleared. Another smaller demonstration took place a few days later with a similarly violent outcome.[55]

If the tabloid press impugned and exaggerated the actions adopted by the squatters, many other newspapers also criticised the heavy-handed tactics used by the police. This did not, however, stop them from regrouping and, in the early hours of the morning of 4 April, a police operation to evict the occupants of Kettenhofweg 51 finally began. Over 700 officers were mobilised as the phone lines between occupied houses were cut and the surrounding area was sealed off. A bailiff entered the house at 4:09 am accompanied by a team of police commandos. To their surprise, however, they did not encounter any resistance and the ten occupiers were peacefully led out to be processed at the local police station. They were released five hours later without being charged and returned to a house whose interior had, in the intervening hours, been completely stripped and demolished by the landlord and a team of hired labourers. The squatters had to sift through the debris and wreckage to locate many of their belongings.[56]

A few days later, a solidarity march was held in Frankfurt with over 4,000 participants, including a small militant faction who led the protest through the city. They dressed in black and wore motorcycle helmets as well as scarfs to cover their faces.[57] There were a number of scuffles with the police that later were used by the media to ratchet up their criticism of the growing violence adopted by the squatters. For the local press, Frankfurt's remaining squatted houses were little more than 'strong points' for 'waging civil war' in West Germany's big cities. In the eyes of many activists, however, the question of direct action and the squatters' own fixation on militant defence was beginning to overshadow other political possibilities. Particular attention was drawn to the city's migrant communities, where tensions between the moderate conciliatory stance adopted by Unione Inquilini and the radical position advocated by Lotta Continua and many of the squatters connected to Revolutionärer Kampf were undermining efforts to sustain and support the city's floundering rent strike movement.[58] For the former Maoist activist Gerd Koenen, the struggle had if anything been reduced, as he later (and rather sardonically) recalled, to nothing more than 'a system of fortified bastions which defiantly flew red and black flags as well as torn banners displaying a raised fist'.[59]

Against this backdrop of rising militancy and violence, the *Häuserkampf* ultimately began to fracture and unravel. In the case of Hamburg, the eviction of squatters on Ekhofstraße in May 1973 broke the back of the movement in the city.[60] It was only the rapid development of the anti-nuclear movement in response to the planned construction of nuclear power plants across West Germany, including one near Brokdorf-Wewelsfleht, that brought new life to the radical scene within Hamburg in the late 1970s.[61] In Frankfurt, the housing struggle limped on for another year, though the squatters were ultimately unable to defend buildings that they had occupied.

On 21 February 1974, one of the last major squats, a series of houses at the corner of Bockenheimer Landstraße and Schumannstraße ('Block'), was cleared in a surprise police operation involving over 2,500 officers. The buildings were immediately demolished and the large demonstrations that ensued saw some of the worst street violence in West Germany since 1968. Over 200 activists and seventy-seven police officers were injured in the protests that took place on 24 February 1974. A further 192 arrests were made.[62]

The Frankfurt Häuserrat defended the actions of the squatters in a special issue of the radical Sponti magazine, *Wir wollen alles*. As they argued, 'violence, or more precisely violent resistance ... has never, for the Häuserrat and all who are in solidarity with its goals, been an end in and of itself (*niemals Selbstzweck gewesen*)'. 'The first squats [in Frankfurt],' they insisted, 'were not hell-bent on conjuring up a battle with the authorities, but were carried out because affordable housing was urgently needed.'[63]

For many including Daniel Cohn-Bendit, then a leader of Revolutionärer Kampf, now a prominent member of the European Parliament, the fault lines were far starker. 'You have to decide,' he concluded, 'either you are on the side of those who commit torture [the police] or you are on the side of those who get tortured [the squatters].'[64]

The spectre of criminalisation and the problem of violence, more generally, appeared to many as the cause for the fracturing and splintering of the anti-authoritarian left in the early 1970s in Frankfurt and West Germany. Some Frankfurt-based activists, as in the case of Hamburg, embraced the militancy of groups such as the RAF and the June 2nd Movements. Others increasingly looked to the formation of new tactics as a source of renewed action and solidarity. Nevertheless, for much of the 1970s radical politics in West Germany was unable to resolve the problem of violence and what the historian Jeremy Varon has called 'the importance of being militant'.[65]

In the end, despite their success in preventing the demolition of many old Gründerzeit buildings in Frankfurt's Westend, the

Sponti scene in the city quickly dissolved into a range of small splinter groups. At the same time, the violent actions of the RAF and other groups only intensified, though the period also bore witness to a new landscape of alternative practices, which, in turn, promoted the cultivation of a much wider range of activist spaces: bars, bookshops, cafés, kindergartens, music venues, rural communes, workshops, etc.[66]

By the end of the decade, these developments had triggered a new major wave of squatting, first in Freiburg, than in West Berlin, and which served, in turn, as a major source of inspiration for housing activists across the country, most notably perhaps in Hamburg where low-income residents struggled to find affordable housing in the face of rampant property speculation and uneven urban redevelopment. Local authorities were afraid that the new movement might gain a foothold in the city, prompting Hamburg's Senate to adopt the so-called '24 hour rule', according to which no house in Hamburg was to be occupied for more than twenty-four hours. All subsequent attempts at open occupation were brutally suppressed by the police.

Activists were forced therefore to adopt new 'quiet' or 'covert' squatting that drew little if any attention to the spaces they occupied.[67] In the autumn of 1981, a number of empty houses on Hafenstraße and Bernhard-Nocht-Straße were, in this way, squatted. The squatters quickly went to work on the city-owned houses that had, with the exception of a few older tenants and students, been empty for up to ten years and were badly run down. The squatters represented a broad cross-section of the city's youth. They included students, apprentices, artists and musicians but also runaways, sailors and unemployed labourers some of whom worked intermittently in the city's docks.[68]

The actions of the squatters, while largely undetected, were known to city officials who were unable to distinguish between the remaining tenants and the squatters who went public with their actions in February 1982 in an open letter to the senator responsible for housing, Volker Lange. While 'the new residents of Hafenstraße and Bernhard-Nocht-Straße' were threatened with immediate eviction, the squatters restated their own demands, insisting that there would be no expulsions and that negotiations should take place over the use and self-administration of the houses.[69] With a local election looming and fearing the outbreak of riots, the ruling SPD backed down. In June 1982, eighteen days before the election, the squatters were granted a 'status quo promise' ('*Status quo-Zustand*') and the right to stay until the end of 1986. There would be no evictions on the condition that the houses be examined by building inspectors who were to produce a detailed report outlining the costs for repair and restoration. The costs would, in turn, serve as the basis for the 'temporary use' contracts issued to the occupying squatters. Needless to say, many in the movement remained suspicious of the city's proposals.[70] The results of the survey were made public in July 1982, and showed that the cost of renovation was far less than the proposed redevelopment of the area under the auspices of the city-owned housing association SAGA.[71]

The houses at Hafenstraße quickly became a centre of the autonomous, anti-fascist and anti-imperialist Left in West Germany. They played an important role within a broad landscape of protest that connected the anti-nuclear and peace movements with solidarity support networks for RAF hunger strikers as well as other anti-imperialist initiatives. An anti-fascist centre – the Störtebeker Zentrum, named after a fourteenth-century North Sea pirate – was set up by the squatters as part of repairs to stabilise the foundations of one of the houses.[72] Beginning in 1986, the occupants were also responsible for the organisation of the Hafentage, one of the largest gatherings of the autonomous Left in West Germany.[73] It is perhaps unsurprising that the houses soon became a major flashpoint within a wider politics of housing in West Germany representing, for many, an intense, turbulent and highly localised revival of the *Häuserkampf* of the 1970s.

The occupants of the twelve houses on Hafenstraße, of course, had other pressing commitments. During the bitter winter of 1981/2, it became clear that the houses required significant mending and repair. Rooms, attics and basements had to be cleared. New pipes and wires were fitted while toilets, sinks, stoves and coal ovens were installed, often using parts that were rescued from other houses in the neighbourhood that were empty and slated for demolition.

As creative destruction gave way to radical resuscitation, the conflict between the houses and Hamburg city authorities, if anything, intensified. Negotiations over the cost of repairs began almost immediately and raged on until 1987. While the squatters received financial support (over 260,000 DM) to cover the most pressing renovations in 1983 and short-term contracts in 1984, the city was still keen to evict the squatters and to revive some of the original redevelopment plans for the area.[74] A number of strategies were adopted by the authorities who were looking for any excuse to move in on the houses. Police harassment and intimidation was used, in particular, as a means to criminalise the residents of Hafenstraße and, in September 1982, the houses were raided for the first time by officers looking for explosives.[75]

The raids and arrests continued over the course of the next four years. The police actions were supported by a relentless media campaign that brought the question of squatting and violence once again into the public eye. Even the liberal *Tageszeitung* (*TAZ*), a newspaper which had historically supported squatters across West Germany, ran an interview with the former chief of the Hamburg office of the Bundesamt für Verfassungsschutz, West Germany's domestic security agency, in which he described the Hafenstraße as far more than a meeting point of the city's '*Lumpenproletariat*'. The situation has fundamentally changed, he argued, and the houses have become, in his eyes, a far more dangerous environment conducive to the clandestine activities of the RAF. While the offices of the *TAZ* were vandalised by a group of Hafenstraße squatters in response to these allegations, others were worried that they would only hasten their eviction. Some were even willing to exchange their existing contracts for housing elsewhere.[76]

Over the course of 1986, a number of brutal police assaults on the houses took place. In August, a raid on Bernhard-Nocht-Straße 22 and 24 led to the partial eviction of one house (number 24) and the demolition of a number of flats. A few weeks later the squatters received notices terminating their rents on 31 December 1986. The authorities did not, however, wait until the end of the year. 'Evacuation titles' for a number of houses were issued on the pretext that social services had stopped making rental payments to SAGA on behalf of the squatters and that they were now, as a consequence, in arrears.[77] So on 28 October 1986, a major operation to expel the residents from six houses began. Over 500 officers from the MEK police commando unit were deployed to provide support to the court-appointed bailiff. In the end, six houses were forcibly evicted. Household goods and furniture were thrown out on to city streets, toilets, sinks and appliances were ripped up and smashed, doors broken, food spoiled, and cups and bedding sprayed with CS-gas. A spontaneous solidarity march took to the streets, though the 2,000 protesters were prevented from reaching Hafenstraße by the police. The surrounding neighbourhood was declared a restricted area (*Sperrgebiet*) by Hamburg's interior minister, Alfons Pawelcyzk.[78]

While the squatters responded with their own militant resistance, they also sought out new alliances within the city through the work of the newly founded group Initiative Hafenstraße as well as a number of smaller solidarity organisations which had been formed across the city. On 12 December 1986, thirty-five different organisations came together as over 12,000 people marched in support of Hafenstraße under the banner: 'Solidarity with Hafenstraße. No evictions. No demolitions. An end to police terror.' The protesters were unwilling to tolerate a rolling police kettle, a new strategy recently devised in West Germany to manage and incite demonstrators. The 1,000-strong Revolutionary Bloc which led the march pushed back against the MEK police units who tried to break up the protest and were ultimately chased away. Despite the militant tactics adopted by many of the marchers, the demonstration did not split or fracture the broad Hafenstraße coalition. As one commentator concluded, 'the state's attempt to divide the movement by repression had failed'.[79]

More importantly perhaps, the actions of the squatters and their supporters secured the remaining houses beyond the date of their scheduled eviction. City officials feared further escalation and once again backed off. Activists seized the opportunity and organised a series of coordinated protests in the spring of 1987 (known as Tag X). By the summer, a number of the houses that had been cleared the previous year were once again occupied. The squatters released a flyer demanding that the 'Senate should ... abandon its plans for eviction and demolition as well as the terror of the past year'.[80]

Negotiations with the Senate, which had been ongoing throughout the year, broke down in November 1987. The squatters were aware that their eviction could take place at any moment and had already fortified the houses on Hafenstraße. They now went public with their decision to defend themselves. A new pirate radio station, Radio Hafenstraße, was launched that quickly became a key source of information for the squatters and their growing number of supporters. On 12 November, a series of barricades were thrown up across Hafenstraße blocking access to the houses. As tensions rose, negotiations between the squatters and the city resumed and, within a week, a compromise agreement was finally reached with Mayor Klaus von Dohnanyi despite efforts by certain circles within the police to unlawfully evict the squatters, a 'putsch' that was quashed by other officers.[81]

The barricades were swiftly removed and the new contract was finally signed. At the same time, the squatters released a statement proclaiming that:

> the Hafenstrasse was officially secured. We recognize that the struggle continues and that this is only the first step ... Our real aims have not, however, been met by the contract. We will

continue therefore to work towards the assembling of collective, self-determined and autonomous lives while building resistance against all forms of oppression.[82]

The new rental contract was, as the squatters feared, tied to the criminal code which left them vulnerable to future actions by the authorities. Despite a series of police operations – most notably in 1990 – the twelve houses were not cleared, and in 1995 they were reluctantly sold by the city to a co-operative set up by the squatters for a fraction of their market value.

In the end, the turbulent and violent history of the Hafenstraße squats and their eventual legalisation represented a rather different outcome than the *Häuserkampf* of the 1970s, where the struggle over urban space produced, in the eyes of many activists, mixed and limited results. The history behind the houses on Hafenstraße also helped to shape and support a broad range of struggles around housing, autonomy and self-determination in Hamburg. This includes the creation of the Rota Flora social centre in an abandoned theatre in the Sternschanze neighbourhood that was first squatted on 1 November 1989, and that remains an important autonomous space within the city.

It also encompasses the historically working class Gängeviertel, whose run-down houses and courtyards were squatted by activists and artists in 2009 as a response, on the one hand, to gentrification, rising rents and living costs, and the city's exploitation of cultural production and social work, and as a direct challenge, on the other hand, to Hamburg's wholesale acceptance of the 'politics of neoliberal urban competitiveness and welcoming of the so-called "creative class"'. In response to the occupation, the buildings in the Gängeviertel were bought by the city and are now undergoing renovations carried out by SAGA, Hamburg's infamous housing development agency. While many activists and artists have embraced the Gängeviertel as a space for alternative cultural, political and social activities, others are worried that these developments represent nothing more than another form of institutionalisation and co-optation that will ultimately erode the neighbourhood's radical inventiveness.[83]

The debate about the future of the Gängeviertel is, of course, just a single episode in a much broader history of squatting in Germany; a history where the 'housing question' ('*Wohnungsfrage*'), more often that not, became an intense and often violent 'struggle over housing' ('*Häuserkampf*'). This was a struggle that testified to the very real and immediate violence which the capitalist form of accumulation often inflicts upon us and our ability to secure a roof over our heads. But it is also a struggle shaped by disagreements *between* squatters that were, in many cases, divisive and violent in their own right. Squatted spaces were, in the end, both sites of liberation and possibility and sources of intense conflict and dissent.

For many squatters who lived through the occupation of Hafenstraße, for example, the experience was one of permanent crisis. 'We lived in a crisis zone (*Krisengebiet*),' one later recalled, 'everyday was a crisis.'[84] The atmosphere of intense and relentless pressure that was felt by the squatters was captured to good effect in a 1988 documentary film, *Irgendwie, irgendwo, irgendwann*. The emotional work of squatting not only took its toll on many activists but often relied on power structures that were, if anything, conspicuously traditional. For many women, in particular, the fetishism of militancy and the recourse to counterviolence only served to reinforce 'male-dominated behaviours and patterns'.[85] Patriarchal structures persisted and squats, including the houses on Hafenstraße as well as earlier spaces in Frankfurt and Hamburg, were often the site of sexist speech and behaviour as well as serious sexual and physical violence. 'The permanent violation of intimacy,' as one squatter concluded, 'was incredibly hard to take.'[86]

It was the violent sexual assault of a woman by three other squatters (one man and two women) in a house on Hafenstraße in June 1984 that brought these dynamics into sharp relief.[87] The assault and the rough summary justice that the perpetrators received created a storm of controversy that crystallised the debate about sexism and violence within the autonomist scene across West Germany. The fallout was widely discussed and eventually prompted many women to seek out 'separatist' alternatives that provided a base for the articulation of autonomist spaces that were ostensibly free from the spectre of patriarchal violence.[88]

And yet, despite the rich history of these developments, many accounts of the squatting movement in West Germany have continued to focus on the heroic actions of some squatters while overlooking the modest material and emotional practices that were often central to the endurance and survival of squatted spaces. The *Häuserkampf* was an undeniably brutal and violent struggle over affordable housing which brought squatters into direct contact with the violent predations of capitalist accumulation. But it was also a struggle shaped by the desire to live *differently* and to produce forms of shared city living – an urban commons of sorts – shaped by new understandings of care and generosity, protest and resistance.

Reassembling the City: Makeshift Urbanisms and the Politics of Squatting in Berlin

> We didn't just occupy buildings, we occupied the substance of buildings.
>
> Group of Freiburg squatters[1]

> We did not squat to simply secure housing. We wanted to live and work together again. We wanted to put an end to the separation and destruction of communal living. Who in this city is not familiar with the agonising loneliness and emptiness of everyday life that has arisen with the ceaseless destruction of traditional relationships wrought by urban renovation and other forms of urban destruction?
>
> Squatters in West Berlin[2]

In early April 2015, a team of artists, activists and academics travelled with a group of six pensioners from Berlin to London where they met with the British architectural firm Assemble. The pensioners were part of a larger group of seniors who had squatted a community centre and recreation home in 2012 in the Berlin district of Pankow after the local council said that they would have to make way for a new luxury real estate development. The 'squatters', aged between 63 and 96, paid a monthly membership of one euro in order to use the space for a range of activities. The space had become a site of care, gathering and refuge for many older Germans from the former East who found themselves unemployed after the *Wende*.[3] The pensioners occupied the centre for over 111 days and, in the process, they were able to assemble a wide network of support across Berlin and elsewhere in Germany. They even adopted aspects of the action repertoire used by Berlin's longstanding squatting scene. Banners were unfurled and draped from the centre with well-recognised slogans such as 'this house is occupied' (*'dieses Haus ist besetzt'*) and 'we will stay' (*'wir bleiben alle'*) and the group soon became part of a wider network of protests against gentrification and housing scarcity across Berlin. In the face of growing popular support, the local district council (grudgingly) agreed to begin negotiations over the centre's leasehold contract. A temporary use contract was issued which allowed the pensioners to run the house as an autonomous self-organised collective. However, the long-term status of the house remains unresolved, and for the former squatters who run Stille Straße 10 as a social centre, the struggle to avoid eviction is ongoing.[4]

The pensioners were teamed up with Assemble as part of an exhibition in Berlin on the 'Housing Question' (*'Wohnungsfrage'*) which took place at the Haus der Kulturen der Welt between October and December 2015. The exhibition focused on the recent history of housing inequality in Berlin and its relationship to the changing logics of capitalist urbanisation and the recurring cycles of creative destruction and accumulation by dispossession which have traditionally condemned significant numbers of Berliners to misery and prompted many to seek informal and often precarious forms of housing and shelter.

Recent winners of Britain's Turner Prize, one of the country's most prestigious contemporary art awards, Assemble is a London-based architectural collective made up of fourteen architects, designers and artists. Much of their work addresses what they describe as 'the typical disconnection between the public and the process by which places are made'. Assemble champion an 'expanded architectural concept' that connects architectural form with public infrastructure.[5] At stake for them, is the development of a working practice that is collaborative and that seeks to involve the public in the ongoing and continuous realisation of the collective's work. This can be seen, for example, in their recent collaboration with the Granby Four Streets Community Land Trust in Liverpool to restore ten derelict terraced houses on

Cairns Street in Toxteth. The collective worked closely with local residents using DIY methods and low-cost materials in transforming the houses into affordable community-owned homes.[6]

The organisers of the *Wohnungsfrage* exhibition first contacted the volunteer committee that ran the Still Straße social centre in the summer of 2014. The pensioners were asked to devise a model project for 'self-determined and communal living for older people'.[7] A few months later in early 2015, Assemble joined the project, despite some reservations from the pensioners who had expected a more specialist team. Over the course of the year, a series of joint workshops were held, first in Berlin and than in London. Members of Assemble travelled to Berlin to meet with the users of the social centre. They also conducted site visits to a number of their apartments. Stille Straße's return visit to London in April 2015 introduced the centre's volunteer committee to a number of projects undertaken by Assemble as well as other community designed spaces across the city.

During the workshops, it became clear that the members of Still Straße were highly critical of the kind of housing available to pensioners in Berlin and the effect that recent urban development in the city has had it on local communities and the resources traditionally available to residents on fixed incomes. 'There has to be space for community and communal experiences', they argued. 'How people organise that exactly is up to them.' They also argued that a balance needs to be struck between notions of self-organisation and solidarity, on the one hand, and specific individual needs, on the other.[8]

In late April 2015, Assemble presented the pensioners with their final proposal. They came up with a model for a multi-storey building that would include over twenty residential units and a communal area that would encompass the entire first floor and included a kitchen, a workshop and storage space. Each residential unit would be subdivided into two sections: one that was to be used as a privately owned apartment with conventional doors and windows, with the other having folding doors and glazed windows across the entire breadth of the room. The second section could be used either privately or collectively. It would be owned by the co-operative responsible for the construction of the building and be administered by a committee chosen by the residents themselves. Basic fixtures would be provided, though the residents would have considerable autonomy in completing the rest of their home according to their own needs and wishes.[9]

A final 1:1 model was constructed in September 2015 for the *Wohnungsfrage* exhibition. While the model, and the process underpinning its design, must be seen within the context of a growing housing crisis in Berlin, they also speak, in turn, to a much wider history of self-build housing and planning in Berlin. This is a history, as the organisers of the *Wohnungsfrage* exhibition were acutely aware, that connected architects and planners with students, workers, local citizen initiatives and tenant groups. This is, moreover, a history embedded within a constellation of struggles over social inequality and housing insecurity that stretch back to at least the early nineteenth century. Squatting and the everyday practices adopted by squatters have always occupied an important place within these struggles. Not only have squatters contributed, in this context, to the emergence of new social movements in the city, but they also responded to acute housing needs through the *assembling* of spaces that served as alternative forms of dwelling and self-organisation.[10]

For many Berliners, squatting was, in other words, far more than a simple act of protest and resistance or a basic expression of immediate housing needs. It also encompassed a series of practices through which a radically different sense of shared city life – a *makeshift urbanism* if you like – was (quite literally) constructed. If squatters were often forced to carve out the most precarious of urban existences, this depended in no small part on a modest politics of adaptation, mending and repair. Squatters confronted abandoned or run-down spaces that required significant renovation and they quickly developed (and shared) a wide range of skills and tactics through which these spaces were slowly and incrementally brought back to life.

The recent history of squatting in Berlin – both in the former West *and* East – can be traced back to the late 1960s. This was, in the first instance, a period which bore witness to the emergence of the New Left in West Germany and the extra-parliamentary opposition (Außerparlamentarische Opposition, or APO) that grew out of the student movement. Activists increasingly turned, in this context, to a host of new tactics from teach-ins and happenings to experiments in communal living and working. Unlike earlier forms of contention and dissent, the protest techniques adopted by the APO were *anticipatory*. They actively prefigured the alternative society that they imagined. In the German Democratic Republic, a much smaller circle of dissidents adopted a similar set of practices that reflected the growing influence of the West on the development of an oppositional milieu in the East.[11]

In both cases, however, access to housing also remained a pressing issue. While architects and planners working in the immediate post-war period were obliged to situate themselves 'physically and aesthetically along Cold War divides', plans to demolish Berlin's famous tenement houses, or *Mietskasernen*, played an equally important role despite the city's geographical partitioning.[12] Early showcase developments such as Stalinallee in the East and the Hansa Viertel in the West were contingent on the further destruction of an existing urban fabric and, along with it, thousands of homes that could have provided much-needed housing.

In the West, urban regeneration depended on an official renewal policy that favoured the demolition of older *Mietskasernen* and an emphasis on the construction of new housing. Large-scale housing estates were constructed on the outskirts of the city, offering cheap rent through direct state subsidies. The majority of the tenants were '*Sanierungsopfer*' ('victims of renewal') who had been 'decanted' from inner-city tenements.[13] These new developments also targeted Berlin's remaining self-built settlements – many dating back to the 1920s and 1930s – that continued to house thousands of residents (often illegally) on the city's allotments. As one architectural historian recently observed, 'modern Berlin was literally built on the memories of informal neighbourhoods'. Many were cleared to make way for modernist tower blocks including the Märkisches Viertel in Reinickendorf, the Falkenhagener Feld in Spandau and the Gropiusstadt in Neukölln.[14]

An economic recession in the 1960s quickly brought an end to the building of massive modernist satellite cities in the West. High rent costs and expensive financing prompted a *reurbanisation* of capital and a preoccupation with the renewal of inner-city neighbourhoods including Kreuzberg, Wedding, Neukölln and Schöneberg where there remained a high concentration of older housing stock. It was in this way that public housing developments were 'transplanted into previously multipurpose *Gründerzeit* districts "replacing" those historic districts with monofunctional modern districts'. This policy, known as 'clear-cut or area renovation' (*'Kahlschlag- oder Flächensanierung'*) involved the demolition of entire blocks of older low-rent housing in favour of new construction, which ultimately served the interests of developers, private investors and city-owned housing associations.[15] It was, moreover, these policies that formed the immediate context to the major wave of squatting that erupted in West Berlin in the late 1970s.

Housing in the GDR was, as in the West, highly politicised, with the state assuming principle responsibility for its construction, maintenance and allocation.[16] This is hardly surprising, perhaps, given the parlous state of housing in the wake of the Second World War. In the 1950s, central heating was available in less than 3 per cent of residences. Only 20 per cent of residences had a toilet and 22 per cent a bath. Over 45 per cent of housing in the GDR had been constructed before 1900.[17] By the early 1970s, official policy had only exacerbated the dereliction of older housing stock across East Germany and, despite an ambitious building programme undertaken during the Honecker era, an acute shortage of housing persisted, especially in inner-city neighbourhoods as ideological priority was given to large industrially manufactured estates on the outskirts of cities.[18] The cost of demolition and construction could not, in turn, be met by the state and, as a result, thousands of properties fell into ruin and remained empty. As waiting lists grew, some residents chose to bypass the official allocation process and occupy properties illegally, a practice which became known as *Schwarzwohnen*.[19]

On either side of the Berlin Wall, squatting thus came to represent both a struggle against housing precarity as well as a series of practices aimed at building a different kind of city. While squatting depended, in this context, on an illegal act of occupation, it was the figure of the commune that ultimately served in the late 1960s as a key point of reference. As many activists later recalled, the creation of free communal spaces in Berlin provided a template for alternative forms of collective living and other self-organised projects that would later assume a more radical and illegal form.[20] It was the student leader Rudi Dutschke who first advocated the formation of communes in the 1960s. As he observed in a December 1966 radio interview with Heinrich von Nußbaum on SFB Radio Berlin, 'the commune – as both an open form of political cooperation and the direct co-existence of free individuals – may come to represent the only adequate response to our times'.[21]

At the time of his interview on SFB, Dutschke was no longer actively involved in plans for the development of an alternative commune in West Berlin. On the very day that he spoke on SFB Radio, however, a meeting was held by a number of other activists in Berlin including the artist and agitator par excellence Dieter Kunzelmann. The group decided in the early hours of the morning of 1 January 1967 to establish a commune that would later became known as Kommune I.[22] The group moved between a couple of flats in the West Berlin district of Friedenau before moving into their own shared apartment, a large six-and-a-half-room flat at Kaiser-Friedrich-Strasse 54a.

The founding of Kommune I has acquired something of a mythical status within a broader history of the extra-parliamentary opposition in West Germany in the late 1960s. Press coverage at the time was largely caricatural in tone, mingling scandalous biographical detail with casual impressionistic accounts of commune life. The commune's political activities were, more often than not, reduced to a collection of colourful episodes and anecdotes that were of a piece with the commune's putative bohemian status. This was, of course, a self-image that was cultivated by members of Kommune I whose political tactics and ensuing court cases guaranteed celebrity treatment.[23]

And yet, these were tactics that did matter; as was the idea that the commune was a particular kind of *constructed* social and political space. Recalling his first visit to Kommune I in May 1967, the activist Peter Schneider described the main room as 'a manifesto in furniture'. 'It announced,' he continued, 'the cancellation of the standard division of labour that we find in the "bourgeois apartment". Books, packages, dishes, chairs, desks, beds, everything was very confused. The room only lacked a toilet bowl.'[24] According to one of the original members of the commune, the flat was organised around two large rooms. One was used as a library, the other as a workroom and dormitory with mattresses spread on the floor. There were two smaller rooms and a room originally used by servants. Most of the 'communards' slept in the large room that served as the main dormitory while others worked around them on political posters and pamphlets.[25]

In the summer of 1968, the commune moved into an empty warehouse at Stephanstraße 60 in Berlin-Moabit and began renovations of the three-storey building. Eventually, the three floors were divided between a discotheque, a floor for visitors and the main space of the commune. The move, if nothing else, served to highlight the growing divisions between various members of Kommune I. As public happenings and interventions became less frequent, some members, most notably Rainer Langhans, advocated a shift away from the group's emphasis on agit-prop provocation, histrionic protest and strident militancy. In its place, they turned to a lifestyle politics that drew inspiration from a wide network of subcultural practices (DIY publishing, underground music, drug use, etc.).[26]

These disagreements and tensions were ultimately responsible for the dissolution of Kommune I in November 1969 in a wave of anger and acrimony. Other communal projects were nevertheless founded in West Berlin during the same period and pointed, if anything, to a much wider and intense field of communal political action. A number of communes were dotted across the city (Linkeck-Kommune, Bülow-Kommune, Anarsch-Kommune, etc.). They were, in many cases, short-lived and often pushed the boundaries of communal living to new extremes.[27]

The experimental ethos cultivated by Kommune I in the West also spawned an imitator on the other side of the Wall. Kommune I-Ost was founded in 1969 by a group of intellectuals including Frank, Florian and Sybille Havemann who were the children of the well-known scientist and dissident Robert Havemann. Kommune I-Ost was first established in a three-room apartment on Samariter Straße in Berlin-Friedrichshain, though it occupied a number of different apartments in the city until 1973.[28] It was described by the Stasi, the official security organ of the GDR, as a 'meeting-place for negative youth' and the commune's organisation was, according to another Stasi report, closely modelled on their predecessors in 'West Berlin and West Germany'.[29] The commune became a site of 'oppositional sociability' in a city where such spaces did not, for the most part, exist. It was unsurprisingly less successful, however, in forging a connection between 'internal and external space, between private and public revolution'.[30]

The expansion of communes in the West pointed, in contrast, to a further deepening of the repertoire of direct action developed in the late 1960s by the extra-parliamentary opposition. The very nature of the commune as a radical political space was a subject of intense debate. The literary journal *Kursbuch* published a dossier on 'Concrete Utopias' which called for the development of a 'permanent process' of communalisation.[31] A year later the same journal published a commentary by the sociologist Heide Berndt, a former student of Theodor Adorno. While Berndt was highly critical of the narcissistic and often sexist behaviour of members of Kommune I, she nevertheless called for the further development of 'concrete communes', through which she believed the form and content of a radical future would be born.[32]

Berndt's observations were part of a wider critique of postwar urbanism that she developed in a series of texts in the 1960s that combined the psychoanalytical with the sociological while acknowledging the influence of prominent American scholars including Jane Jacobs and Kevin Lynch.[33] While Berndt's work has received little attention outside of Germany, it contributed to the flourishing of a radical architectural milieu that emerged in Berlin and elsewhere in West Germany and Europe in the 1960s. At stake here for many was the articulation and exploration of a different politics of habitation that prompted many young architects and planners to re-examine their understanding of Berlin's urban fabric.

It was in this context that, in the spring of 1968, a group of young professionals met in room 507 of the Faculty of Architecture at the Technische Universität (TU-Berlin) in West Berlin to challenge the planning policies that had been adopted by the city. They formed Aktion 507 and proclaimed that they were for 'direct democracy' and 'better public control of the structural development of urban areas'.[34] The group advocated the formation of an alternative public sphere and called for the participation of all those affected by the city's top-down planning process. In a major 1968 exhibition, *Diagnose zum Bauen in West-Berlin*, the group painstakingly documented the impact of displacement and relocation on inner-city residents and the socio-psychological effects of living in newly constructed satellite estates with little if any social infrastructure. They also used the exhibition as a forum for discussing urban renewal with tenants and for creating a space for collective resident-led planning.[35]

A focus on grassroots urban planning also prompted many architects in West Berlin to link up with the so-called

'*Basisgruppen*' ('rank-and-file groups') that emerged as the student movement dissolved in the late 1960s.[36] These were groups that were rooted in various West Berlin neighbourhoods as many young students sought to extend their own struggles within the university to the city at large. Their attention was primarily focused on the factory as a space of political mobilisation, though they gained little support from workers who questioned the students' commitment or their understanding of the needs and desires of workers.[37] Other groups were more successful by placing particular emphasis on concrete local struggles around the provision of youth services, affordable housing and urban regeneration.[38]

They also turned to the wider repertoire of contention (agitprop, happenings, teach-ins and street theatre) that had accompanied new forms of political protest in West Germany in the 1960s. In the West Berlin district of Kreuzberg, a *Basisgruppe* made up of architects, planners and workers joined the local street theatre troupe to perform *Komfort in Günstige Lage oder Die Sanierung* (*Comfort in an Affordable Location or The Renewal*), a play that was conceived to raise awareness of the impact of 'clear-cut redevelopment' on the neighbourhood.[39] Others, including the social worker Helga Reidemeister, turned to the medium of film and worked closely with local residents in the Märkisches Viertel to co-produce a series of documentaries on everyday life on the estate. 'My main project,' she later recalled in an interview, 'is to make films for the people who are in them and who recognise themselves in them.'[40]

Throughout the late 1960s and early 1970s, the Märkisches Viertel thus remained a key site of activism for a number of political groups in West Berlin, many of whom were involved alongside residents in a series of grassroots struggles around housing and infrastructure.[41] It was also in the Märkisches Viertel that Berlin's first squat was (briefly) set up. On the evening of 1 May 1970, a small theatre troupe began an impromptu performance in the middle of a shopping district in the estate. The troupe, Hoffmann's Comic Teater, were a radical theatre ensemble that were formed in 1969 by three brothers Gert, Peter and Ralph Möbius. Wearing colourful costumes and masks and accompanied by a live band, they developed a reputation for staging politically daring events that took place in the streets of West Berlin and in the city's many youth homes.[42] The performances focused, in particular, on the everyday conflicts that shaped the lives of Berlin's working-class residents. Audience participation was actively encouraged by the troupe, who developed an engaged agitprop style. Scenes were improvised while spectators were invited on to the 'stage' to play out scenes from their own lives.

The performance by Hoffmann's Comic Teater focused, unsurprisingly, on the experience of the estate's residents and their anger at the lack of social infrastructure and the unwillingness of state-operated landowner and developer GESOBAU to provide 'free spaces' (*'Freizeiträumen'*) for local youth.[43] It concluded with a scene that dramatised the recent closure of an after-school club (*Schülerladen*), after which the participants and spectators were encouraged to occupy a nearby building as a symbolic protest against GESOBAU. They were prevented, however, from doing so by the police who had been following the performance and had already secured the site. A group of over one hundred activists, performers and other local residents were nevertheless able to stage an occupation in an adjoining factory. As they began discussions over the formation of an autonomous self-organised youth centre, the factory hall was stormed by riot police and the occupiers, who included the journalist Ulrike Meinhof, were brutally evicted. Three protesters were seriously injured and taken to hospital.[44]

In the immediate aftermath of the eviction, a small group of local activists initiated a discussion about the future direction of political mobilising in the Märkisches Viertel. A strategy paper was produced and circulated by the group, who criticised the new housing estate and its developers for their insufficient attention to the needs and desires of its tenants.[45] One of the authors of that unpublished paper was Meinhof, who only two weeks later would take part in the breakout of Andreas Baader from the reading room of the Social Studies Institute of West Berlin's Free University (Freie Universität), an event which led to the formation of the Red Army Faction (Rote Armee Faktion or RAF).[46] Hoffmann's Comic Teater continued to produce engaging performances in the wake of the occupation and also turned their attention to children's theatre.[47] Members of the group were later involved in the formation of Ton Steine Scherben, one of the most important bands within the radical scene in West Berlin and whose history is largely inseparable from the evolution of the anti-authoritarian Left in the city.[48]

While the factory occupation in the Märkisches Viertel was itself short-lived, it was nevertheless the first squatted space in a city where the radical politics of occupation assumed a new and enduring significance. There have, in fact, been at least 610 separate squats of a broadly political nature in Berlin between 1970 and 2014. The majority of these actions took place in the city's old tenement blocks, though they also encompassed a range of other sites from abandoned villas, factories and schools, to parks, vacant plots and even, in one case, a part of the 'death strip' that formed the border between West and East Berlin.[49] As a form of illegal occupation, squatting typically fell under §123 of the German Criminal Code ('Trespassing'), though many magistrates in Berlin were reluctant to charge squatters as a rundown apartment did not satisfy, in their eyes, the legal test for an apartment or a 'pacified estate' ('*befriedetes Besiztum*').[50]

The main impulse for squatting in the early 1970s in West Berlin and elsewhere in West Germany was the emergence of a movement for independent and autonomous youth centres and the desire among young people to escape the unyielding predetermination of their lives and establish their own autonomous self-determined spaces. For many young people, the choice to squat represented far more than a simple act of resistance. It was an opportunity to resituate their own struggles on the terrain of everyday life. These were struggles over the right to autonomy and self-organisation, and were shaped by the lack of facilities and services available to many marginalised youth. But these were also conflicts over 'the disposition of urban space'.[51] If young people seized, occupied and transformed buildings in ways that reflected their own needs and wishes, they were spaces that were actively *remade* as part of a wider movement against housing speculation, rent hikes and unfettered urban redevelopment.

The occupation of a factory in the Märkisches Viertel was soon followed by other actions. On 3 July 1971, over 300 students, activists and youth workers occupied two floors of an abandoned factory at 13 Mariannenplatz in the district of Kreuzberg with a view to creating a centre for disadvantaged and unemployed youth.[52] The occupation followed a concert at the Technische Universität Berlin by Ton Steine Scherben where the lead singer, Ralph Möbius, implored the crowd to take action against the lack of youth services in the neighbourhood. Despite initial clashes with the police, municipal authorities eventually supported and legalised the initiative which became known as the Kreuzberg Youth Centre (*Jugendzentrum*).[53]

The relationship between political performance and direct action assumed an even more spectacular form only a few months later. On 8 December 1971, a teach-in was held at the Technische Universität to protest the death of the militant activist Georg von Rauch in a shoot-out with the police. While a teach-in on the status of the Bethanien, a recently abandoned hospital complex in Kreuzberg, had already been planned for that day, it was now accompanied by another concert by Ton Steine Scherben. After the concert a large group of youth, including many involved in the creation of the Kreuzberg Youth Centre a few months earlier, took the opportunity to squat in the abandoned Martha-Maria-Haus, a former residence for nuns and a part of the Bethanien complex. Around 300 concertgoers were able to enter, occupy and secure the house despite police efforts to prevent them. A large banner was quickly unfurled and draped along one side of the building. It read, 'BESETZT' ('occupied').[54]

The founding of the Georg von Rauch-Haus by a group of students, young workers and runaways remains one of the defining moments within the broader history of squatting in West Berlin and was famously celebrated at the time by Ton Steine Scherben in the cult hit Das Rauch-Haus Lied with its rousing rhyming chorus: *'Ihr kriegt uns hier nicht raus – Das ist unser Haus'* ('You can't toss us out – This is our house'). A preliminary contract was signed with the Berlin Senate on 31 December 1971, though negotiations over the long-term use of the space did not begin until April 1972. While some local politicians attempted to force the closure of the house, arguing that it was being used to support left-wing militants, negotiations continued with municipal authorities, including the Kreuzberg councillor for youth and sport (Stadtrat für Jugend und Sport), Erwin Beck. A five-year extension to the lease was agreed in January 1973. The new lease recognised the house project as a socio-pedagogical experiment. Notwithstanding changes to the original contract, the space has served as an autonomous housing project for more than forty years.

The Georg von Rauch-Haus was ultimately one of a small number of self-organised youth projects that emerged out of the first wave of squatting in West Berlin in the early 1970s ('The Drugstore', 'Putte' and the Tommy Weisbecker-Haus). These were spaces that spoke to the needs of many working-class youth. They quickly became major 'scene' locations for young runaways, drug users and radicals from a variety of political groupings. And yet, as successful examples of political squatting, they were relatively small in number. It was only in the late 1970s that a major wave of squatting erupted in West Berlin as small-scale opposition to urban renewal and displacement gave way to a series of escalating struggles over the right to housing.

Between 1979 and 1984, over 265 separate sites were squatted in West Berlin as activists and other local residents responded to a deepening housing crisis by occupying apartments, the overwhelming majority of which were located in the districts of Kreuzberg and Schöneberg. At the high point of this wave in the spring of 1981, it is estimated that there were at least 2,000 active squatters in West Berlin and tens of thousands of supporters. A total of 169 houses were, in turn, occupied.[55] There was considerable public sympathy for the new squatting 'movement'. In 1981, the prominent polling agency, Allenbach, conducted a survey which showed that over 53 per cent of the West German public believed that squatters were right in their criticism of urban development and 'clear-cut renovation' ('*Kahlschlagsanierung*').[56]

The period between 1979 and 1984 represented the high point for the squatting movement in West Berlin. This was undoubtedly a struggle *against* urban renewal, housing insecurity and social inequality. But it was also a struggle *for* the creation of new spaces that challenged dominant understandings of home, family and work. While it may have, in other words, been architects and planners who first rediscovered the value of Berlin's historical inner-city housing stock in the 1960s and 1970s, it was squatters and other housing activists who rebuilt and re-animated these spaces. To therefore claim the right to a different city was not limited to the seizure and occupation of buildings. It centred on what those buildings might become as spaces that promised a different form of life.

It is perhaps not surprising that the new wave of squatting adopted the motto, 'it is better to squat and mend than to own and destroy' ('*lieber instabd(be)setzen als kaputt besitzen*').[57] The occupiers also used, for the first time, the term *Instands(be) setzung* to describe their movement; the term itself a clever combination of the German for maintenance (*Instandsetzung*) and squatting (*Besetzung*). In the words of one squatter, 'we wanted to show that it is cheap to repair apartments. So we tidied up, painted and repaired windows.' 'The constructiveness of our approach,' added another, 'lies in *what we do* with flats.'[58]

The language (and practice) of repair must be seen in a context where whole neighbourhood blocks in inner-city districts such as Kreuzberg had fallen into serious disrepair as owners 'waited' for the city to implement renewal plans. Owners had no incentive to undertake even the most basic of renovations, and this intentional neglect only served to further diminish the quality of housing in the neighbourhood such that demolition remained the only option while assuring generous pecuniary benefits for owners.[59] Even attempts by West Berlin authorities in the mid-1970s to roll back on the worst excesses of urban renewal were muted while efforts to promote greater citizen engagement were often overlooked.

In the face of official intransigence, local citizen initiatives in Kreuzberg had no choice but to take the matter into their own hands. On 3 February 1979, two apartments in two separate buildings were squatted. As the occupants made clear in a widely distributed flyer:

> In our district, hundreds of apartments are empty and falling apart. Cheap apartments are demolished because landlords no longer put them up for rent. This is against the law. On the 3rd and 4th of February, the citizen's initiative SO36 [after the local postcode] wants to restore the lawful condition of rental accommodation. Starting at 10 o'clock we will occupy and restore one apartment in Luebbener Straße and another on Goerlitzer Straße.[60]

The squatters intended to use the occupations as symbolic sites of protest, drawing public attention to the effects of urban renewal and the acute shortage of housing in Kreuzberg. The city's official renewal policy nevertheless continued. Empty flats were bricked up by city-owned and private housing associations, while suspicious fires were started in a number of vacant properties. In at least one instance, a block of abandoned flats were used as a training ground for US soldiers stationed in Berlin to practise the latest urban combat manoeuvres.[61]

With growing public support, the number of squatted houses rose steadily to eighteen over the course of 1980. It was, however, local government corruption and police brutality that ultimately served as a catalyst for the wider housing movement in West Berlin. The attempted occupation of an apartment building in Kreuzberg at Fränkelufer 48 on 12 December 1980, and the violent crackdown by the police in its wake, was seen by many squatters and their supporters as a deliberate provocation. The squatter's council which had been set up a few months earlier made it clear in a prepared statement that the ongoing housing crisis required new forms of housing and shelter. To occupy, in their view, was to seek out spaces for self-determination and emancipation. 'We want to determine our lives at home just as we do at work', they proclaimed. 'We believe that squats are a disruptive possibility, an imaginative cog in the wheel of the state.'[62]

The period that immediately followed the events of 12 December became a high point for squatting in Kreuzberg and West Berlin more generally, as the scene grew rapidly and moved into other neighbourhoods with similarly old and empty housing, including Schöneberg, Charlottenburg, Moabit, Neukölln and Wedding. By 6 February 1981, over fifty separate apartment blocks were occupied across the western half of the city. Three weeks later the number had risen to one hundred. Occupations peaked on 15 May 1981, at which point 169 houses were occupied in West Berlin.[63]

It is against this backdrop that many activists shifted their attention to the spaces they were occupying and the possibilities that they offered. In an article published in the journal *Kursbuch*, the *TAZ* reporter Benny Härlin recounted his life as a squatter in West Berlin in 1981. For Härlin, the early moments of an occupation were described in pioneering expeditionary terms. He recalls a 'triumphant but also oppressive feeling, to wander for the first time through the long, echoing hallways'. 'You are an intruder,' he continued, 'a stranger in this dead world.'[64]

And yet, if a house appeared, on first inspection, to be 'dead', it was slowly brought back to life, as Härlin argues, through a makeshift process of mending and repair as materials and infrastructures were incrementally added to satisfy new needs and possibilities. The very act of occupation was therefore understood as a form of 'resuscitation'. Makeshift materials and do-it-yourself practices combined with the sharing of food and other resources to provide the material support for collective self-management. As Härlin noted, 'our rule was "learning by doing"'.[65] Occupation and renovation thus moved in a series of stages. As squatters entered into a vacant building, the first task was to remove any immediate dangers. Fallen debris was cleared while dry rot and mould was identified and removed from apartments. Once this was done, squatters secured rooms that could be immediately occupied, and cleared further debris and garbage from apartments and courtyards. Only then did they turn to the task of repairing structural problems that were a result of the owner's neglect and, in many cases, deliberate vandalism.[66] Härlin recalled how old manual handbooks such as *Der Heizungstechniker* (*The Heating Technician*, 1929) and *Die Neue Bauwirtschaft* (*The New Construction Industry Manual*, 1946) did the rounds between occupied houses as windows were repaired or replaced, old and exposed electrical wiring was fixed, and proper plumbing was restored.[67] After this, squatters turned their attention to damaged floors and roofs. Repairs would often take months, and in some cases years, to complete.

The squatters who thus occupied three apartments on Cuvrystraße on 26 December 1979 encountered spaces 'full of garbage and refuse'. Over the next few months, the houses were painstakingly renovated. Electricity metres were acquired from the local utility company, new wastewater pipes were installed and existing water pipes were repaired. In the early summer of 1981 a new roof was finally completed. Repair and rehabilitation also depended on the sharing of materials, practices and know-how between squatters and their supporters across Kreuzberg and West Berlin.[68] As the squatters who occupied a building on Manteufelstraße pointed out, once the 'junk was out' and they were in, a long and difficult road of labour-intensive work began.[69]

It was, in fact, the squat on Manteufelstraße which set up the Bauhof Handicraft Collective (Bauhof Handwerkskollektiv) as a place where squatters and other locals could learn basic construction skills and techniques from other squatters many of whom had completed an apprenticeship in a trade or were attending a vocational school in West Berlin.[70] The Bauhof took on a key coordinating role within a wider activist milieu in Kreuzberg that encompassed a growing number of handicraft collectives that had emerged during the 1970s as part of an expanding network of radical self-help activities. The Bauhof supplied squats with inexpensive building materials that were either recycled or purchased cheaply in bulk. It also ran a series of articles in the *Instand-Besetzer-Post*, one of the chief publications of the squatting scene, that provided detailed DIY instructions on a host of repair-related issues.[71] Ultimately the Bauhof became a site where squatters and architectural professionals often met to debate, discuss and experiment with new and innovative approaches to participatory design and adaptive reuse.

In this way, squatters in West Berlin in the early 1980s were able to cultivate an ethos of self-determination and self-help – a radical form of DIY that transformed the ways in which people, materials, ideas and resources came together. Squatters were also acutely aware, in this context, of the complex set of actions, connections and forms that sustained the spaces they lived in. 'Well, on such premises, there is always something that is not working', noted one squatter in 1981. 'And if there is nobody else,' they added, 'you develop a kind of relation to it which you could call responsibility. You know where the cables run, as much as you know the sounds of the environment, the people, *it is all interconnected*.'[72]

For many Berlin squatters, it was the built form that ultimately served as a guiding frame for the creation of new sustainable structures of organising, working and living. If the traditional Berlin tenement house (*Mietshaus*) was widely seen as a key symptom of creative destruction, for squatters it also offered an alternative to the 'organized inhumanity' of the modernist tower block.[73] As the historian Brian Ladd once noted, 'a hallmark of the *Mietskaserne* [is] its flexibility'. The existing building structure only encouraged squatters to maximise communal spaces. Over half of all squats in West Berlin contained collective self-managed spaces as the permeability of buildings was increased and re-engineered to suit the changing needs and wishes of their inhabitants. Walls were therefore removed in order to increase the size of social spaces including kitchens, while stairwells were created to produce a new geography of movement through buildings, now connected and held together by a network of doors, passageways, courtyards and vestibules.[74]

In the end, each squat adopted its own approach to the organisation of everyday life and the development of common spaces. Separate floors were, in some cases, designated for different activities (with workspaces on one floor and bedrooms on another). In many other squatted spaces, walls were torn down in order to create communal kitchens and dining rooms. In other houses, large common rooms were designed and used for general meetings (*Plena*) and other cultural activities including parties, gigs, theatre performances and films. At the same time, these were spaces that were embedded within the local neighbourhood. Across West Berlin and in Kreuzberg, in particular, squatters responded to a lack of social services by developing new social spaces 'designed to help shape and maintain the living environment to best serve all neighbourhood residents'.[75]

Taken together, the broad spectrum of sites and activities developed by squatters in West Berlin played a significant role in the consolidation of a radically different kind of infrastructure than the one routinely explored by contemporary urbanists. This was an infrastructure that assumed a number of forms including alternative cafés (Café Krantscho, Lokal Lummerland and Das Besetzereck), concert venues (Bobby Sands Pub and Café Knüppel), day-care centres, workshops and youth centres as well as a children's petting zoo, a Turkish bath and a homeopathic clinic.[76]

Some of the larger squatted spaces, including the *Regenbogenfabrik* on Lausitzer Straße and the *Kerngehäuse* on Cuvrystraße, became social centres in their own right. Both sites recalled an earlier history of mixed use in Kreuzberg, while hosting a wide range of initiatives that blurred the boundaries between 'new forms of living' and 'new ways of working'.[77] For the squatters that occupied an abandoned chemical factory now known as the *Regenbogenfabrik*, 'occupation' represented far more than an act of rehabilitation and renovation. It was also widely understood as an ongoing 'process' through which a meaningful social infrastructure was assembled, sustained and extended. As was the case with many squats, the *Regenbogenfabrik* placed particular emphasis on horizontal decision-making and collective self-management and applied these practices to both the day-to-day life of the squat and to projects that supported a larger community (cycle repair shop, carpentry workshop, day-care, cinema, hostel and community 'info shop').[78]

As the squatting scene blossomed in the early months of 1981, each new squat in West Berlin was greeted with a sense of exhilaration and elation. The countless posters, flyers and magazines produced by squatters during the period celebrated the makeshift urbanism that they endeavoured to create. The constant assemblies, meetings, performances, gigs, open houses, demonstrations and eviction resistances generated, in turn, a sense of openness and spontaneity and convinced many squatters that they were moving out of a society shaped by the logics of competition and consumerism and into an alternative city that still held, in their eyes, the potential for collective living and social transformation.

While squatted spaces were, in this way, seen as sites of liberation and possibility, they were also sources of intense conflict and struggle, especially as the pleasures and intensities of occupation gave way to conflicts over the organisation of everyday life. Tensions within houses were compounded and amplified by the pressures exerted from both within (sexism, petty crime and drug use) and without (criminalisation, eviction), as squatters became increasingly divided over wider movement goals. Should they negotiate with local authorities to secure legal status and funding to support renovation and rehabilitation?

The prospect of negotiations were greeted by many activists with feelings of anger and betrayal. Others felt that there was no choice but to secure some form of legal contract, especially in the face of a new hard-line policy (the '*Berliner Linie der Vernunft*' or the 'Berlin Line of Reason') rolled out by the Berlin Senate in the spring of 1981. It proscribed and vigorously policed any further attempts to squat in West Berlin and was supported by a 'law and order' approach that culminated in a wave of searches, arrests and evictions.[79] Many 'projects' that were able to guarantee long-term use of a building fell under the *Behutsame Stadterneuerung* programme later ratified by the Berlin House of Representatives in 1983. Under this programme, houses could apply for public funds to repair and modernise their properties through what became known as the *Bauliche Selbsthilfe* (Structural Self-Help) initiative. As a result, over a hundred houses were legalised through a combination of rental and purchase agreements. The remaining 'non-negotiating' houses were cleared out between 1982 and 1984. On 8 November 1984, the last squatted house in West Berlin was evicted.[80]

As the squatter movement in West Berlin waxed and waned in the early 1980s, on the other side of the Wall a growing number of East Berliners were adopting similar tactics. While the East German government had begun an ambitious programme of housing construction in the 1970s, older properties in cities such as East Berlin, Dresden, Leipzig and Halle were largely neglected and many fell into a state of dereliction. Levels of vacancy doubled in the 1970s, and by 1981 there were over 200,000 empty apartments across the GDR, either scheduled for demolition or waiting for repairs.[81] In East Berlin, waiting lists for housing had risen up to eight years.

It is against this backdrop that many citizens elected to occupy dwellings illegally. What the historian Udo Grashoff has recently described as '*Schwarzwohnen*' ('illegal living') or '*wohnen in Abriss*' ('living in ruins') was not a marginal phenomenon but involved thousands of 'squatters' in the 1970s and 1980s in East Berlin and other major cities.[82] By 1982, a report put the number of people illegally occupying buildings in the Berlin district of Prenzlauer Berg alone at 800. A few years later, the number had risen to almost 1,300. Throughout the 1980s, it is estimated that there were at least 1,000 cases per year in East Berlin.[83]

The archival footprint left by *Schwarzwohner* in East Berlin is modest, however, and it remains difficult to fully gauge the geographical extent of squatting across the city. What is clear, is that for many former squatters, *Schwarzwohnen* had little in common with its Western counterpart and far more to do with basic housing needs and a desire to take control of one's life (in most cases squatters did pay some form of rent). If anything, the rise of *Schwarzwohnen* in the 1970s and 1980s was part of a growing body of informal practices and tactics used by citizens in East Germany in response to housing scarcity (subletting, house swapping, bargaining with authorities, etc.). What they did share with squatters in the West was a commitment to make-shift do-it-yourself practices that gradually transformed squatted flats into liveable spaces and that were, in turn, a product of a wider shadow economy based on practices of informality and reciprocity. Floorboards and pipes were replaced, roofs were repaired, and courtyards were transformed into small community playgrounds.

And yet, if *Schwarzwohnen* pointed to the different ways in which citizens in the GDR found a way to carve out an alternative personal space, many squatters were also connected to a wider network of opposition and dissent and saw their actions in terms that were constitutively political.[84] Wolfgang Rüddenklau, a former occupant of a squatted house in Prenzlauer Berg at Fehrbelliner Straße 7 explained that: 'The islands of occupied flats and houses ... grew together to form an alternative social structure. They affirmed a self-determined lifestyle and developed a common culture.'[85] The connection between underground political activism and *Schwarzwohnen* was also echoed by Jörg Zickler, a former member of the Kirche von Unten, an oppositional movement in the GDR that was closely connected to the Protestant Church. As he later noted, 'from my own political understanding, [*Schwarzwohnen*] was far more than an attempt to simply occupy an apartment. Rather it was an attempt to create a free space for people, against or parallel to the state. In my view, "squatting" was the more appropriate word.'[86]

It was clear therefore that a number of political activists did establish themselves in illegally occupied flats and houses and that an action repertoire more commonly associated with the West had been adapted and reimagined by dissident groups in the GDR.[87] The occupied house on Fehrbelliner Straße was widely known to security services as a 'non-conformist centre for resistance', while the squat at Lychener Straße 61 was home to eight different groups.[88] Both houses played an important role in the alternative infrastructure – social, cultural and political – that emerged in East Berlin in the 1970s and 1980s, and that was centred on the district of Prenzlauer Berg. It was, in turn, dissidents based in Prenzlauer Berg that were responsible for the underground publication and distribution of the most important samizdat publications in the GDR such as *Grenzfall* and the *Umweltblätter*.[89]

It is in this context that an anonymous report appeared in the East German underground magazine *Umweltblätter* describing the plight of a group of squatters who had occupied Lychener Straße 61 in the Berlin district of Prenzlauer Berg. In the squatters' own words, they had 'occupied the house in order to overcome the contradiction between, on the one hand, the many vacant and decaying houses [in Berlin], and on the other, a growing number of people in search of housing'. As 'squatters (*Instandbesetzer*),' they proclaimed, 'we will resist the further cultural and spiritual devastation of the country.'[90]

The occupants of Lychener Straße 61 were under surveillance, and perhaps unsurprisingly subject to a number of police raids. The eventual eviction and demolition of the house in September 1988 was greeted by an unusually open display of defiance by the squatters, who dropped a banner from the roof of the house proclaiming that 'this house has been ruined by the KWV'. Additional banners were added with the words 'rebellion, resistance, Lychener is fully in our hands', and 'we might be out, but we will continue'.[91] If these words seem prophetic, it is worth noting that, for most *Schwarzwohner*, occupation was still viewed less as an act of official political resistance and rather as an attempt to remake their home as a locus of autonomy and freedom. In the end, squatters never posed a serious threat to the

GDR and its apparatus of control. And yet, it is nevertheless clear that the spectrum of alternative practices and tactics developed by squatters in East Berlin spoke to the importance of housing and the city for the development of oppositional cultures and infrastructures in the GDR. It was these practices – informal, makeshift and underground – that laid the groundwork for the new wave of squatting that erupted in the eastern half of the city in the winter of 1989.

What is widely seen as the second major wave of squatting in Berlin has its immediate origins in the covert occupation of houses in the months before the fall of the Wall. In the spring of 1989, for example, a series of flats in a backyard apartment block on Prenzlauer Allee were illegally occupied by a group of *Schwarzwohner* who only made public their activities as 'squatters' in January 1990. It was, however, another nearby house in Prenzlauer Berg at Schönhauser Allee 20/21 that became the first 'official' squat of a new movement. While the house was first occupied in August 1989, it was on 22 December that the occupants chose to publicise their actions by dropping banners from the roof.[92]

The second major wave of squatting in Berlin was characterised by three main phases. The first phase, from December 1989 to April 1990, was largely confined to the districts of Mitte and Prenzlauer Berg, where over seventy houses were eventually squatted. As in the case of Schönhauser Allee 20/21, houses were squatted openly with banners, secured windows and barricaded doors to protect the occupants from attacks by groups of neo-Nazis who had begun to organise in large numbers in the final years of the GDR and were themselves occupying a series of houses on Weitlingstraße in Berlin-Lichtenberg.[93]

The second phase of squatting lasted from the end of April 1990 to July 1990 and shifted to the district of Friedrichshain. The number of squats rose to over 130, especially in the wake of an article published in the autonomous magazine *Interim* which drew attention to houses in Mainzer Straße that had been left vacant since 1987. The magazine put out a call to 'occupy these houses before it was too late'. In the following weeks, the occupation of abandoned houses in the East intensified and, on 30 April 1990, eleven vacant houses on Mainzer Straße were squatted by activists mainly from the West Berlin autonomous movement.[94] The 'Mainzer' became the centre of the Friedrichshain squatting scene and was characterised by a range of political activities and housing projects: no. 3 was a woman's only squat with a café; no. 4 housed the latest incarnation of the 'Queerhouse' ('*Tuntenhaus*') and an antiquarian bookstore (the Max-Hoelz-Antiquariat für DDR-Literatur) on the ground floor; no. 5 was the home of the neighbourhood information centre (or *Infoladen*) and no. 6 opened a popular pub; there was a late-night shop in no. 7 and no. 9 was responsible for a community kitchen which was open to the public; another communal kitchen and cinema would later open in no. 22.[95] In the end, over 250 squatters made Mainzer Straße their home in the summer of 1990.[96]

The third and final phase of squatting began in July 1990 and lasted until the violent eviction of the Mainzer Straße squatters in November in a brutal police operation involving 3,000 officers, ten water cannons and a squad of helicopters. During this period, the number of houses dropped as authorities in East Berlin adopted their own version of the '*Berliner Linie*'.[97] Municipal authorities vigorously proscribed the further occupations of houses and other spaces across the eastern half of the city. At the same time, existing negotiations between the squatters and the East Berlin city council (Magistrat) stalled as it became clear that the Magistrat was simply buying time until the problem of squatting came under the jurisdiction of authorities from the West.

In more practical terms, the second major wave of squatting in Berlin drew on a sedimented history of contentious politics that encompassed both the modest acts of 'rebelliousness' undertaken by *Schwarzwohner* during the GDR and an action repertoire that was developed in West Berlin and elsewhere in West Germany and Europe during the 1970s and 1980s. As in the case of their earlier counterparts, squatters that occupied houses in Berlin in the months following the collapse of the East German state were motivated by a desire to build a radical makeshift infrastructure that linked pressing local issues around housing insecurity to wider articulations of autonomy and self-determination.

A brochure produced in the summer of 1990 by squatters from a group of houses that formed part of the wider squatting network highlighted the range of practices and strategies adopted by their occupants. Echoing tactics first developed by Western activists in the 1970s, the introduction to the brochure describes a 'growing movement' of young people who, in their own words, 'want to realize their own ideas of collective living and working'. 'We want to break through the traditional structures of isolation,' the authors added, 'and build a self-determined neighbourhood infrastructure that prevents liveable homes from remaining empty and falling into disrepair.'[98]

The various squatted houses profiled in the brochure not only signalled a further extension of existing occupation-based practices in Berlin, they also drew attention to the differences between squats in terms of their respective goals and motivations. For the eight activists occupying one wing of an apartment block at Prenzlauerallee 203/204, squatting represented far more than simply an opportunity for collective living. As they pointed out, 'we started with the renovation of the house and repaired the roof. But we still have a lot in front of us to do ... We want to take control of the house's energy needs according to sound ecological principles.' In the case of another house at Rosenthaler Straße 68, it was three well-known bands from the underground scene in East Berlin – Ich-Funktion, Firma and Freytag – that were behind the occupation. According to the founders of what became known as the 'Eimer', 'our wish is to build a permanent centre for art, culture and communications that enables a self-determined exchange with local and foreign groups while facilitating the development and exploration of various art forms'. 'Our own way of life,' they concluded, 'is to re-function the ruins of a vulnerable world and to create, in the process of living and working, our own culture.'[99]

While squatted centres such as the Eimer, Kule ('Kultur und Leben') and Tacheles undoubtedly played a decisive role in the reimagining of Berlin's empty spaces in the early 1990s, other squats documented in the brochure focused, in particular, on the development of local self-help initiatives.[100] The activists who squatted a house at Kastanienallee 85/86 described the occupation as a 'colourful and lively self-help project' with plans to expand the attic, open a print shop, a record store and other workshops. Similar plans were proposed by the squatters living in a house on Schliemannstraße. 'We want to realise in our house,' they proclaimed, 'a collective form of life and work that preserves and extends existing neighbourhood structures. We intend to achieve this with the establishment of a children's club, a bicycle repair shop and a café.'[101] Another group of squatted houses on Kreutziger Straße in Friedrichshain drew up plans for a social centre, while a house on Lottum Straße was transformed into a radical meeting place for groups that had already been active in East Berlin in the final years of the GDR.[102]

The act of occupation was widely framed, in this context, as a politics of adaptation as squatters tackled derelict spaces that (once again) required significant repairs. The squatters occupying a house on Tucholsky Straße described, for example, how they entered a house 'gray, dirty and dusty. The building structure is good. All the beams are solid holding everything in place. Step-by-step, we carried off all the dirt in order to make the house breathe again.'[103] Improvised materials and do-it-yourself practices were, in this way, combined with grassroots political organising to revive a makeshift urbanism that offered an alternative understanding of city life in a period of social and economic change. Many squatters also saw their actions as offering a direct challenge to the rapid privatisation of the housing market in the former East of the city as unification offered, for many, a new 'spatial fix' for the further urbanisation of capital and the creative destruction of earlier forms of socialist property.[104]

The violent clearance of the 'Mainzer' marked a major turning point, however, in the wider history of squatting in Berlin and led to the fragmentation of the scene into a complex archipelago of accommodation, resistance and experimentation. Few squatters were willing in the aftermath of the Mainzer Straße evictions to reject a negotiated settlement with local officials. Over 75 per cent of remaining squatted houses were contractually safeguarded as squatters turned to structural improvements and repair work, often under the auspices of public funding programmes. Houses unwilling to negotiate were cleared, the last wave of evictions taking place between 1996 and 1998 under the direction of former Bundeswehr general, CDU hardliner and local politician, Senator Jörg Schönbohm.

The legalisation of squats in the former eastern half of Berlin had a number of consequences. Houses soon doubled as social centres within a stable yet fragile infrastructure of alternative practices that subsisted in neighbourhoods undergoing rapid change. While many squatted spaces were quickly subsumed within the wider logics of urban regeneration, there were also other sites that that became crucibles of intense cultural experimentation. Houses such as Kastanienallee 77 (K77), Auguststraße 10 (KuLe), Kleine Hamburger Straße 5, Lychener Straße 60 and Rosenthaler Straße 68 (Eimer) were part of an informal network of houses to which the development of shared cultural spaces and activities was a common cause. At stake here in particular was an understanding of squatting as a radical cultural practice, a form of architectural activism that combined community design and participation with a wider understanding of the built environment as a source of continuous invention.[105]

And yet, the makeshift urbanism cultivated by squatters and the 'use' of abandoned buildings, temporary spaces and disused lots for the development of alternative practices and events has also played a decisive role in Berlin's ongoing neoliberal restructuring. As a number of commentators have noted, many of the city's temporary spaces have, in recent years, been 'captured' and harnessed into 'urban development policies and city marketing campaigns'.[106] Such spaces were often transformed into 'branding assets' that contributed to the refunctioning of the city as a site attractive to economic investment, marketisation and hyper-gentrification.[107]

It is perhaps unsurprising therefore that a number of prominent house projects in Berlin were cleared by the police between 2009 and 2012 including Brunnenstraße 183, Liebig 14 and the Kunsthaus Tacheles. Others including Brunnenstraße 6/7, Linienstraße 206 and Rigaer Straße 94 remain under threat of eviction.[108] The heavy-handed tactics recently adopted by the police in a series of brutal operations involving Rigaer Straße 94 – not to mention the leaking of confidential information about the house's occupants to far-right groups – point to the enduring existential threat facing the city's squatter movement.[109]

While Berlin's longstanding squatter movement undoubtedly faces serious challenges, the recent emergence of new oppositional movements in the city, from struggles over refugee rights to protests over gentrification, rising rents and forced evictions, shows that the spaces they created and the practices they deployed still resonate for many activists (and former squatters) for whom a more socially just urbanism persists as an unfinished project. Nowhere is this more in evidence than in the recently established Kotti & Co tenants' initiative in Kreuzberg. Formed by a group of social housing residents, including many from the local German-Turkish community, the makeshift protest camp at Kottbuser Tor has become a neighbourhood social centre and a key organising base in citywide struggles against housing inequality and enduring forms of structural racism.[110]

This is, admittedly, an increasingly fragile project, especially as a new generation of urbanists, planners and geographers have shifted their attention to the dense network of logistics, platforms, routines and systems that sustain and structure our cities. For Keller Easterling these practices produce what she describes as 'infrastructure space'. Easterling is largely concerned with retracing the so-called 'operating system' that provides the material support for a new globalising urbanism.[111] The longstanding history of squatting in Berlin and the makeshift urbanism it produced suggests, however, that another more radical and fragile 'infrastructure space' has also occupied an important place in the history of the contemporary city, bringing people, ideas and resources together in new constellations of care, solidarity and hopefulness. Squatters in Berlin did not simply claim space. They radically transformed it.

6

Seizing the City:
Autonomous Urbanisms
and the Social Factory

Let's take the city! (*Prendiamoci la città!*)

Slogan of Italian autonomists

Metropolitan revolt is always a refoundation of the city.

Antonio Negri[1]

The recent history of urban squatting is full of stories that begin with acts of occupation and resistance and end with tales of eviction and loss. This is, however, a story that begins with an eviction. On the morning of 25 May 2015, Davide Cassarini, a fifty-six-year-old religious studies teacher at a local high school in Bologna gathered together his class of twenty students. He took them outside and across the street to an abandoned commercial centre which had been occupied by squatters and was in the process of being evicted by the police, the Carabinieri and special branch officers from the Digos (Divisione Investigazioni Generali e Operazioni Speciali) Unit. By the time Cassarini and his students arrived, the occupants of the building had already been forcibly evicted and were being processed and identified by the authorities. Most of the 150 occupiers were refugees, many with families. They had occupied the former shopping mall, empty since 2012, on 22 May 2015 and were supported by activists from the grassroots union AS.I.A USB (Associazione inquilini e abitanti), members of the Lazzaretto Social Centre as well as representatives of the International Coalition of Migrants and Refugees Without Papers (Coalizione internazionale migranti rifugiati e sans papiers).[2]

According to Cassarini, the forced eviction was a lesson in 'reality' for his students. 'I don't see what's so strange in bringing the kids here', he added. 'Exposing them to current events is something we are trying to do more of as a school. There is an academic culture that you learn in books. But we also must teach our students to be attentive to what is happening around them.'³ The 'reality' that Cassarini had in mind is the ongoing and protracted economic crisis in Italy that has left a generation of Italians facing a precarious future without jobs or affordable housing. More importantly perhaps, it is a 'reality' shaped by an ever-intensifying refugee crisis in Europe as thousands of people continue to make the dangerous journey across the Mediterranean on cramped fishing boats and shabby dinghies. While many who manage to reach the shores of Italy are ultimately granted asylum and permission to stay (*permezzo di soggiorno*), basic access to housing and other social services is often restricted. Refugees are thus forced to rely on the support of poorly funded, short-term government initiatives characterised by widespread corruption and non-existent services as well as racist intimidation and violence.

It is in this context that refugee groups have linked up with squatters and other housing rights activists in Italy. Together, they have begun to occupy empty buildings across the country, most notably in cities such as Bologna, Milan, Rome and Turin.⁴ If these actions points to the forging of a radical politics of care and hospitality, local authorities have responded in less sympathetic terms. Evictions – whether driven by spurious security concerns or increasingly corporate forms of urban regeneration – are commonplace, forcing many migrants, precarious workers and pensioners onto city streets. For an increasing number of squatters, the very articulation of an alternative right to the city had, in fact, become a battle to realise a more basic fundamental right to *be* in the city.

The recent revival and intensification of squatting and other occupation-based tactics in Italy is only the latest chapter, however, in a much wider history of protest and dissent. While this must undoubtedly be seen as a response to a serious and intensifying housing crisis, it also points, at the same time, to an even richer story of political activism and resistance. This is a story that brings autonomous politics and urban squatting together. At its heart is a longstanding commitment to self-organisation and self-management that depended, in turn, on the collective, non-institutional control of urban and public space.

The very language of autonomy and self-determination can be traced back to political struggles that were first born in the large factories of northern Italy in the early 1950s. 'Autonomy at the base' ('*autonomi di base*') was originally devised by migrant workers from the south in defiance of their union bosses – backed by the Communist Party – who did not, in their eyes, represent them or their needs and desires. Autonomy, and the Autonomia movement it later spawned, soon moved beyond demands for higher wages to question the very nature of the relationship between labour and capital.

But the movement for Autonomy did not end here. As it challenged the idea of labour, it also began to extend the struggle from the factory floor to the 'city' as a whole while 'insisting upon the direct appropriation of urban space'. At stake here was a deep shift in the nature of social conflict in Italy as the everyday spaces of the city became both increasingly 'embattled terrain' as well as a series of laboratories for political and social experimentation.[5] This is a history of intense resistance and violence shaped, in turn, by 'moments of explosive richness and inventiveness' that prepared the ground for a different kind of urban politics.[6]

The 1950s were a period of profound social and economic change in Italy. The Second World War had left much of the country in a state of complete disrepair. Industrial output plummeted, agricultural productivity languished while the transport infrastructure lay in ruins. Within just over a decade, however, the economy had rebounded with dramatic rises in output and productivity. Already by the late 1940s, industrial production had returned to pre-war levels; by 1953, it had risen by over

64 per cent and it almost doubled again by the early 1960s.[7] Italy's 'economic miracle', unlike its Western European counterparts, was not carried out, however, with full employment or social welfare primarily in mind. Rather, successive governments pursued a policy of deflation and the containment of consumer demand through the suppression of wages and high unemployment. State expenditure focused on new infrastructure projects that were supported by generous funding from the Marshall Plan, 75 per cent of which was channelled into the country's steel industry. This only reinforced an earlier industrial geography of production that clustered around the northern cities of Genoa, Milan and Turin. It also promoted a wave of recruitment and a new generation of workers, many of whom had little experience of factory work or unionism. While an expanding workforce at first drew on employees that came predominantly from the north, it also promoted a wave of mass migration as over 3 million Italians moved from the south to work in factories in the north in the two decades that followed the Second World War.[8]

The main beneficiaries of Italy's rapid transformation were industrialists and small sections of the middle class. Modest rises in overall consumer expenditure were largely attained on the back of high rates of productivity and low wages that were insured, in turn, by the complete ineffectiveness of organised labour. Further industrialisation, if anything, deepened existing divisions between the financially advanced north and the semi-feudal Mezzogiorno. Despite their earlier role in the Resistance and the defeat of fascism and Nazism, the 1950s were, for many working-class Italians, a period in which they appeared 'markedly weaker and more divided than that of a decade before'.[9]

While post-war economic inequalities were a direct product of government policies that favoured laissez-faire initiatives, a sharp deflationary environment and systemic wage repression, the transformations that had changed the composition of the Italian working class had also 'radically altered its housing and living conditions'.[10] The movement of millions of Italians from the south to the north created a demand for housing and basic infrastructure that the government was simply unable to cope with. The right to decent affordable housing unsurprisingly became a key rallying point for a new wave of working-class struggles.

These were admittedly struggles with a much longer historical arc. Informal urban settlement and the occupation and squatting of land played a significant role in the history of urban development in Italy throughout the twentieth century. In the case of Rome, for example, new areas of housing for the working class were, from the 1920s, located on the urban periphery in neighbourhoods known as *borgate* that were constructed during the fascist administration as part of the *sventramenti* which displaced families from the historic centre. Between 1924 and 1937, twelve new *borgate* were constructed around Rome. They were cut off from main transportation routes and they lacked, in many cases, amenities such as running water, drains and basic sanitation. This can be seen in a number of films shot in Rome in the post-war period including De Sica's *Ladri di biciclette* (1948), Rossellini's *Europa '51* (1952) and Pasolini's *Accattone* (1961). While the *borgate* were state-sanctioned housing projects often used to disperse the potential of organised working-class protest, there were other types of informal precarious housing in Rome and elsewhere. This included *borghetti*, small clusters of make-shift jerry-built dwellings, and *baracche*, simple shacks that were constructed using found materials such as loose bricks, planks and corrugated iron. The *baracche* were often grouped together to form small informal settlements or shanty towns known as *baraccopoli* (cities of shacks).[11]

At the end of the Second World War, there were thirty-five legal *borgate* and eighty-seven illegal *borghetti* in the city.[12] Many of the landlords and real estate speculators that thrived during the dictatorship were still active and closely connected to a municipal government that they largely controlled. The new housing law of 1962 did little to ameliorate the situation, and nor did the new Urban Master Plan for the city. Tower blocks built on the city's eastern and south-eastern fringes at the end of

1960s were as marginalised as the informal housing they were meant to replace. By 1970, it was estimated that over 200,000 people in Rome were still living on the urban margins in self-built informal settlements as well as the *borgate ufficiali* erected under the auspices of the fascist government. Another contemporary study suggested that upwards of one-third of the city's population were precariously housed in what Pasolini once described as those 'limitless places (*luonghi sconfinati*) where you think the city ends, and where instead it begins again'.[13]

These developments were not limited to Rome. In the early 1950s in Milan, migrants, first from the north and later from the south, were often forced to construct their own housing in peripheral zones on the edge of the city. The new self-built neighbourhoods were widely known as '*coree*', a term that gained currency due to the dwellings bearing a certain resemblance to images appearing at the time from the Korean War. A number of these zones were constructed in the 1950s and early 1960s and they were, by 1965, home to over 100,000 residents. If the *coree* became symbols of urban informality and marginality, they were far from illegal. Most were self-constructed on small plots of land that had been subdivided and sold to migrants.[14]

Many *coree* lacked infrastructure and services, though this evolved as the neighbourhoods were increasingly formalised. As one recent study concluded, 'the history of the *coree* is an extremely complicated one, which cannot be pigeon-holed into the categories of marginality, poverty, exploitation and peripheralisation. This was a rich history, sited in particular geographical and economic spaces which redrew the map of the city.' *Coree* inhabitants were not, in fact, at the bottom of the 'immigrant ladder' as was often suggested. The ability to purchase land, construct a house, buy building materials and then rent out parts of that house presumed a certain level of wealth. *Coree* construction depended, moreover, on a complex chain of entrepreneurs, speculators, mediators, surveyors and other specialists through which homes were built, rents secured and neighbourhoods consolidated.[15]

The overwhelming majority of migrants to the industrial cities of northern Italy were not so lucky, so to speak, and were forced to live in appalling conditions. They found lodgings in overcrowded basements and attics, in apartments slated for demolition and in other vacant buildings. Flats were often restricted to non-southerners with posted warnings such as 'Non si affitta a meridionali' ('not for rent to southerners').[16] Public housing construction did not, however, meet the growing demand for affordable housing. Between 1949 and 1971, GESCAL, the main state agency, built roughly 390,000 housing units, including 3,254 apartments in 1971 when there were 138,931 families on its waiting list. The construction of new housing units was lower in Italy in the 1960s than anywhere else in Western Europe, while rents doubled during the same period.[17]

At the same time, planning regulations were regularly ignored and even adapted to facilitate profiteering and speculation. In Turin, local residents, municipal employees and veterans were given preference in the allocation of public housing often on land purchased by the city from private developers at inflated prices.[18] Not only was corruption endemic throughout the country, GESCAL was also routinely outbid by private developers who later charged rents that consumed up to 40 per cent of a worker's wages. In Italian cities, over 80 per cent of tenancies were unprotected during the 1950s which, in turn, led to rent hikes that disproportionately affected working-class residents. The remaining 20 per cent were, in most cases, professionals who enjoyed frozen rents (affitto bloccato) and other privileges. Another study in 1969 showed that over 70 per cent of all residents in the country's larger cities were renters; the number rose to almost 80 per cent in Turin.[19]

If the housing 'question' for many working-class Italians spoke to the uneven geographical development of Italian cities and the urbanisation of capital, it did so in ways that were increasingly connected to the political struggles of the period. By the late 1950s, many left-wing activists in Italy had already begun to question whether the dogmatic Marxist narrative propounded by the Italian Communist Party really applied to the struggles of the Italian working class. Workers, they argued, were able to organise *autonomously*, whether they belonged to a union or not.[20] They also initiated a series of groundbreaking studies of factory workers that focused on ordinary experiences and struggles that had been hitherto overlooked by the official organisations of the labour movement. As Danilo Montaldi, a member of one of the many dissident circles in Italy, concluded:

> The worker is first of all someone who lives at the point of production of the capitalist factory before being the member of a party, a revolutionary militant or the subject of coming socialist power. It is the productive process that shapes his *rejection of exploitation* and his capacity to build a superior type of society.[21]

These observations increasingly assumed a new urgency and form, spawning a series of publications in the early 1960s (*Mondo Operaio, Quaderni Rossi*, etc.) in which 'many of the themes central to classical *operaismo* [workerism] were to receive their initial nourishment'.[22] It was in the pages of these journals that writers such as Raniero Panzieri, Romano Alquati and Mario Tronti began to trace the emergence of a working class whose needs and desires were no longer compatible with either those of the labour movement or of capital. To do so, they cultivated an approach – a militant participatory form of research known as *conricerca* or co-research – that zoomed in on the experiences of the 'mass-worker' and their collective capacity for obstinacy, rebelliousness and resistance.[23]

It was against this backdrop that an uprising of factory workers in Turin in July 1962 first brought the work carried out by *Mondo Operaio, Quaderni Rossi* and Italian workerism more generally, under intense scrutiny and pressure. After a series of strikes at Mirafiori and elsewhere around Turin, the UIL (Unione Italiana del Lavoro), one of the more conservative trade unions, chose to sign a separate agreement with Fiat management.[24] In response, a large group of factory workers staged an immediate walk-out. They attacked the 'scab' union headquarters on Piazza

Statuto, a large square in the centre of Turin where a three-day confrontation with the authorities began. According to Antonio Negri, 'the workers took over the streets – on their own, but maintaining and renewing for a couple of days the composition of the pickets, operating their own system of shift work on the pickets, matched to the shift times in factories – clashing violently with the police and the various peacemongers'.[25] In the end, the riots were brutally suppressed. Over 1,000 protesters were arrested while many suffered injuries in clashes with the police.

The workers were roundly impugned by the Communist Party and the Italian General Confederation of Labour (CGIL) union (representing many of the metalworkers) who accused them of sabotaging ongoing negotiations with Fiat. For many workerists including Tronti, however, a new political outlook was needed that was capable of grasping 'the total viewpoint of the worker'. Writing in the first issue of *Classe Operaia*, a new journal that he helped to found, Tronti demanded an approach that acknowledged the 'emerging autonomy of the working class with respect to capital, that is, its power to generate and sustain social forms and structures of value independent of capitalist relations of production, and similarly the potential autonomy of social forces from the domination of the State'. At stake here, as Tronti added, was a form of working-class self-organisation that *refused* to 'function as an articulation of capitalist society' and to therefore 'act as an active partner in the whole social process'.[26]

What the 1962 protests at Piazza Statuto made clear was that such a 'strategy of refusal' pointed to an expansive ecology of protest that moved 'from the factory *to the streets*'. As Negri, one of the most important protagonists of the 1960s and 1970s, later proclaimed, 'the measure of the struggle is born ... from the refusal of work, and then it extends positively in the social programming of equality and of the development of productive forces. From the factory to the social, from Mirafiori to Piazza Statuto ... Piazza Statuto [showed] the workerist how irreversible and all-encircling passion is.'[27] While Negri's reflections, written almost two decades later in the Rebibbia Prison as he awaited trial on charges of political subversion, belie something of a retrospective romanticism, they also point to a class struggle that operated, so Negri insisted, on the terrain of the city more broadly, and within the sphere of social reproduction in particular.[28] The right to decent affordable housing was at the very heart of these struggles.

The Italian state responded to these challenges and pressures by, on the one hand, depressing the value of these wages through artificially induced inflation. On the other hand, they targeted the sphere of social reproduction, raising the cost of public housing, transportation and utilities. As one radical daily concluded at the time, 'any gains made inside the factories have been countered by the bosses' use of inflation and property speculation ... In this situation the struggle in the community becomes crucial, and working-class people are forced to discover new forms of self-organization, tactics, and demands.'[29] These were 'forms' of contention that focused on the city as a sphere of social reproduction in an attempt to extract 'political prices for those commodities and services necessary for the reproduction of the working class'.[30] It is also, in this context, how a more expansive and radical urban politics acquired its legitimacy. New practices of mass illegality emerged in the late 1960s, including the auto-reduction of basic needs (the unilateral reduction of rents, bills and transportation) and the mass squatting of housing.

These practices dovetailed with the emergence of a large and militant student movement (Movimento Studentesco, or MS) in the late 1960s. University occupations and demonstrations had already become a common feature by the mid-1960s as students agitated against moves to rationalise higher education. And yet, the major unrest that characterised campus life in the United States and in West Germany, and which came explosively to the fore in France in May 1968, arrived belatedly in Italy. In so doing, however, the Italian 'year of the students', unlike its various counterparts, sparked an extended wave of social conflict that only peaked during the 'Hot Autumn' ('*L'autunno caldo*') of 1969.[31] Students not only rebelled against a paternalist approach to their problems, they also forged alliances and solidarities with workers that had lasting effects on the practices and tactics they developed.

While student politics in the early 1960s tended to reflect those of the national parliament, there were already signs of change. It was, in fact, architecture departments that became important early sites of radical student activism. In 1963, all faculties of architecture were briefly occupied by students protesting against an antiquated system and curriculum, and the widespread 'misuse' of architecture and planning in the ongoing redevelopment and transformation of Italian cities. In Milan, faculty at the Polytechnic (Politechnico di Milano) were involved in the formation of study groups that placed particular emphasis on the political functions of architecture, the failures of urban planning and the need to improve the quality of working-class housing.[32] In 1967, in opposition to government attempts to streamline and rationalise the study of architecture, students occupied the faculty for fifty-five days. All decisions made during the occupation – around questions of 'collective living, debate and shared work' – were reached through the use of general assemblies; a move that led, on the one hand, to the introduction of a new experimental curriculum which blurred the boundaries between student and professor, campus and city, but also anticipated, on the other hand, new forms of political organisation that swept aside the tactics adopted by the traditional student unions.[33]

Events in Milan were overshadowed, however, by student protests in Pisa in February 1967, as student activists disrupted a meeting of university leaders and occupied a number of buildings including the Sapienza as part of a series of nationwide protests. Official student unions were largely ignored, while the activists released a manifesto (partially reformulated in 1968) which became a key theoretical text of the new student movement. The *Tesi della Sapienza* (also known as the *Pisan Theses*) was the first major document to examine the class position of students 'in terms of the struggle between capital and labour'.[34]

The *Tesi* drew inspiration from the recent insights of journals such as *Quaderni Rossi* and *Classe Operaia*, arguing that the very nature of capital's socialisation meant that the student must also be understood within the production process and, in particular, as a 'labour-power in qualification'.[35]

By locating students within the complex circuitry of capitalist accumulation, the *Tesi* pointed to an emerging workerist position which pointed to new political possibilities and solidarities far beyond the factory. This was characterised, in the first instance, by an intensification of student agitation and a further commitment to occupation-based tactics. In November 1967, a new series of student occupations erupted in Genoa, Milan, Trento and Turin. By December, the occupations had spread to the south. There were soon thirty-six in total across the country, though by the end of February 1968 they had all been brutally cleared by the police. Clashes between students and police in Rome, on 20 March 1968, only served to radicalise the student movement further as students countered a ban on demonstrations by driving the police off the streets in what became known as the battle of Valle Giulia. A few days later, attempts to end a lock-out of students at the Catholic University in Milan led to brutal confrontations with the police. Over sixty students were imprisoned, and forty-eight were charged with serious offences.[36]

If the student movement in Italy became a mass movement in early 1968, it also did so in no small measure as a struggle over space and territory. Students attempted with varying degrees of success to link the battle for political autonomy with the reappropriation of institutional space. In the case of the State University in Milan, students were able to refunction the university and the surrounding neighbourhood into a base for their movement and as the centre for a new form of sociality.[37] These tendencies were unable, however, to scale up the student protests in the same explosive way as their counterparts in France in May 1968. For many commentators, '1968' in Italy was less an event than a prolonged and incremental trajectory often described as Italy's 'creeping May' (*'maggio strisciante'*).

By early 1969, a growing assertiveness among many Italian workers in the north lent a new urgency to struggles within the factory and beyond. The events of the French May, if anything, reminded workers of the untenable nature of existing tactics and the need to take matters into their own hands. Already in the summer of 1968, workers in some factories (Pirelli most notably) had formed their own autonomous rank-and-file committees known as *Comitato Unitario di Base*. New connections were forged with other groups on the Left, including tenant unions that had only recently sprung up in response to rapidly rising rents. At the same time, workers adopted practices within the factory aimed at reducing production while resisting union interference. As the student movement fractured and split during the course of 1968, a number of groups that encompassed both students and workers also began to emerge.[38]

Workerist thinking and practice turned its attention (once again) to Fiat and the Mirafiori plant with its 50,000 workers, 60 per cent of whom were originally from the south. Tensions had been simmering over the course of 1968 as many of the plant's semi-skilled workers were unwilling to accept modest wage hikes that corresponded to specific piecework rates and other bonuses tied to production. They clamoured instead for flat wage increases in line with some of their more specialised colleagues. Lightening stoppages, wildcat strikes and other forms of disruption including reductions in output (*autoriduzione*) were thus organised along various points in the assembly line, while many of the workers joined assemblies and meetings organised by students and other activists. They were drawn, in particular, to an emphasis on immediate material needs (higher wages, affordable housing, access to basic public services, decent education, etc.) and 'a desire to live, to do something' and escape the predeterminations of factory work.[39]

It was perhaps the writer and activist Nanni Balestrini who best captured these demands in his remarkable 1969 novel, *Vogliamo Tutto* (*We Want Everything*). The novel draws on a range of primary materials (interviews, flyers, pamphlets, daily bulletins) in order to capture the experiences and struggles of the factory floor as well as the meetings, demonstrations and barricades that transformed Turin into a veritable theatre of protest in the summer of 1969. As the main protagonist of the book – a worker from the south who made his way to the Mirafiori plant – explains, 'the problems of the factory were connected to the problems outside the factory'. He draws particular attention to the parlous state of housing that many working-class families faced in Turin in the book's characteristic declamatory tone: 'More or less complete absence of services. Rents continually rising. Constant blackmail by the landlords, with the threat of eviction.' 'These concrete material objectives of the struggle,' he added, 'got right around the city, because they were things that concerned everybody, that touched everyone directly.'[40]

While the struggle in Mirafiori began in May, it was the lack of housing and rising rents and their connection to low wages that finally prompted the union to call a strike on 3 July. However, as one worker in a general assembly (recorded by Balestrini's worker-activist) proclaimed, 'it wasn't the unions who realised that the workers couldn't cope with the rents any more. It was the workers with their acts of rebellion, *outside* every union and political line, who showed they'd had it up to here with increases in the cost of living and in rents.' 'It's about taking our strike, our struggle,' added another, 'outside and that's why we have to organise ourselves.' 'Some of you,' shouted another comrade, 'may have doubts about the risks, about the fact that there could be serious clashes at the march. But we say right away that the march is not a provocation but that it has the job of explaining the struggle in the factory to the city. To let it be known what has been going on in the workshops for more than a month and why.'[41]

The strike at Mirafiori on 3 July was the event that finally ushered in the Hot Autumn of 1969, the third-largest strike movement recorded in history. What began as a trade union demonstration over housing turned into a march organised by workers to the main gates of Fiat which, in turn, escalated into a series of street battles with the Carabinieri that took in surrounding suburbs and lasted well into the early hours of the morning. 'The struggle,' recalled Negri, 'ran from Mirafiori to the Valentino to Nichelino – a ribbon of Molotov cocktails and thousands upon thousands of militants.' In the months that followed, unrest circulated in numerous factories across the country, from Milan to Porto Marghera, as workers threw the assembly line and the production process into complete chaos. Negri's retrospective gloss on the protests is again instructive here: 'a massive pivotal moment of workers' struggles was being built ... It held solidly the large metropolitan areas of the North, then stretched in an endless variety of experiences and multiple activities ... to the South.'⁴²

The Hot Autumn with its widespread strikes, protests and disruptions seemed to confirm conclusively the workerist thesis that the factory no longer stood over society but had completely absorbed and transformed it 'into an *articulation of production*'.⁴³ And yet, this was also the moment in which Italian workerism itself fractured into a number of different and, in many cases, competing groups and organisations. It was in the latter half of 1969, for example, that Potere Operaio first emerged as a countrywide organisation (as did a publication with the same name) from its base in Padua, in the factories of Porto Marghera and at the University of Rome.⁴⁴ Activists associated with the student-worker assemblies in Turin also came together with other students to form the group Lotta Continua. The first issue of the group's eponymous newspaper appeared in November 1969. In the same year, a dissident branch of the Communist Party associated with the radical newspaper, *Il Manifesto*, attempted to gather its sympathisers into the semblance of an organisation. As a diagram produced by the activist and bookseller Primo Moroni in the late 1980s shows, the extraparliamentary groups that formed in this period (Avanguardia Operaia, Potero Operaio, Lotta Continua, Il Manifesto) and the broad array of journals they spawned did not correspond to any single cohesive movement. They pointed, if anything, to the emergence of a complex and uneven landscape of protest and resistance – an 'archipelago' in the words of Giorgio Bocca – that fuelled the development of Autonomia in the 1970s.[45]

What these protests did share, however, was a commitment to an expanded form of socialisation that took the fight into the city, and into working-class neighbourhoods in particular. The very first issue of *Lotta Continua* featured a major article on rising rents and the struggle against housing insecurity which, by the 1960s, had already become a major source of political agitation in many marginal and informal urban communities.[46] If the PCI played an important role in mobilising against poor housing conditions and illegal building practices in the 1950s and 1960s, it was Lotta Continua which launched a campaign in 1971 in Turin, Milan and Bologna called *Prendiamoci la città* (Let's Take Over the City) in which many of the same tactics of mass action that had proved successful in the factories were adopted.[47] Activists called for the picketing of supermarkets that refused to lower their prices, for the withholding of fares on public transport, and most importantly perhaps for the occupation of empty apartments and houses. They also helped to organise the collective auto-reduction of rents as well as rent strikes, many of which began spontaneously in apartment blocks in response to growing inflationary pressures. For Lotta Continua, it was imperative that the struggle of workers became a 'general struggle'.

It was during this period that Italian activists (in Lotta Continua but also in many other groups) attempted to organise prison inmates, hospital nurses, mental health patients, tenants and even army recruits. These struggles dovetailed with the anti-authoritarian and anti-institutional impulses that characterised the extra-parliamentary Left. This also included the radical anti-psychiatry movement and the work of Franco Basaglia whose assemblies in the Gorizia asylum became models for the open-style meetings that would dominate the Hot Autumn, from factories to universities to housing estates to schools.[48] While these new tactics served as key stepping-stones in the 'long march' through (and against) various institutions of power, many other actions and tactics were more prosaic, and as such focused on local issues and their impact on predominantly working-class neighbourhoods. Activists helped form local committees in various cities that coordinated the auto-reduction of utility bills, while at the same time protecting those taking part from either bill collection or the disconnection of their services. Rises in transport fares were widely ignored by workers who simply refused to pay. New after-school clubs and leftist medical clinics were also created as was the Soccorso Rosso Militante, which provided legal aid to striking workers and other activists involved in extra-parliamentary struggles.[49]

In the end, the most successful aspect of these struggles was the widespread turn to rent strikes as well as the organised squatting of inner-city and suburban buildings in Rome, Milan and Turin and the various efforts made by the occupants to resist eviction. 'Rent strikes have developed,' according to one article in *Lotta Continua*,

> not as symbolic acts of protest against government policies, but as a direct response to the tyranny of rent ... The strikes are organized block by block, staircase by staircase, with regular meetings, newsletters, wall newspapers, leaflets, and demonstrations. In the course of the struggle people begin to take control of their project or building, asking themselves why they should pay rent, how much they should pay, if any, and what it should be used for. At the same time they make sure that the rent collector and the police can't carry out their jobs. Anti-eviction squads are set up, and contacts are established with workers in nearby factories who can be brought out immediately.[50]

In the case of squatting, an earlier phase of occupations in Rome was already targeting unassigned public housing in the mid-1960s in the neighbourhoods of Trullo, San Basilio and Tufello. A much larger wave of squatting first erupted in 1969 as earlier protests against housing insecurity 'converged with broader national protest movements'. These were 'mass collective actions involving hundreds of people'. The squatters focused on the development of new 'collective ways of living' that, in turn, revolved around an infrastructure of shared services: day-care centres, health clinics and communal kitchens.[51]

Between 1969 and 1975, over 20,000 apartments were thus occupied across Italy in one of the largest squatting campaigns in Europe. The squatters were supported by the metallurgical unions (the Federation of Metallurgical Workers [FLM] in particular) and various extra-parliamentary groupings including Lotta Continua, Avanguardia Operaia and later Il Manifesto.[52] Rome, in the two years up to 1971, bore witness to the mass occupation of empty houses, peaking on 29 October when 3,300 apartments were occupied by over 13,000 families. The number would rise to 4,000 apartments a few years later during another wave of protests. Hundreds of families also camped out in front of the city hall in 1974 for sixty-eight days demanding immediate access to affordable housing.[53]

In Turin, in neighbourhoods such as Nichelino, Falchera and Valleta, the shortage of accommodation was such that residents squatted new public housing blocks before they were even completed. A mass movement for the auto-reduction of basic utilities also erupted in the city in 1974, and at one point over 150,000 families in Turin and surrounding area had auto-reduced their electricity bills.[54] Similar tactics were mobilised in Milan, where tenant unions (*unione inquilini*) were formed as early as 1968. Rent strikes and resistance to evictions quickly became a common feature of housing struggles in the city in the late 1960s and early 1970s.[55] In Quarto Oggiaro, local supermarkets were picketed while secondary students went on strike over the price of their textbooks. Many families also turned to squatting as a necessary protest against housing scarcity, and in January 1971 a modern block of apartments owned by the state housing agency was occupied on the Via MacMahon.

A few months later, in June 1971, a series of protests centred on the Via Tibaldi bringing tenants, students and workers together in a sequence of occupations, protests and demonstrations. As

German writer and activist Peter Schneider noted in a special issue of the journal *Kursbuch*, the more than forty families involved in the occupations on the Via Tibaldi were simply exercising a right to housing that they had been repeatedly denied.[56] To do so they seized a series of new and unfinished properties on the Via Tibaldi in the early morning of 2 June 1971 with the help of activists from Lotta Continua.[57] The occupations pitted homeless families, students and workers against bosses, unions, housing officials and the police. Over the course of a week, what began as an occupation of an empty block of apartments had turned into a major insurrection as the occupants took to city streets, occupied city hall and later the faculty of architecture at the Politechnico in Milan.

The state responded through a wave of repression as thousands of police officers were mobilised against the occupations. On 8 June 1971, a police operation to remove the squatters from the Via Tibaldi began. After long negotiations the squatters agreed to leave, though they quickly moved to the Politechnico in response to an invitation by students in the faculty of architecture. By that evening an even larger police force had been assembled to evict the families and the students that supported them. They encountered fierce resistance and, while they were able to gain access to the building, the protesters were able to escape and regroup. By this time, the police had run out of tear gas and were forced to strike a retreat. The next morning, the families returned to the faculty of architecture. It was agreed by the faculty board that a permanent seminar on housing would be set up in collaboration with the squatters.[58]

The police returned a few days later in the early morning of 11 June 1971, and were finally successful in evicting the families and their supporters. Public support for the squatters was growing, however, and the mayor of Milan, Aldo Aniasi, was forced to back down and offer a series of major concessions. Over 200 apartments were ultimately allocated to the families from the Via Tibaldi as well as a number of other precariously housed residents in the city. Each family received 100,000 lira in compensation and an additional 15,000 lira for each member of the family. The usual obligation to provide three months' deposit in advance was waived. All rent arrears were also frozen by the city council.[59]

The success of the Via Tibaldi squatters galvanised activists across the country. Some turned to the occupation of private housing. Others connected longstanding neighbourhood struggles over housing inequality with a new-found desire to reinvent the city as a space of creativity and experimentation and as a site of resistance and solidarity. These were intense and often violent conflicts with tenants, squatters, students and workers on one side and the police, pliant union officials, local authorities as well as far-right militants on the other. Fascist crimes were often used by the state as an occasion to stoke tensions (the infamous *strategia della tensione*) and initiate repressive counter-measures against the Left who were, more often that not, blamed for the violence. Assassinations and bombings were commonplace, and in at least one instance a left-wing activist, Fabrizio Ceruso, was shot dead by police in Rome after they attempted to evict families squatting a high-rise block in the outlying working-class district of San Basilio.[60]

At the same time, the sheer scale of the struggle over housing in Italy in the early 1970s pointed to the further transformation of Italian workerist ideas and tactics. By mid-1973, splits within Potero Operaio had led to the break-up of the organisation and the emergence of new groups and collectives that came to represent Italian Autonomia. In the face of growing state repression and deadly far-right violence, many former members were drawn to armed resistance and the 'clandestine organisation of a proletarian military apparatus' which led to the formation of the Brigate Rosse (Red Brigades) and the Gruppi Armati Partigiani.[61] While the Brigate Rosse began as an organisation whose actions were largely symbolic, their tactics – as well as those of other groups such as Prima Linea – became increasingly militant in the mid-1970s, and ultimately played a decisive role in the brutal dissolution of the Autonomia movement in the late 1970s.

In the wake of Potero Operaio, it was a number of new collectives, committees and base structures (the so-called small groups or *piccolo gruppo*) that came to form the extensive yet loose network of Autonomia Operaia.[62] The first groups date back to 1972, when both the journal *Rosso* in Milan and the Via Volsci collectives in Rome were founded. It was in 1975, however, that autonomous assemblies and collectives in neighbourhoods first spread throughout the country. These were developments that reinforced a profound shift in the nature of radical politics in Italy as technological restructuring and strategic reforms began to roll back the gains achieved in the workplace.

The fulcrum of social conflict had shifted, and for many the factory was no longer the only determinate site of struggle as the era of full employment ended and a new precarious and marginalised workforce emerged. This process was known in Italy as 'metropolitanisation' and was responsible for the recomposition of an urban working class that now included elements that were 'traditionally outside the classical Marxist definition of productive labour: students, the unemployed, and women'. It was from these layers, however, that a more 'diffuse' Autonomia movement would draw its strength. What was widely understood in 1969 as the articulation of a worker's separation from his or her own institutional infrastructures had, by 1977, become a rejection of that identity altogether.[63]

This was moreover a movement, as Balestrini argued, that increasingly *connected* forms of political radicalism with 'creative production' ('*pruduzione creativa*') and 'cultural self-management' ('*culturale autogestita*').[64] At stake here, as his contemporary Franco 'Bifo' Beradi later recalled, was a commitment to social autonomy that was brought about through a process of intense cultural experimentation that promised to revive an alternative form of life that operated in direct opposition to the economy. 'Automony,' he concluded, 'is the ability to give an adequate rule to Desire (*regola adequata al Desiderio*), and not the art of begrudging the world.'[65]

It was, in this context, that Bifo founded the radical magazine

A/traverso in Bologna in 1975, promising a new form of political organising from below, 'from everyday life, from relationships and friendship, from the refusal of wage labour to the pleasure of solidarity'.[66] He was also heavily involved in the free radio movement, and helped to establish Radio Alice in Bologna in 1976. While these new cultural impulses shaped the emergence of the countercultural agitprop strand of the Italian Left in the 1970s, the diffuse form of Italian Autonomia that first appeared during this period was still shaped by a commitment to a practice of mass 'illegality' through squatting, the occupation of public spaces and the self-reduction of cultural and social costs.[67] Immediate physical needs had, however, given way to a host of new desires that were, in turn, indebted to two further developments: the impact of Italian feminist struggles on the objects and methods of radical political action and the concomitant rise of a distinctively militant youth politics 'hostile to all codified ideologies'.[68]

It was Antonio Negri who argued that 'without the women's movement, Autonomia would never have taken off in Italy'.[69] For many Italian women, the emergence of radical social movements in the late 1960s did little to address the male domination of political organisations or the deeply entrenched inequalities that structured the sexual division of labour at work and in the home. The feminist movement which emerged at the same time as the factory struggles and student protests of the late 1960s not only challenged these tendencies, it also promised new political trajectories that were grounded in women's own experiences and based on the transformation of their everyday social lives. For many, autonomy meant separation, and it was a sustained critique of the radical Left – its unwillingness to engage with the needs and differences of women – that prompted many women in Italy to form their own self-managed organisations and collectives in the early 1970s. They also played a prominent role in the dissolution of other political formations such as Lotta Continua in 1976, after male members of the group attacked an abortion rally on 6 December 1975.[70]

The first women's collectives emerged between 1969 and 1971 in many major Italian cities. They included Rivolta Femminile (based in Milan and Rome), Anabasi (Milan), Lotta Femminista, an offshoot of Lotta Continua (Padua and Rome), and the student group Cerchio Spezzato (Trento). There were many other groups that formed in the years that followed, such as Col di Lana (Milan) and Collettivo Femminista Romano (Rome). Meetings took place in private homes, new women's centres as well as squats. In the case of Milan, the Collettivo Femminista di via Cherubini became a key meeting place for a number of different groups across the country, largely thanks to its journal, *Sottosopra*, which was launched in 1973.[71] A couple of years later in the same city, a group of women – some formerly associated with Avanguardia Operaia – squatted a housing complex on the Via Mancinelli that had been previously occupied by other leftist groups in the city. They set up a social centre while another group established a Women's Library (*Liberia della donne*) on the Via Dogana.[72]

While many of these groups focused on single issues such as women's reproductive health, sex work, sexual violence and domestic labour, they also played an important role in the creation of a radical urban infrastructure that encompassed daycare centres, health clinics, bookshops, printing presses, radio stations, theatre groups, shelters and squats. Such spaces were, in most cases, autonomist, separatist and relational insofar as their physical separation from men became the necessary starting point for consciousness-raising practices (*autocoscienza*) geared at shaping feminist political subjectivities. There were practices that, in other words, provided the physical ground *and* social space where women's personal desires and differences could be openly acknowledged and explored.[73]

At the same time, there were spaces and practices that also refunctioned the home as a radical domestic space. Not only did many Italian feminists seek to challenge its traditional, routinising demands, they also focused their attention on the material exploitation of women in the home. Members of Lotta

Femminista, including Mariarosa and Giovanna Franca Dalla Costa and Leopoldina Fortunati, began a campaign known internationally as 'wages for housework' in which they developed a workerist approach to unpaid domestic labour. They argued that the family, and social reproduction more generally, represented an important aspect of the wage system by keeping wages lower and hours longer than they would otherwise be if such activities were purchased as commodifiable services. Other feminists disagreed, however, arguing that such a demand was tantamount to the further ratification of domestic work, not to mention the conditions of other forms of labour and the very idea of work more generally. As one contemporary article in the journal *Rosso*, on women's domestic and salaried work, concluded: 'our struggle, is against factories, ... offices, against having to sit at a check-out counter all day ... We are not fighting for such an organisation of work, *but against it*.'[74]

Whatever the case, it was clear for many feminists that the fight for women's liberation was a decisive component in a wider revolutionary struggle. The tactics and practices that they developed resonated, after all, with a youth movement which emerged in the same period and whose actions culminated in the cycle of struggles that marked the 'movement of 1977'. This was a movement that constituted, as the writer and activist Sergio Bologna argued, 'a totally different way of conceiving of the *relation* between life and politics'.[75] It was a movement, moreover, that challenged, and in many ways rejected, the law of value as the main mediator of its needs and desires. It presumed, and indeed depended, on a mass of young people who found themselves marginal to mainstream society, whether socially by lack of employment or culturally by a kind of existential disaffection. 'They were,' as one historian has argued, 'stylistically rebellious, while living and working inside distinctive collective arrangements and informal economies.'[76]

For many young Italians, existing forms of political resistance such as squatting and auto-reduction now took on a new and heightened significance. And yet, where earlier forms of squatting had (quite understandably) focused on struggles around housing, the wave of squatting that accompanied the autonomist movement in the mid-to-late 1970s was, like its counterparts across Europe, predicated on a wider interpretation of the cultural and political needs of squatters who not only occupied homes but also other buildings with a view to living 'differently from families'.[77] At work here, as Balestrini and Moroni later concluded, was 'a swarming process of diffused organisation whose real protagonists were young proletarians, marginal to the organised autonomous groups, but inserted into dynamics of spontaneous, magmatic, uncontrollable aggregation'.[78]

It was in this period that a number of proletarian youth clubs and new social centres sprang up for the first time in cities across Italy, particularly in Milan. Many young students and precarious workers had found themselves living on the city's margins in districts such Quarto Oggiaro, where the effects of the mid-1970s economic crash were most acutely felt.[79] The clubs were set up as meeting places for youth deprived of services by the city council. There were over fifty clubs operating between 1975 and 1976, though these were usually confined to a single room and were quickly superseded by larger social centres allied in most cases with the Autonomia movement and its various offshoots – spaces that tended to bring activists from many different groupings together. These centres often squatted vacated industrial factories, warehouses and sheds on the city's fringes. While many were evicted by the police or fell into disuse during the heroin epidemic of the late 1970s and early 1980s, a small number, including Leoncavallo and Cox 18, remain active today.

The former was first occupied in October 1975 and consisted of a small building on the Via Mancinelli as well as a large and abandoned warehouse structure overlooking the Via Leoncavallo in the city's north-east. The complex was slowly restored and eventually encompassed a series of workshops, a printing press, a theatre, a 'people's' school as well as other neighbourhood services. The original complex was evicted in 1989 and a new centre was finally established in 1994 on the Via Watteau. While attempts have been made to regularise the status of the new building, it remains under threat of eviction. In the case of Cox 18, the social centre on the Via Conchetta in the Ticinese district of Milan was first occupied in July 1976 by a mixed group of anarchist activists and local families protesting the poor state of housing in the neighbourhood. Despite numerous evictions, the centre is still active. It is home to a number of groups as well as the Primo Moroni Archive and the Calusco City Lights bookstore.

By the late 1970s, there were also a number of other squatted spaces in Milan in the Piazza XXIV Maggio, on Via Gentilino, Via Bergognone, Via Gorizia and Via Pontida. A women's only centre and squat was located on Via della Pergola while a punk-inspired venue was founded on Via Orti.[80] In Rome, local 'neighbourhood committees' were active across the city and assumed a similar role to the social centres that had sprung up in northern Italy. Groups associated with Autonomia were based throughout the period on the Via dei Volsci, while squatting also continued in many neighbourhoods such as Primavalle, San Basilio and Spinaceto. There were also a number of small squatting initiatives that persisted in other cities such as Bologna, Naples and Turin. All of these actions were, in turn, supported and sustained by a wide infrastructure of collectives, bookshops and free radio stations including Radio Popolare and Radio Onda d'Urto in Milan, Radio Onda Rossa, Radio Proletaria and Radio Città Futura in Rome, Radio Sherwood in Padua, and Radio Alice, Radio Kappa and Radio Città in Bologna.[81]

The turn to squatting and other occupation-based tactics within the wider Autonomia movement testified to a desire to build bases of worker autonomy in the city. But it also formed part of a new urban geography that treated the whole city as a stage for radical happenings, spontaneous encounters, creative interventions and other insurgent practices which, in their eyes, pointed to a new urban movement for the creation of 'free spaces'.[82] It was the emergence, in particular, of the 'metropolitan indians' ('*indiani metropolitani*') as a new radical grouping of sorts, first in Rome then elsewhere across Italy, that would eventually come to symbolise an autonomist movement whose actions were simultaneously political *and* aesthetic.[83]

It was a group known as Geronimo (formerly the ex-Cassio Collective) that, in December 1975, began to organise a series of spontaneous neighbourhood 'events' in Rome that included 'happenings' as well as occupations in parks and partially abandoned buildings.[84] This was, more generally, a movement that increasingly drew on forms of action that had little to do with work and were, in many cases, conspicuously 'anti-work'. It found particular inspiration in a series of alternative countercultural events organised by youth groups looking for new experiences, identities, intimacies and a sense of togetherness (*stare insieme*). In 1976, for example, a number of groups in Milan organised a Festival of the Spring in the city's Parco Lambro as part-carnival and part-pop concert with plenty of drinking, dancing and dope-smoking.[85] Many so-called *indiani metropolitani* wore face paint at such events and celebrated a popular if fanciful imagination of North American indigenous peoples that showed, in turn, little real knowledge of the societies they romanticised.[86]

The *indiani metropolitani* also first appeared at a time when squatting in Italy was 'extending its scope from providing space to live to establishing places of cultural activity'. Many of the actions and interventions that were developed during this period belied an irreverent and self-consciously Dadaist impulse, and as such drew on the network of alternative bookshops, radio stations and social centres that were established at the same time. Other actions were adapted from existing strategies such as auto-reduction and were applied *en masse* to various cultural events including the cinema and, in one instance, the La Scala Opera House.[87]

From January 1977 onwards, many of the students that were involved in the movement also began to agitate against education reforms which would have introduced a quota system at universities.[88] A new wave of university occupations began in Rome and, in the wake of violent fascist attacks, spread quickly across the country to Bari, Bologna, Cagliari, Florence, Naples and Perugia. As one activist recalled:

> People thronged to the university from every neighbourhood – school students, the unemployed, youth from estates on the urban periphery, druggies, gays [sic], young workers in the black economy. This was the 'movement' which exploded. It had scarcely seen daylight before it began to bawl out loudly and ever yet more loudly causing, even if it was only for a few moments, the pillars of the social contract to shake.[89]

Another commentator writing in *La Rivoluzione*, a Maoist-Dadaist newspaper based in Bologna, described the February movement as 'the *conquest* of a mass social terrain and the central territory of the university by a subject incarnating the refusal of work'.[90] This was a view supported by an article in *A/Traverso* which concluded that the 'great wave of struggles, discussions, mobilisations that encompassed the university' were unlike 1968 insofar as they 'came from the neighbourhoods, the thousand collectives, the places of precarious work' and did so to put 'the actuality of the revolution on the agenda'.[91]

For many, the very idea of 'conquest' was now shaped by an increasingly violent confrontation with authorities, and in many cases the Communist Party (PCI) itself, whose 'historic compromise' with the right-wing Christian Democrats was widely impugned by many on the autonomous Left. On 17 February 1977, the PCI sent union leader Luciano Lama to remonstrate with the occupying students in Rome. They were unwilling, however, to back down and in the riot that followed chased Lama and his supporters from the campus shouting that 'this is our space and you will not succeed in taking it from us so easily'. At this point, the police surrounded the university and proceeded violently to evict the students whose makeshift barricades were quickly cleared by a new fleet of armoured cars.[92] Protests soon spread to other cities, and on 11 March 1977 a serious conflict broke out in Bologna at the university as a group of autonomist activists attempted to prevent a meeting of a right-wing youth organisation. The rector of the university called in the police and the Carabinieri, and in the violence that ensued a small detachment of officers began to fire indiscriminately into the crowd of protesters killing one of them, Francesco Lorusso, an activist who had been formerly involved in Lotta Continua.[93]

The city exploded into a wave of protests that turned the university quarter into a 'liberated zone' from which stores, banks – even gun shops – were raided. The police once again dispatched special units and tanks to clear the barricades which were largely constructed from the desks and chairs that usually filled the lecture halls and seminar rooms of the university.[94] Radio Alice, which had become a vital source of information for the protesters, was also closed down in a police raid on 12 March that took place during a live broadcast.[95] The editors were either arrested or forced to go on the run, as were many other activists involved in the struggle in Bologna. On the same day, a large protest took place in Rome as over 100,000 students, workers and other residents marched through the city while many thousands of young people were engaged in running street battles with the police. March 1977, as Bifo later recalled, was *the* 'moment of greatest intensity in the explosion of the struggle for autonomy'. It was also the moment, he noted, when 'the State was forced to resort to brutal repression'. Over the next few years, hundreds if not thousands of Italians were arrested while radio stations, journals, publishing houses and bookstores were closed and searched.[96]

Confronted with a wave of repression, activists in the Autonomia movement began to question their own tactics and many began to reimagine their actions, in turn, as a form of armed struggle, or at the very least embraced the importance of being 'militant'. It is against this backdrop, moreover, that a major international congress was organised in September 1977 in Bologna, the Congress Against the Repression in Italy (*il Convegno contro la repressione*). At least 70,000 participants attended the congress, which represented a defining moment in the history of Italian Autonomia and the high point in an intense period of political, social and cultural experimentation.

During the congress, the entire city of Bologna was effectively transformed into a radical festival as the intense carnivalesque atmosphere blurred the boundaries between the political and the cultural, between protest and performance. Downtown streets were lined with 'uninterrupted waves of people' painting, dancing and singing while the city's squares, parks and public buildings became huge makeshift camps.[97]

The congress in Bologna provided a glimpse into an alternative urbanism shaped by the autonomous organisation of creative, social and political energies that pointed to the creation of new identities and institutions.[98] And yet, it was ultimately overshadowed by the question of violence and its uses within and on behalf of the Autonomia movement. One contemporary journal observed how the question of armed organisation was 'lived concretely in the movement' and that it pointed to a real process within a network of Communist cadres that was spreading rapidly.[99] It was the Brigate Rosse (Red Brigades) and their actions, however, that came to dominate the new forms of violent struggle that emerged in the late 1970s. The Red Brigades had originally formed in October 1970 in the northern industrial cities of Genoa, Milan and Turin and many of their early actions were centred around factory-based conflicts. While many of the grassroots actions of the 1970s (squatting, eviction resistance, tenant strikes, etc.) led to violent confrontations with authorities and the police, the Red Brigades did little to engage with these initiatives, focusing instead on the factory where they targeted bosses and managers as well as union officials. What began as a series of punitive actions based on the tactics adopted by workers soon escalated through the mid-1970s to professional actions (kidnappings, assassinations) carried out, so the Red Brigades insisted, on behalf of the 'masses'.[100]

The 1978 kidnapping and assassination of Aldo Moro, former prime minister and then president of the Christian Democrats, by the Red Brigades not only brought these new violent impulses into sharp relief, it also unleashed a wave of statist repression as activists – most of whom were unconnected with the Red Brigades

– were targeted in a wave of new laws and extra-judicial killings, some of which were carried out by fascist paramilitary groups and organisations. Thousands of activists were arrested and incarcerated often under the most spurious of evidentiary pretences. In April 1979, Antonio Negri, Alisa del Re, Oreste Scalzone and a host of other activists associated with Autonomia Operaia were arrested under orders from the Padua state attorney, Pietro Calogero. They were charged with being the leaders of the Red Brigades and, as such, responsible for the wave of violence that had spread across Italy during the 1970s. Negri was, in turn, indicted by a judge in Rome who charged him with the murder of Aldo Moro and the promotion of an 'armed insurrection against the powers of the state'.[101] Negri was eventually exonerated for the killing of Moro and the charge of 'armed insurrection' was dropped at the last minute. He was, however, convicted for his alleged involvement in the death of a Potero Operaio activist and in the murder of the Carabinieri Lombardini during a bank robbery. During his lengthy trial, Negri was elected to the Italian parliament as a member of the Radical Party. He was granted immunity and was able to leave Rebibbia Prison, at which point he fled to Paris where he lived until 1997 protected from extradition by the Mitterrand government. Negri was subsequently sentenced *in absentia* to thirty years in prison. He later returned to Italy to serve out the remainder of his sentence which had been reduced, in the meantime, to thirteen years.[102]

In the eyes of many, the brutal crackdown on Autonomia ushered in the final defeat of Italian workerism as both a political project and social movement. Thousands of activists were incarcerated by the authorities while others greeted the end of the movement with feelings of anger, loss, despair and hopelessness. Many struggled to cope and left the wider scene. Drug abuse was rampant, especially as heroin addiction became an increasingly serious problem within many Italian cities. And yet, the political repression of the late 1970s and early 1980s was never all-encompassing or wholly depoliticising. Anger and loss, if anything, was equally constitutive of new social, political and aesthetic relations, however fragile and precarious. As the French activist, philosopher and psychoanalyst Félix Guattari noted in a 1982 interview with Sylvère Lotringer, 'that the Italian Autonomia was wiped out proves nothing at all. From time to time, a kind of social chemistry provides us with a glimpse of what could be another type of organisation.'[103]

It was around questions of housing and in a growing network of squatted social centres that a different kind of 'organisation' endured. During the 1980s and 1990s, a new wave of social centres were set up across Italy that helped to nurture and sustain a radical urban milieu in a number of Italian cities, especially in the northern half of the country. Many of these spaces – disused industrial premises, deconsecrated churches, unused schools and movie theatres – were initially squatted with their occupants adopting the abbreviation CSOA (Centro Sociale Occupato Autogestito). By 1998, over 50 per cent of these spaces had entered into some kind of arrangement with their owners (becoming Centro Sociale Autogestito, or CSA).[104] As self-organised spaces, they often enjoyed a prominent place in local neighbourhoods, offering space for activists and artists while hosting initiatives associated with other closely related campaigns and practices (tenant activism, anti-fascist organising, migrants' and precarious workers' rights, urban gardening schemes, etc.).[105]

Social centres were, in this way, embedded within a local ecology of practices and knowledge. They also supported a range of political groupings that emerged in the wake of the Autonomia movement. Some remained close to Autonomia; others were connected to anarchist groups. A significant number supported the Disobbedienti movement that emerged in the wake of the anti-G8 protests in Genoa in 2001. Others still were linked to the Italian rank-and-file union movement and were supported by 'base unions' such as Federation of Rank and File Unions (COBAS) as well as USB (Unione Sindacale di Base) who remain active in struggles around the politics of asylum and the right to housing (through their tenants' union AS.I.A USB).[106]

Italian social centres were also closely connected to a much wider set of struggles over housing. While a new nationwide law was passed in 1978 to control rents (Equo Canone, Law No. 392/1978), it was largely ignored by property owners who were successful in overturning the law as well as other state-based provisions for social housing and affordable rents.[107] As evictions soared, residents responded through a new wave of occupations that began in the late 1980s in Rome and other cities such as Bologna, Milan and Turin. Where earlier squatting initiatives were largely used as a means to negotiate with authorities, activists were now involved in permanent occupations, squatting empty public buildings and, in some cases, large abandoned apartment blocks that were a product of widespread corruption and speculation. A whole series of radical housing organisations also emerged during this period and became increasingly involved in actions and occupations involving migrants and refugees, many of whom were undocumented and would otherwise have been detained in special temporary detention centres (*Centri di Detenzione Temporanea*).[108]

The recent occupations undertaken by activists, migrants, students and a growing number of precarious workers across Italy ultimately point to the articulation of an alternative right to the city that is, at the same time, an expression of a more basic struggle to find a place in the city. These are actions that point to the further development of radical forms of care, generosity and dwelling and have successfully provided housing for thousands of families across Italy. Not only do they build on the longstanding self-organising ethos of social centres, they also serve to support people who are in desperate need of housing and are largely unaware of the Italian radical Left and its complex history, and the entanglements of the autonomous movement and urban squatting.

And yet, this is also a history whose various afterlives are under constant threat. Numerous social centres and squatted spaces across the country have been evicted in recent years. Even Bologna, a city long known as one of the beating hearts of autonomous politics, has become, as one commentator recently noted, a 'city of evictions'.[109] Most of the city's autonomous spaces have been pushed out in recent years in a series of high-profile police operations that include the ex-Telecom squat and the Casa Nelson Mandela, spaces that housed migrant families in desperate need of housing.[110] It was the recent forced eviction of the Atlantide – a self-managed social space and radical queer centre – in October 2015 that ultimately brought these developments into sharp relief. The former centre was housed in an abandoned nineteenth-century gatehouse on Piazza Porta Santo Stefano and had become a major site within a wider landscape of community organising in the city.[111]

The loss of the Atlantide and many other spaces across Italy have been acutely felt. But there is also reason for hope. The recently re-elected mayor of Naples, Luigi de Magistris, has approved the legalisation of a series of seven squatted spaces in the city on the grounds that they represent 'structures and facilities' dedicated to the 'common good'. There are now thirty-three social centres in Naples and, if the autonomous city of Italian workerism has any purchase today, it does so – as the ongoing actions of squatters, workers and migrants show – as an inescapably necessary place of endurance, hospitality and survival.[112]

7

Mudflats Living and the Makeshift City: Settler Colonialism, Artistic Reinvention and the Contradictions of Squatting in Vancouver

They are taking down the beautiful houses once built with
    loving hands
But still the old bandstand stands where no band stands
With clawbars they have gone to work on the poor lovely
    houses above the sands
At their callous work of eviction that no human law
    countermands

Malcolm Lowry[1]

We resist
person by person
square foot by square foot
room by room
building by building
block by block

Bud Osborn[2]

It was in the fall of 1946 that the author Malcolm Lowry and his wife, the actor and writer Marjorie Bonner, first made a trip to Gabriola Island, one of the many small idyllic islands off the coast of Vancouver Island.[3] The Lowrys had been living in North Vancouver since August 1940, having rented a small squatter's cottage on the North Shore of Burrard Inlet at Dollarton before buying another nearby shack eight months later. When that shack burned down in 1944, the Lowrys were unable to salvage the many manuscripts that Malcolm was working on at the time, with one exception – a novel that would famously appear a few years later as *Under the Volcano*. The Lowrys were able, however, to rebuild the shack on the beach in 1945, though the small informal community of squatters that they belonged to was soon threatened with eviction by municipal authorities intent on transforming their beachfront homes into a public park named after a family of tugboat operators.[4]

While the threat of dispossession and eviction prompted Lowry to write a number of short stories celebrating the precarious existence he and his wife had come to love (including 'The Forest Path to the Spring'), they nevertheless decided to visit Gabriola to see if the island might offer an alternative to Dollarton. The Lowrys took the ferry over from Vancouver to Victoria and then, after spending a day in the city, they took a bus to Nanaimo from where they boarded the local ferry to Gabriola. The couple stayed for half a week at the Anderson Lodge. They went on long walks, visited friends and looked into the possibility of moving to the island. As with other trips, they also brought with them a small notebook which they used to record impressions, ideas and thoughts, including the preliminary sketches for a short story which would later become the basis for Lowry's unfinished novel, *October Ferry to Gabriola*.[5]

In the end, the Lowrys chose to ride their luck and stay in Dollarton, though by 1950 city officials had redoubled their efforts to clear the beach and evict the squatters. Lowry's own fragile mood darkened. The prospect of imminent eviction terrified him. 'My love for this place and my fear of losing it,' he wrote, 'has begun to exceed all bounds.'[6] Lowry returned to the draft of *October Ferry*. A simple short story about the search for a new home now became, in the author's own words, 'a huge and sad novel'. 'It deals,' Lowry later noted, 'with the theme of eviction, which is related to man's dispossession [*sic*], but this theme is universalised.' An 'outer world of makeshift and homelessness' had, in other words, been transformed into an epic quest for spiritual and moral redemption.[7]

By the time of his death in 1957, the manuscript for Lowry's *October Ferry* had gone through seven separate drafts which, taken together, now fill six boxes in the Lowry Collection at the University of British Columbia and consist of over 4,000 pages, some typewritten, others handwritten and heavily edited by both Malcolm and Marjorie. As with each of his other novels, Lowry almost always added new text. He rarely made any cuts, and it was only in 1970 that a collated version of *October Ferry* was published by Marjorie, though many of the hundred or so pages written in the last year of Malcolm's life were omitted from the final printed version of the novel.[8]

For Ethan and Jacqueline Llewellyn, the main protagonists of *October Ferry*, paradise was, in some measure, regained as they chose to abandon their own squatter's shack and start a new life on Gabriola. For the Lowrys, however, there was no such happy ending as Malcolm's drinking and increasingly poor health finally prompted a move in August 1954. The beachside cabin at Dollarton was left behind and, in 1958, it was demolished by the District of North Vancouver, as were a number of other foreshore shacks that clustered around Roche Point on the north side of Burrard Inlet.

The history of Lowry's shack did not, however, end with its demolition. In 2010, a replica of the original structure was reconstructed as part of an art installation by the Vancouver-based artist Ken Lum. The site-specific piece, entitled *from shangri-la to shangri-la*, was created for the Vancouver Art Gallery's outdoor public art space, Offsite. It consisted of three scale replicas of squatted shacks from Vancouver's North Shore: the Lowrys' Roche Point cabin, a second structure that was occupied by Dr Paul Spong (who would later become the leader of the Greenpeace 'Save the Whales' campaign) and a dwelling that was constructed by the artist Tom Burrows who, like Spong, was part of a community of squatters who lived on the intertidal Maplewood Mudflats to the west of Roche Point in the late 1960s and early 1970s. Lum's installation, located at the base of the Living Shangri-La tower, a mixed-use skyscraper and the tallest building in Vancouver, was on display during the 2010 Winter Olympics and until September of the same year.⁹ While the shacks were slated for demolition, they were donated, in the end, by the artist to the District of North Vancouver and rebuilt on stilts in a tidal slough off the Dollarton Highway, only a hundred metres from the original location of the Maplewood squats.¹⁰

The reconstruction and subsequent restitution of the rustic shacks – in this case as aesthetic placeholders rather than as objects of dwelling and necessity – brings together a number of issues around which the story of squatting in Vancouver is usually organised. It would be tempting to detect in Lum's architectonic reproductions, a modest historical remainder of a different urban imagination – experimental, makeshift and precarious – that played an important role in the recent transformation of the Lower Mainland. Lum's installation represents, according to this view, just the latest episode within a much longer history of creative practice in Vancouver; a history in which artistic intervention and radical urban politics are indelibly intertwined.¹¹ And yet, while Lum invites us to imagine the stubborn endurance of alternative architectures and other informal urbanisms, the relationship between squatting, urban development and artistic practice in Vancouver is hardly straightforward. It is, if anything, shaped by a series of basic and largely unresolved contradictions: between the city and the surrounding countryside; between the occupation and resettlement of British Columbia, and the dispossession and displacement of its indigenous inhabitants; between forgotten histories of informal housing and recurring cycles of creative destruction; between tactics of care and survival, and new forms of creative resistance and subversion.

It is only out of the open and indeterminate space marked out by these contradictions that a history of squatting in Vancouver may be meaningfully assembled and narrated. It would, in other words, be misguided to plot a strongly vectored historical narrative that connects the network of early colonial landholdings and squatter settlements in the Lower Mainland with the various communities we know today. After all, and as a number of geographers and historians have argued, the *resettlement* of this region was an uneven and violent process in which 'the Canadian Dominion struggled to manage the appropriation of legal, social, and physical space'. Squatting provides not only a *minor history* of these struggles, but a privileged point of view for understanding the various entanglements of capital, law and violence that underpin 'the making of Vancouver'.[12] This is a history of makeshift cottages, boathouses and shacks, precarious and informal urban settlements, experimental housing initiatives and radical autonomous communities. It is a history shaped by a complex patchwork of customary beliefs and rights, the improvised use of materials and skills, and the development of emergent forms of dwelling, sociality and cooperation, where the figure of 'the squatter' was itself a source of multiple imaginings.

In retracing the contours of this history, it would be wrong to posit a blithe romanticism about squatting or sidestep the sheer precarity and insecurity that many Canadians faced in seeking adequate forms of housing and shelter. One also needs to remain alert to the historical sediments of settler colonialism and their constitutive role in shaping the recent development of the Lower Mainland. To do so demands an attentiveness to the specificities of the concept of the 'squatter' that can be traced back to its usage in nineteenth-century colonial Canada and where colonisers laboured 'to establish a cultural, political and legal context for land rights in various frontiers'. More often than not, squatters rights were a category that was 'used to impose the colour of title to the appropriate class of settler and remove the remainder'.[13] There is, in fact, considerable historical evidence to show that – even before confederation – land officials across the Canadian Dominion were mobilising the concept of squatters' rights as, on the one hand, a way of introducing market-based private property rights and, on the other hand, as a sort of Trojan horse that could provide entry for settlers to land that was initially ceded to indigenous communities.[14] Officials also used legal preemption as a way of negotiating the growing number of squatters on Crown land and, in many other instances, settlers 'violently displaced Aboriginal people from their homes without even the formality of filing a pre-emption'.[15]

Such complex legal geographies, as well as the micropolitics of violence they often subsumed, take on a heightened significance in British Columbia where aboriginal title was never officially extinguished and where settlers, in the wake of the Land Ordinance of 1861, could pre-empt any Crown-claimed land that was not an 'Indian' reserve and did not contain 'Indian improvements' so long as they improved the land and resided on it permanently without being absent for more than two months.[16] As the historical geographer Cole Harris has long reminded us, most British Columbians are not only immigrants but the 'occupiers of spaces that recently belonged to others'. In British Columbia, 'land', according to Harris, 'was the new opportunity; life here was about occupying, controlling and managing it, about establishing who could do what where. In the process settlements were created and space was reconfigured.'[17] The resettlement of British Columbia, to borrow Harris' felicitous phrasing, thus depended on the radical refashioning of pre-colonial native spaces not only through the creation of a patchwork geography of small scattered Indian reserves, but through a process of violent dispossession and land-grabbing. 'Native space,' in the words of one historian, 'had to be *unmade* as much as it had to be made.'[18] 'One human geography,' added Harris, 'was ... superseded by another, both on the ground and in the imagination.'[19]

In the case of Vancouver, this new 'geography' represented 'the final act in a one-sided drama whereby newcomers claimed the city for themselves – *and only for themselves*'.[20] The creation of the city saw the obliteration of native geographies and the erasure of complex social lifeworlds, longstanding patterns of resource extraction as well as deeply sedimented understandings of property and kinship. Nevertheless, the relationship between colonialism and the making of a settler city remains something of a blind spot within much of the literature on squatting, which has often exonerated the 'pioneers' of settler colonialism from the various predations and displacements of colonisation and proprietary injustice. There is, in other words, another story still to be told here that speaks to a conspicuously uneven and unsettled process of occupation and resistance, gathering and subversion. At the heart of this story is an understanding of Vancouver as an urban landscape where competing understandings of land, property and dwelling clashed, and where squatting was used as *both* an agent of dispossession and a basis for alternative political claim-making and creative resistance.

This is a story that returns briefly to the Lowrys and the tiny North Shore squatter community that they were part of. The community became known in a number of Malcolm's published stories and novels as Eridanus in a deliberate reference to the underworld river in Virgil's *Georgics*. 'We poor folk,' he wrote, 'were ... Eridanus, a condemned community, perpetually under the shadow of eviction.'[21] And yet as the writer Stephen Osbourne has argued, in mapping the Old World on to the New, Lowry ultimately overlooked the shoreline's original namers, 'whose descendants, members of the Tsleil-Waututh Nation, were sequestered on an allotment bordering Lowry's beach (mentioned in passing in his stories as "the Reserve"), and whose eviction from that beach several decades earlier had failed to lodge in his imagination'.[22]

The transformation of 'wilderness' into territory and real estate and the concomitant alienation and erasure of aboriginal lands depended on the subdivision of Crown land into discrete sections that were distributed through sale or pre-emption.[23] Cole Harris is undoubtedly right to detect, in the imposition of a Western property system, a powerful tool of discipline and control and one in which racism was built into the very 'landscape of settlement'.[24] At the same time, the effects of colonial power were never absolute and were, if anything, shaped by uneven and contradictory geographies of encounter and contestation. For Renisa Mawani, the colonial contact zone was 'a space of racial intermixture – a place where Europeans, aboriginal peoples, and racial migrants came into frequent contact, a conceptual and material geography where racial categories and racisms were both produced and productive of locally configured and globally inflected modalities of colonial power'.[25] If Mawani focuses, in particular, on the emergent practices of racial governance in British Columbia, it is also clear that squatter settlements and informal communities (and the ways in which these terms were mobilised and understood) were part of the colonial contact zone that she has in mind and that in these settlements we find the kind of 'counter stories and mappings' that 'complicate the certainties of the settler city'.[26]

Mawani is, in this context, one of many commentators drawn to the history of Vancouver's Stanley Park, the genealogies of the families who once lived there – aboriginal, Hawaiian, mixed-race and European – and the various stories of their dispossession. The park, as with so many aspects of Vancouver's recent history, was 'imposed on existing ways of life'. 'It was intended from the beginning,' according to Jean Barman, the park's most accomplished historian, 'to serve one set of interests at the expense of others: its creation was a consummately colonial enterprise.' And yet, for Barman, other histories of the region encompassed by the park do still exist; histories that linger and cluster around three sites: the prominent indigenous Coast Salish settlement at Whoi Whoi which predated the appropriation of the peninsula by the colonial government in 1858; the Kanaka Ranch at Coal Harbour which was established by Hawaiian settlers in the 1860s outside the official boundaries of the park; and a group of mixed-race families who had settled in Brockton Point and who were pejoratively described as 'squatters' by the City of Vancouver while refusing to be relocated from their homes.[27]

Whoi Whoi or Xw'ay Xw'ay (the former the spelling adopted by Major J.S. Matthews, Vancouver's first city archivist) was the largest Coast Salish settlement on the Stanley Park peninsula between its northern and eastern tips, and has been identified by anthropologists as one of the oldest indigenous settlements along Burrard Inlet. Xw'ay Xw'ay, which translates as 'a place for making masks', was the site of a sacred burial ground. It also held a number of large gift-giving ceremonies known as *potlatches* well into the late nineteenth century. Such an indigenous presence was conspicuously erased, however, by colonial authorities who reappropriated and reterritorialised the land – as was so often the case in settler societies – under the auspices of *terra nullius*, that is as empty land open for development and permanent 'occupation'. Indigenous inhabitance was widely seen, in contrast, as temporary and seasonal and not in keeping with Western understandings of law, land and sovereignty.[28]

It is against this backdrop that a military naval reserve was allegedly created on the peninsula in 1858 by then Governor Douglas, though it is now clear that this was never publicly proclaimed or 'gazetted'. While the legal status of the reserve remained murky, colonial authorities were more than happy to use it as a pretext to evict and relocate indigenous peoples to newly formed Indian reserves on the northern shore of Burrard Inlet and up Howe Sound. A small number of families nevertheless remained at Xw'ay Xw'ay until 1888, while many others continued to live east of the village at Brockton Point. In an 1876 report, Malcolm Sprott, one of the Joint Reserve commissioners in British Columbia, observed that there were still 'thirty or forty Skwamish [*sic*] squatting on the Government Reserve between Coal Harbor and First Narrows, Burrard Inlet'. Another commissioner added that 'they have several small cottages but have made little improvement otherwise'.[29]

With the establishment of Stanley Park in 1888, the remaining aboriginal inhabitants of Xw'ay Xw'ay were resettled on Indian reserves while a small Chinese community at Anderson Point was cleared the following year. The Hawaiian settlers at Kanaka Ranch were, however, more fortunate. They had first set down in 1869 on three acres of land at Coal Harbour. 'Our buildings ... were not much,' one later recalled, 'just a couple of small houses on the beach beside a creek.'[30] As squatters, they were eventually threatened with eviction in 1889, though they claimed the right to remain under adverse possession. The City of Vancouver required only twenty years' residence to claim adverse possession and the residents at Kanaka Ranch were successful in court as they satisfied the city's own measure. In the case of Brockton Point, the families were relatively undisturbed until the early twentieth century, though they were routinely impugned as 'wrongfully and illegally occupying the land and [that they] should be evicted'.[31] It was only in the early 1920s that the City of Vancouver initiated eviction proceedings, as they feared that many of the Brockton Point families would be eligible to claim adverse possession under both the terms required by the city and the Dominion government (sixty years).

At the beginning of April 1923, the Federal Department of Justice instructed the City of Vancouver's legal department 'to take all necessary steps in the name of the Dominion government and the City of Vancouver to institute proceedings in the Courts for the ejectment of the squatters'. Three separate lawsuits were filed against eight families. Despite compelling and detailed eyewitness testimony, city officials argued that the residents had only moved to the land after it had been 'discovered' and transferred to the Crown in 1858.[32] The British Columbia Supreme Court ruled in their favour, arguing that the families had not settled in the park before April 1863 with the evidentiary particulars of an 1863 Survey Map of Burrard Inlet superseding the testimony of four aboriginal men. Many of the families appealed to the British Columbia Court of Appeal, which overturned the original decision and ruled that 'they had in fact demonstrated the minimum number of years to claim adverse possession'.[33] Justice Matthews, one of the three presiding judges, described the word of the aboriginal witnesses as 'remarkable and beyond expectation precise'. In an even more startling passage, Justice McPhillips, one of the other appellate court judges, concluded that:

> it can reasonably be found that title was acquired by the Defendant to the land in question by continued possession adverse to and in derogation of that of the Crown. *There being no express*

extinguishment of the Indian title in British Columbia the question whether there was earlier possession in the Crown than that
of the Defendant and those under whom he is entitled to claim
possession, is brought up somewhat graphically and it might rea-
sonably be said that there could be no prior possession of the
Crown to the possession shewn [*sic*] by the Defendant.[34]

The implications of these remarks for questions of native title
in British Columbia were not lost on the Crown, which made
a final appeal to the Supreme Court of Canada – the appellate
court's decision was quickly overturned and the initial verdict
that the Brockton Point residents were, in fact, 'illegal squatters',
was reinstated. The residents were finally evicted in 1931, with
the exception of one family who were allowed to stay until their
deaths in the mid-1950s. At the same time, a number of squatters living on nearby Deadman's Island were themselves forcibly
expelled.[35]

There is, of course, much more to be said about the multiple
understandings of 'indigeneity' in the case of Brockton Point.
A close inspection of the government correspondence that
preceded the trials highlights the degree to which the families'
'racial designation and colonial otherness was never fully established nor disestablished'. Rather, they were variously referred
to as 'a family of Indians', 'Indian squatters', 'half-breeds' and,
in the final instance, 'squatters'. If the courts situated the families *between* colonial categories, they did so with a recognition
that territorial claims and identities were closely intertwined. It
is perhaps not surprising that the one family that could claim full
aboriginal ancestry received compensation from the Parks Board
commissioner in exchange for relinquishing their land, while
the remaining mixed-race families were described as unlawful
'trespassers' and 'squatters'.[36] In early twentieth-century British
Columbia, it was therefore clear that what it meant to be a 'squatter' was connected to questions of identity and 'indigeneity'. At
stake here were very real material demands for land, resources
and rights, and the slippages between these terms dramatised the

complex configurations of law, identity and violence that shaped British Columbia's 'colonial contact zone'.[37]

The recent history of squatting in Vancouver remains, in this way, haunted by the memories and residues of another more violent form of 'occupation'. Of course, struggles over land and housing assumed a number of different forms during the city's early history. Housing informality and urban marginality were key features of Vancouver's development, and it was in fact the makeshift flimsy and jerry-built shack which had, by the 1890s, already come to serve as a potent symbol of social marginalisation.[38] 'Shacks' – usually dwellings located along the shorelines of Burrard Inlet and False Creek – sprung up with considerable frequency such that there were, according to one source, over 364 shacks on the city's various foreshores in 1894. While many of the squatters' homes were destroyed, other communities endured, including Finn Slough whose homes in the intertidal flats off Richmond remain to this day.

As Rolf Knight has shown in his wonderfully evocative account of the Vancouver waterfront and the history and social geography of the No. 20 Tram Line which ran from Victory Square along Cordova and Powell Street all the way to Exhibition Park, the developing industrial and working-class districts in the city's East End were emblematic of a modernity shot through with contradictions. Development was, if anything, uneven and the East End remained a fractured landscape of railway yards and overgrown industrial wastelands intermixed with pensioners' bunkhouses and squatters' shacks, many of which existed well into the 1940s and 1950s.[39] Shacks, floathouses and other forms of precarious housing were remarkably resilient as new dwellings quickly sprang up in the wake of demolitions and evictions.[40]

In general, low-income households in the centre of Vancouver faced a 'continuous shortage of adequate, affordable housing'. Recurring cycles of creative destruction and the vagaries of a resource-based economy condemned significant numbers of the city's residents to misery and prompted many to seek out alternative forms of shelter even during the pre-Depression years.

While lodging houses, rooms, shacks and tents represented the first choice for the poor, the jobless and the elderly, other institutions including missions and hostels, as well as the city's first public library, were also used to provide shelter for the city's homeless population. With economic depression came further immiseration and 'the inability of many urban residents to afford adequate housing'.[41] A floating surplus population of jobless and homeless single men wandered in and out of the city, and by the summer of 1931 over 1,000 homeless men – their relief payments slashed – had occupied four East End 'jungles', the most significant of which bordered Prior Street near the Canadian National Railway (CNR) yards. The informal encampments were soon cleared, however, in response to a typhoid scare. At the same time, the burden for housing Vancouver's transient population increasingly fell to the provincial and federal governments who provided shelter for homeless men, first in provincial road camps and later in Department of National Defence relief camps.[42]

It is in this story of housing insecurity that the various twists and turns that shaped the imaginative geography of Vancouver's East End can be traced. The area surrounding Hastings Street east of Cambie was widely stigmatised by civic authorities, while many others saw the neighbourhood as a potent source of political activism. One historian describes, for example, the strategic significance of the neighbourhood's streets and parks as sites of working-class sociability and resistance which, in the 1930s and 1940s, became a key crucible of agitation and dissent. During this period, Hastings Street was the main thoroughfare for marches and demonstrations supporting full employment, as well as strikes organised by the city's longshoremen.[43] In May 1935, the Carnegie Library (now the Carnegie Centre) was occupied by hundreds of young men in protest against the relief work camps set up by the federal government, while three years later a cut in the relief projects that had replaced the work camps prompted scores of unemployed young men to occupy the Hotel Georgia, the Vancouver Art Gallery and the city's main post office. The month-long occupation was brutally suppressed by police on

19 June 1938. At the same time, the city's chronic shortage of housing intensified as overcrowding, substandard housing and the eventual demobilisation of returning military personnel in 1945 led to a wave of popular protests which culminated in the occupation of the old Hotel Vancouver by a group of veterans on 26 January 1946.[44]

If these actions speak to a wave of housing-based activism in Vancouver, the late 1930s and 1940s also bore witness to a further rise in the number of squatted shacks along the various foreshores of Vancouver (Burrard Inlet, False Creek and along the Northern Arm of the Fraser River). According to city officials, there were 538 people living on the waterfront in 1937. On Burrard Inlet, there were ninety-three houseboats and sixty-six shacks, a number that rose to 205 total dwellings in 1939. In False Creek, there were 108 boats and eighteen shacks, while there were sixty-two shacks on the North Arm of the Fraser River between Main Street and Boundary Road.[45] While efforts were made as early as 1938 to report on the sanitary conditions of the houses – undoubtedly as a pretext to their demolition – many of the communities remained largely intact until the 1950s even as efforts to formalise their housing arrangements were firmly rejected. Local government authorities, on the one hand, argued that 'definite steps be immediately taken to prevent the placing or erection of any additional houseboats or shacks'. They were, on the other hand, challenged by the health inspector for the City of Vancouver, who described the foreshore squatters as 'respectable, law-abiding citizens and worthy of every consideration. Most of them are there to meet the high cost of living with such small incomes and are enjoying much better health there than when living in stuffy, overcrowded rooming houses or insanitary homes in town.'

Many of the homes also exploited the legal ambiguities of intertidal squatting. In Canada, private property as regulated by municipal zoning laws only extends to the mean high-tide mark, while the intertidal zone was and remains the jurisdiction of the federal government. There were attempts by local politicians in the 1940s to amend the Navigable Waters Protection Act and legislate against intertidal squatting. These were, however, unsuccessful. It was only in the autumn of 1958 that the shacks were finally (and in many cases illegally) destroyed and their inhabitants evicted after a new round of health inspections that 'recommended that the shacks and float houses ... be declared a nuisance and dangerous to public health and safety'.[46] The 1958 demolition of the Lowrys' Dollarton home and the wider North Shore community that they belonged to was also part of the clearances authorised by the City of Vancouver and other local municipalities in the late 1950s.

The District of North Vancouver building inspector who oversaw their demolition was not, as it turns out, finished. He returned just over a decade later and was responsible for the fiery (and equally illegal) destruction of a new squatter community that had sprung up in the late 1960s on the Maplewood Mudflats, just a kilometre west of the Lowrys' original shack at Roche Point. As much as the experiences of the Lowrys were therefore of a piece with an older history of occupation, settlement and dispossession, they also served, in this context, as an important point of reference for a more recent wave of activism that speaks far more directly to the action repertoire at the heart of this book. Like many other cities in Europe and North America, the 1960s and 1970s in Vancouver represented a period of intense urban restructuring and development which were, in turn, challenged by a host of new community-based groups and grassroots organisations, particular in inner-city districts such as Kitsilano, Grandview, Mount Pleasant and Strathcona. Where local planners, developers and politicians – often they were the same person – saw opportunities for growth and profiteering, city residents saw rising rents, greater insecurity and the prospect of imminent displacement.[47]

In August 1968, a group of around seventy local tenants came together in a Kitsilano apartment to form the Vancouver Tenant's Council. The council used a variety of direct action tactics, including rent strikes, to lobby for rent control and other regulations to protect tenants against unscrupulous land-lords. The council also campaigned successfully for the right of Vancouver tenants to vote in municipal elections and other changes to the Landlord and Tenant Act. While tenant-based activism in Vancouver enjoyed a modicum of success, other local residents – undoubtedly inspired by the new social move-ments and countercultural impulses of the late 1960s – turned to a more radical repertoire of contention. In 1970, the student branch of International Workers of the World at Simon Fraser University met up with a group of hippie radicals from East Vancouver and Kitsilano. Both groups shared a commitment to rejecting the tired pieties of traditional Marxism in favour of new spontaneist, anti-authoritarian impulses. The meeting led to the formation of the Vancouver Yippie as a Canadian offshoot or 'Northern Lunatic Fringe' of the Youth International Party that was formed in the US in late 1967.[48]

The group 'organised' a range of actions and practices that reflected their youth-based militancy, from the founding of autonomous communes in the city to drug-fuelled 'smoke-ins' and other improvised happenings. On 29 May 1971, the group and a host of other activists occupied the proposed site of a new Four Seasons Hotel next to Stanley Park.[49] The proposed hotel was supported by then mayor and developer Tom Campbell, though it was opposed by the city's Park Board. Despite police efforts the protesters were able to occupy the site, which they transformed into the 'All Seasons Park'. An act of protest thus became a self-organised protest camp of sorts with hundreds of inhabitants, some politically motivated, others just crashing for the fun (and drugs). Over time, many of the original activists drifted away from the squatter encampment and, by February 1972, the hotel development was dead. A small group of squatters nevertheless remained until the spring when their makeshift huts and shacks were demolished by the Vancouver Port Authority.[50]

A new alignment of radical youth politics, creative protest and alternative forms of living found its most concrete expres-sion, however, in the squatter community that was created on the Maplewood intertidal mudflats. While a number of shacks already existed on the site and were evidence of an earlier history of foreshore squatting, the community that briefly thrived in the late 1960s and early 1970s pointed to a radically different sense of shared city living. The prominent Canadian artist, Tom Burrows, who moved to the mudflats in late May 1969, described the older community as one with a 'traditional relationship to coastal BC. Shake bolt and boom chain salvagers; crab fisher people.'[51] By the late 1960s, many older residents had left their shacks or had been forced out by L&K Lumber who purchased the land in 1961. At the same time, a new generation of artists, activists and other bohemians moved in including Burrows, the collector Willy Wilson and the cetologist and Greenpeace activist Dr Paul Spong.

The Maplewood squatters cultivated a modest ethics of mending and repair, as salvaged materials and do-it-yourself practices provided the main material support for their community. Burrows describes how he slowly and incrementally transformed an abandoned partially built structure into his own home. 'There was,' he noted, 'ample building material, in a boom at the very far western edge of the flats where flotsam from Vancouver harbour was corralled before it was chipped. I had weekends and the long summer evenings to work on our new home.' 'With no power I had to build the house with handsaws', he added. 'We had candles and gas lamps that were kind of scary.'[52] As an experimental makeshift community, the Maplewood squatters represented, it would seem, the very antithesis to a city whose neighbourhoods were being 'razed for condo high-rises'.[53]

In a highly influential essay on the history of the Vancouver art scene in the 1960s, Scott Watson describes how the intertidal squatters lived in 'active polemical opposition' to the recent transformation of the city. The high-tide mark that their community straddled was far more than a simple line in the sand between competing notions of property, between the house as a commodity and the home as a place of dwelling and refuge.

It also pointed to a wider precarious existence, both urban and rural. 'It was,' writes Watson, 'a bit of country ringed by the city. Backed by a liminal forest that separated it from the growing bedroom suburb of North Vancouver, it faced the Shell Oil refinery located across the waters of Burrard Inlet'; the same Shell refinery that in Lowry's *October Ferry* had lost the S on its sign only to blaze a lurid 'HELL' across the inlet.[54]

Everyday life on the mudflats was the subject of two contemporary films. *Mudflats Living* (1972) was a National Film Board of Canada production, one of many radical forays by the board into community-based documentary as part of the Challenge for Change Programme which ran from 1967 to 1980. The second, Sean Malone's *Living in the Mud* (1972), was an independent documentary that was more polemical and poetic in tone. Both films were, nevertheless, indebted to the wave of experimental film-making that thrived within the Vancouver art scene during this period.[55] They also pointed to a form of dwelling that self-consciously blurred the boundaries between life and art. For the artist Tom Burrows, the intertidal location of the mudflats provided the supporting context for a new body of sculptural work shaped by the location's own diurnal rhythms. Heavily indebted to the Situationists, Burrows traded in the sandstone cobble and paving stone for the flotsam and jetsam of the tidal flats.[56] As in the case of his new house, Burrows's work incorporated materials that he had found and salvaged. As he later observed in an article published in *artscanada*, 'I have lived within the boundaries of the North Vancouver tidal estuary, the mudflats, for more than two years. Boundaries of environmental setting, source of material, observation ... the machinations of my squatter community, the lunar rhythms of the tide, no telephone, no electricity, few words'.[57]

Burrows's intertidal installations drew inspiration from the drawings of the Russian artist Kasimir Malevich, whose work Burrows had seen while studying in London. They spoke to questions of form and functionality as well as the relationship and place of sculpture within the local landscape. This was art deeply connected to its environment, not imposed on it. It was art subject to the action of the tides and, in Burrows's own words, 'the anarchy of squatters' who often borrowed material from the sculptures 'pragmatically removing glass for a window and wood for a fire'.[58] It is against this backdrop that Burrows began to understand squatting and self-help housing as a form of radical art-making. The protracted court case surrounding the status of the Maplewood squatters only reinforced this view. The case was held – ironically enough – in what is now the Vancouver Art Gallery, and it became clear during court proceedings that a piece of alluvial sediment along the mudflats had not been claimed by either the Corporate District of North Vancouver or the National Harbours Board. In early December 1971, Burrows with the aid of a group of volunteers successfully lowered his house on to the 'no man's land' using driftwood rollers. When the building inspector arrived a few weeks later, court order in hand, to evict the Maplewood squatters, he torched Burrows's house and most of the other shacks on the mudflats.[59]

Despite the fiery destruction of his house, Burrows's working practice remained closely connected to questions of squatting. In 1974, he gave up his job at the University of British Columbia and moved to Hornby Island where he constructed a new studio and residence. Two years later, he participated in the UN Habitat Forum in Vancouver, where he worked as Co-ordinator of Information on Non-Tenured Architecture, a role that brought him into contact with a number of leading experts on self-help housing including the architect and urbanist John Turner, whose now classic book, *Housing by People: Towards Autonomy in Building Environments*, appeared in the same year. Burrows assembled and edited a series of conversations with squatters from London, Amsterdam, Copenhagen, Paris and elsewhere.[60] The original typed transcripts from those discussions still exist and represent a key early document in the emergence of squatting as an urban social movement in the 1970s.[61] They also inspired Burrows, who embarked on a seven-month Canada Council-funded project on squatting and non-tenured housing in Europe, Egypt, India and South East Asia in 1977. The trip led Burrows to produce *Skwat Doc*, a project that consisted of a series of colour photographs with accompanying text for each of the cities he visited. As a combined visual and textual document, the project was completely portable and travelled in an old suitcase which was also exhibited as part of the work. *Skwat Doc* was first shown as a series of slides at the Western Front Gallery in Vancouver in October 1978 and as a photo installation at the Carnegie Centre in 1983. Versions of the work were also exhibited in galleries, squats and housing projects across Europe.

One of the first attempts to explore the emergence of a new squatting movement in the 1960s and 1970s and its relationship to other forms of self-help housing in the Global South thus emerged from one of its more distant outposts. If Burrows became an early interlocutor in the history and development of a new movement, the experiences of those living on the mudflats also points to other competing trajectories. The Maplewood resident and collector Willie Wilson was a major supplier of salvage from old houses and worked as a set decorator for Robert Altman's *McCabe and Mrs. Miller* (1971), a frontier film that transposed the hippie ideals of the period to a more conventional Western setting. Much of the film was shot on the North Shore just as a group of squatters were organising a 'Pleasure Faire' on the mudflats, an 'ersatz village that mirrored the one for the movie that in turn mirrored the squat itself'.[62] The eruption of what Burrows somewhat derisively described as 'late hippy Baroque floridity' demonstrated that the squatter's shack was not immune to the image industry and that, in its commodification, one detected a rather different alignment of art and urbanism. As Burrows concluded, 'considering this all happened in the light of Paris 68, the pleasure fairs had the political awareness of a *Vogue* magazine issue on hippy fashion'.[63]

The dissolution of the squatter community on the Maplewood Mudflats ultimately marked a significant turning point in the recent history of Vancouver and a decisive moment in the evolution of the art scene in the city. Many artists turned their back on art-making while others retreated from the demands of politically engaged work, including many associated with the so-called Vancouver School for whom a return to the 'historical problem of modernism' represented a welcome 'sanctuary'.[64] What artists including Roy Arden, Ken Lum, Jeff Wall and Ian Wallace shared was a common interest in reviving a pictorial tradition that was informed by a close reading and deep understanding of critical theory and a commitment to a form of photo-conceptualism that established a certain image of Vancouver as a key locale in the global art economy.[65] If these distinctions were never absolute, they nevertheless served to widen the gap between 'the aesthetic' and 'the political' and pointed to a rather different sense of what it might still mean to represent Vancouver as an urban space. It is hardly surprising perhaps that Vancouver increasingly became, in this context, the go-to city of 'postmodernist, global lore'; a development documented to good effect by hometown writer Douglas Coupland and reinforced by the city's 'peculiar status as Hollywood's favourite stand-in for the American city picturesque'.[66]

In basic material terms, the period after 1970 was characterised by the transformation of Vancouver's social and economic landscape and the gentrification of the city's downtown core. Since 1989, housing for tens of thousands of new residents – from converted lofts to glittering high-rise condominium towers – has been built; with prices now the most expensive in North America. At the same time, the accelerated pace of redevelopment has placed particular pressure on the city's most vulnerable citizens. This is particularly the case in the Downtown Eastside, long a site of neglect, underinvestment and capital flight which has become just the latest frontier in a city whose very identity was built on the back of an expansionary settler colonialism. As the late Marxist geographer Neil Smith argued, the 'myth of the frontier' carries significant ideological weight in struggles over the meaning of gentrification. According to Smith, 'insofar as gentrification infects working class communities, displaces poor households, and converts whole neighbourhoods into bourgeois enclaves, the frontier ideology rationalises social differentiation and exclusion as natural, inevitable'.[67] Smith shows how the poor and working class are all too easily framed as 'uncivil' and on the 'wrong side' of a dividing line between an urban wilderness and those heroic homesteaders (read gentrifiers) who seek to tame it. As a process, gentrification is therefore neither benign nor innocent. Not only does it describe a process of violent dispossession and reordering, more often than not it erases, as Smith argues, the very social histories, struggles and geographies that it subsumes.

Smith's frontier *mythos* takes us into the heart of Vancouver's social divide and Downtown Eastside as a site of confrontation between 'incoming middle-class settlers' and longstanding residents who live in Single Resident Occupancy (SRO) hotels, rooming houses, basement suites and, in many cases, on the streets themselves.[68] While redevelopment in the neighbourhood has pushed the city's outcast poor – the drug addicts, homeless, pan-handlers and sex workers, many of whom are aboriginal Canadians – into an ever-diminishing enclave, it has also been fiercely contested by area residents. The Downtown Eastside may have been traditionally labelled as Vancouver's 'Skid Row', a blighted space of poverty, disease and crime. But it is also very much a space marked by a long history of grassroots community activism and the formation, in particular, of the Downtown Eastside Residents' Association (DERA) in 1973 which remains a key moment in a wider history of anti-poverty and housing-based organising in the city.[69] DERA was able to score some notable successes, especially in terms of social housing provision, though intensifying gentrification in recent decades has erased many of the organisation's hard-fought gains.

The involvement of non-profit organisations in housing provision heralded a shift in the nature of local community activism in the Downtown Eastside and elsewhere, as the requirements of project management overtook more trenchant forms of community advocacy. Many residents and activists responded by reviving a range of direct action tactics, including squatting. When, for example, low-income rental housing in the Downtown Eastside was threatened by the World Exhibition in 1986, 'the downtown core saw', as *Open Road*, a local anarchist magazine reported, 'some desperate but organized squatting activity'.⁷⁰ While these practices were ultimately unsuccessful, it did not stop a group of squatters from occupying several houses on Frances Street in East Vancouver a few years later. 'These houses,' they proclaimed, 'have been slated for demolition and gentrification. In the face of unregulated rent increases, and out of necessity, we have chosen to squat as one of many viable means of protesting this atrocity. Housing is not a luxury, it is a right, and these houses are available now.' 'New developments,' they concluded, 'must be kept within an affordable price range for all people presently affected by the housing crisis.'⁷¹

Four houses on Frances Street were initially occupied in February 1990. As one of the former occupants recalled, 'the fences separating the houses were the first thing to go'. One of the houses became a women-only space while a free store ('take what you need, leave what you can') was started in the garage of another. A fifth building was squatted a few months later, while tenants living in another building down the street joined the squatters when they refused to leave after having been served an eviction notice. The squatters received a largely favourable response from their neighbours and the local East Vancouver community, with the Grandview-Woodland Area council passing a motion in support of the squatters.⁷² The case ended up in the Supreme Court of British Columbia where the lawyer acting on behalf of the houses' owner summarised the position of his client by stating that 'it's our land, and they've got no bloody business being there'.⁷³ By the end of November 1990, the threat of eviction loomed for all six houses and despite internal divisions, some of the squatters decided on 25 November to throw up a series of barricades across both sides of the street, no doubt inspired by their (recently expelled) counterparts on Mainzer Straße in Berlin. They were nevertheless evicted by the Vancouver police two days later in a military-style operation that involved eighty riot cops, thirty heavily armed SWAT team members, the Royal Canadian Mounted Police bomb squad, dog teams, fire trucks and two earth-moving tractors.[74] In response to growing public concerns about the heavy-handed approach adopted by the police, Mayor Gordon Campbell was quick to exonerate the police, noting that in his view the 'circumstances warranted the precautions taken by the Police'.[75]

In June 1993, a number of the squatters involved in the Frances Street squats occupied two houses at the corner of Broadway and Commercial Drive with a view to creating a 'radical free space for activists to live and work'. The two houses had been used as 'shooting galleries' by local drug dealers, though they were quickly restored by the occupiers. The occupations proved short-lived, however, as eviction notices were posted in late July of the same year. The squatters as well as a number of other activists barricaded themselves into the two houses in anticipation of another large-scale police operation. The police never arrived, and it was left to the City's Board of Engineers to carry out the eviction a few days later. As one squatter lamented in the wake of the eviction, 'I came back the next day to get my stuff. They had torn the staircase down and smashed in every window. They smashed the toilet and knocked over the bookshelf with zines and newsletters and had strewn them around. They trashed people's stuff.'[76]

It was the ninety-two-day occupation of the former Wood-ward's Department Store on West Hastings Street in the Downtown Eastside in 2002 that ultimately crystallised recent struggles for affordable housing in Vancouver. The department store had closed in January 1993 as the city's commercial core gravitated westwards. While attempts were made in the late 1990s to redevelop the building as private luxury condominiums, it remained empty, though it was acquired in 2001 by the provincial government who promised the construction of three hundred co-operative housing units on the site. The spring of 2001 ushered in, however, a new 'avowedly neoliberal' provincial government with former mayor (and developer) Gordon

Campbell as premier. As the new government attempted to offload the building to private developers, a number of activists and homeless residents took matters into their own hands and occupied the Woodward's Building, establishing what became known as the 'Woodsquat'.[77]

The squatters were soon served with a court injunction and enforcement order by the police, who raided the squat a week into the occupation. Fifty-four residents were arrested and charged with civil contempt of court. They were quickly released under the condition that they did not re-enter the building, though they were not restricted from the pavement area immediately outside of the former store which was soon occupied by over 150 squatters.[78] The squatters demanded the redevelopment of the building as social housing and that local aboriginal residents living in the Downtown Eastside, in particular, were allotted a significant share of available units. They also insisted on the reversal of cuts to social housing and services and the drafting of a new civic by-law to seize and convert empty, abandoned buildings into social housing.[79]

While the status of the building and the Downtown Eastside became a key issue in the November civic election, the landslide victory of the progressive candidate, Larry Campbell, did not bring the kind of solution anticipated by the squatters whose encampment had defied the elements for over two months. Campbell publicly supported a successful court injunction which called for the eviction of the protesters. Wishing to avoid confrontation, the city paid a local non-profit housing organisation, the Portland Hotel Society (PHS), to clear the squatters, clean the sidewalk and erect a fence around the Woodward's Building. The PHS was also given upwards of CA$90,000 to house up to fifty squatters for the next four months.[80]

Woodsquat was demolished in December 2002, and many of its occupants found themselves either homeless or back in squalid SRO hotels whose conditions were a key catalyst for the original protest.[81] At the same time, the city acquired the Woodward's Building from the province and began a public consultation process on the future of the site. The winning design, which incorporated parts of the existing structure, included 536 market housing units, 125 single non-market units run by the PHS and another seventy-five family non-market units run by another local housing society. The development, which was finally completed in 2010, also included offices for the National Film Board of Canada and a new satellite annex for Simon Fraser University's downtown campus.[82] In 2008, the artist Stan Douglas unveiled a new large-format image on glass in the atrium of the redevelopment. The photograph was a detailed reconstruction of the 1971 Gastown Riots, when Vancouver police attacked a peaceful occupation and 'smoke-in' organised by the Youth International Party.[83]

It is hard not to detect in the recent history of the Woodward's Building, another episode in the successful co-optation and neutralisation of an alternative and critical urbanism. If the making of Vancouver has been shaped by different and competing understandings of occupation and urban struggle, Douglas's tableau points to a further *reduction* of this struggle to a mere space of representation and to a problem of aesthetics. Of course, the relationship between critical art practices and urban discourses is itself hardly new, nor is the connection between the creative industries and gentrification. The redevelopment of the Woodward's site coincided, after all, with a successful bid by the City of Vancouver to host the Winter Olympics in 2010. The transformation of the Downtown Eastside and other city neighbourhoods has, in this context, only intensified as the frontiers of a neoliberalising city are once again on the move.

But such shifting frontiers also remain sites of struggle and resistance over land, property and alternative forms of shared city life. At stake here is an urban history that is also a history of settler colonialism with its various exclusions and predations. It is finally a history that points, if nothing else, to squatting's 'dark side' as much as they speak to its radical possibilities. Squatting can be both the problem and the solution, a story of dispossession and displacement and a form of dwelling and solidarity. Squatting can be configured as violent and marginalising. It can also be a means to construct new practices of care and subversion. While, for some, it represented an artistic and creative retreat from the social struggles of the city, for others it pointed to different and more socially just ways of organising and sharing urban space. These contradictions may yield no easy answers, though they do point, however fleetingly, to how we might still come to know and live the city differently.

8

Reclaiming New York: Squatting and the Neoliberal City

> They shall rebuild the ancient ruins
> The former wasted they shall rise up
> And restore the ruined cities
> Desolate now for generations
> Isaiah 61:4 (epigraph at the top of Peter Spagnuolo's
> notebook, a former New York squatter)[1]

Squatting creates housing. Squatters take abandoned, city owned buildings that have been neglected for years and turn them into homes. Through our collective initiative, hard work and imagination, we restore buildings that would otherwise be left to rot, or be demolished.

> Flyer, 'The Squatters Are Your Neighbours',
> Lower East Side, New York[2]

In 1975, the City of New York was facing a serious crisis. On 17 October at 4:00 pm, over 450 million dollars worth of the city's debts were due. The city had little over 30 million dollars on hand. If New York couldn't pay those debts, the city would have to declare bankruptcy. At the time, New York's budget was one of the largest 'public projects' in the world. It was estimated that a default could bring down over a hundred banks world-wide and expose many others to liability for selling suspect or fraudulent products.[3]

The city had already run out of money a few months earlier. At the time, the governor of New York, Hugh Carey, had advanced state funds in order to pay the city's bills. The city was forced, however, to hand over its finances to the state. Bonds were issued to cover the city's immediate borrowing needs. Further cuts were also made. Thousands of public sector jobs were lost, wages were frozen, several public hospitals were closed and tuition fees were introduced for the first time at City University.[4]

New York's finances nevertheless continued to deteriorate in the months that followed. By the evening of 16 October, city officials were scrambling to secure the necessary funds to cover the city's debt obligations. Banks were unwilling, however, to market the debt and, despite repeated requests, President Ford refused to offer federal aid. Even the city's unions were reluctant to use their pension funds to purchase bonds. In the early hours of 17 October, a statement was prepared for then mayor, Abraham Beame. It announced that 'the city of New York had insufficient cash on hand to meet debt obligations due today'. 'This constitutes,' it continued, 'the default that we have struggled to avoid. Now we must take immediate steps to protect the potential life support systems of our City and to preserve the well-being of all our citizens.'[5]

The prepared statement was never read by Mayor Beame. In the immediate lead-up to the 4:00 pm deadline, the Teacher's Retirement System – facing possible legal action, job losses and pension cuts should the city default – agreed to reverse course and purchase bonds that would cover the city's shortfall. President Ford, in turn, relented in approving federal support for New York.

In the wake of the crisis, it was New York's 'life support systems' that were targeted as the city underwent a 'regime change' and embraced austerity. A 'social democratic polity' became a neoliberal laboratory in the decades that followed.[6] Cutbacks and privatisation were rolled out by Mayors Beame, Koch and Giuliani respectively. Thousands of police officers, firefighters, teachers and other public sector workers were fired.[7] Social programmes and anti-poverty operations were scaled back and starved of funds.[8] A new 'austerity urbanism' took hold. As the geographer David Harvey has repeatedly argued, New York became the 'center for the invention of neoliberal practices of gifting moral hazard to the investment banks', while at the same time 'making people pay up through the restructuring of munic-ipal contracts and services'.[9]

For Harvey, the financial crisis of the early to mid-1970s was a product of a number of factors. The late 1960s and early 1970s in the United States and elsewhere were, after all, shaped by a period of post-Fordist decline and an intensifying urban crisis which had a devastating impact on New York, and its poorest communities in particular. The crisis, as Harvey has argued, was already gathering momentum at the end of the 1960s. The sprawling urbanisation of the previous two decades produced an uneven geography where suburbs thrived and inner-city neigh-bourhoods stagnated and declined as thousands of industrial jobs left the city. It was these patterns that, according to Harvey, drove a series of inner-city uprisings across the United States in the face of growing disaffection, marginalisation and deep-rooted racial inequality.[10]

The uprisings prompted an influx of federal funding which encouraged cities such as New York to invest in an expansion of the public sector (education, health care, sanitation and transportation), though the whole stabilisation programme was ultimately contingent on the city having adequate funds. By the early 1970s it was borrowing heavily, though the fiscal crisis that erupted in 1975 was as much a product of the city's commitment to budgeting tricks ('magic windows', the move from capital to operating budgets, rollbacks, etc.) and debt-based financing as it was a result of shrinking tax revenues and a growth in the municipal workforce. Even so, it was the latter that ultimately suffered as a new 'crisis regime' was imposed on the city in the late 1970s.[11]

The 1970s also marked, in this context, a major turning point in ongoing struggles over affordable housing in New York. While New York squatters were successful in the late 1960s and early 1970s in opening up alternative political possibilities, they and other housing activists also encountered new challenges in a rapidly shifting and increasingly hostile socio-economic envi-ronment. The 'neoliberal transformation' of New York only accelerated the commodification of land and housing at the expense of low-income New Yorkers.[12] These were, in turn, circumstances that created, as the historian Roberta Gold has argued, 'an opening for propertied interests to advance on turf they had been eyeing for decades: rent control'.[13]

Between legislative attacks on rent regulation and the social fallout of economic contraction, the conditions for transforming New York's housing system proved difficult at best. Many of the tactics and strategies adopted by a new generation of activists were unsurprisingly defensive and concessionary. It was squatters who once again seized the initiative, occupying abandoned buildings across New York – most notably in the Lower East Side – while offering an alternative vision of the city as a space of resistance.

If New York's financial crisis was a housing crisis, it was wholesale abandonment and disinvestment that became it's defining symbol. Land admittedly remained valuable in inner-city neighbourhoods during the 1970s, though hundred-year-old tenements were not, so their owners lamented, particularly profitable. At the same time, weak code enforcement meant that landlords were still able to 'milk' buildings to the point where they required prohibitively costly repairs and were thus discarded. Entire blocks succumbed to abandonment across parts of Brooklyn, the South and West Bronx and the Lower East Side, while many buildings were damaged in suspicious fires as owners cashed in on dodgy insurance settlements.[14] The blocks became the property of the city, entering '*in rem* forfeiture due to unpaid taxes'. The city also created a new Department of Housing, Preservation and Development (HPD) to manage the buildings, though in most cases the buildings were 'warehoused empty rather than repaired and returned to the housing market'.[15]

In 1961, there were roughly 1,000 abandoned buildings in the city. The number had risen to 7,000 in 1968.[16] By 1970, over 200,000 low-income units had been abandoned by their owners, leaving their occupants without heat or water. The pace of abandonment was such that space for an estimated 81,000 people was being lost across New York each year.[17] As the city's tax base shrank, large cuts were made to anti-poverty programmes and associated housing policies. In May 1970, the city introduced a new rent-stabilisation bill that raised controlled rents by up to 15 per cent. The same bill introduced provisions that would allow for rents to be set in accordance with a calculation of operating costs (known as MBR or 'maximum base rent'). Additional measures ('vacancy decontrol') to lift rent limits from apartments when a tenant moved out were also passed.[18]

In the end, the widespread abandonment of housing across New York resulted in the destruction of whole neighbourhoods in the mid-1970s as a devastating wave of fires wreaked havoc on low-income communities across the city. According to geographer Michael Dear, writing in 1976:

> the process of abandonment as it operates in space … suggests an initial broad scattering of abandoned structures, characterized internally by the occurrence of many small groups of abandoned houses. With the passage of time, this pattern is intensified; the broad scatter is maintained, although the small groups now contain a greater number of structures … once abandonment has begun it is likely to be very difficult to stop. It may become almost a self-sustaining process under the force of contagion.[19]

Dear's model of contagious urban decay builds, of course, on an outdated version of urban ecology that risks overlooking some of the major structural forces that were responsible for what was later described as a 'fire and abandonment disaster'. For New York's minority neighbourhoods, it was racial segregation and housing discrimination combined with government mismanagement and the rollback of 'hard' municipal services that played a decisive role in the housing crisis that erupted in the 1970s.[20]

At the very height of the crisis, a fiscal retrenchment programme was introduced by the city's housing and development administrator, Roger Starr. The programme of 'planned shrinkage' advocated the withdrawal of city services from marginal blighted neighbourhoods and a transfer of savings to viable – read white middle class – communities. Starr's programme was widely condemned, though the 'triage' of welfare services and community assistance was largely implemented as part of the austerity measures introduced by the city.[21] During the same period, the city turned to the Rand Corporation and to new forms of systems analysis and management whose origins were firmly rooted in military operations and civil defence planning. The New York City Rand Institute was established in 1969 and it was soon put in charge of managing the city's fire department using the latest in computer simulations to generate recommendations for 'streamlining operations and improving agency performance'.[22]

The results proved catastrophic. In response to false alarms, the fire department began to replace electromechanical fire alarms with less reliable voice-activated boxes in 1969, which only led to a reduction in effective initial responses. The number of fire stations in poor working-class neighbourhoods was cut, thereby making them more dependent upon firefighters based in other parts of the city. Overall, fire department staffing fell from 14,700 to 10,200 between 1970 and 1976. As a consequence, and because blazes tended to cluster geographically and to peak at specific times, fire companies were no longer able to control and manage individual fires quickly and effectively. All of this led to an 'epidemic of conflagrations' that wiped out whole city blocks, spread to contiguous neighbourhoods and leaped to other marginal communities across New York.[23]

In the Bronx alone, seven census tracts lost more than 97 per cent of their buildings to fire and abandonment between 1970 and 1980; forty-four tracts (out of 289 in the borough) lost more than 50 per cent.[24] Not only were large swathes of housing destroyed, but a vast 'transfer of population' within and beyond the city took place as displaced minorities were forced to move into already overburdened neighbourhoods which led, in turn, to another round of suburban flight by the middle class. By the 1980s, abandonment and arson coupled with a crisis in services and an AIDS epidemic meant that the city was facing both a housing and a health disaster.[25]

New York was not alone. In many ways abandonment defined urban America in the 1970s. By 1974, Detroit and Philadelphia each had over 25,000 abandoned properties. Homelessness soared, and while housing activists attempted to extend and recast earlier initiatives, other creative responses were also developed. In the District of Columbia, policymakers experimented, unsuccessfully, with an urban speculation tax that would take up to 70 per cent of the profits made on residential speculation.[26] In New York and other American cities, community groups came together with municipal and federal agencies to form urban homesteading programmes in which low- and middle-income residents received vacant government homes and became home-owners under the condition that they brought the properties up to code – often by means of their own 'sweat equity' – and lived in them for a specified period of time. The federal Urban Homesteading programme, which was set up in 1975, was present in over 110 cities by 1983, while local organisations in New York pioneered their own programmes which were far more successful in rehabilitating homes than their federal counterpart.[27]

In the end, urban homesteading programmes achieved limited success. While they encouraged growing homeownership among African Americans, many commentators argued that they did little to address systemic urban inequality and homelessness. In New York, they nevertheless prompted a wave of housing occupations in the mid-1970s as activists took matters into their own hands, squatting a series of buildings on East 11th Street in the Lower East Side. The squatters teamed up with Interfaith Adopt-a-Building, a citywide sweat equity group, and were able to secure financial assistance to rehabilitate buildings that the city would otherwise have demolished. Other activist groups such as ACORN (Association of Community Organizations for Reform Now) and Banana Kelly (in the South Bronx) adopted similar tactics. As one former homesteader recalled, 'We could just go into these buildings and start gutting them to stake our claim, then back that up by putting in an application for the city [homesteading] program or to get funding from the federal government or state.'[28]

In South Williamsburg in Brooklyn, a small group of predominantly Latino activists began to organise and develop strategies to 'recover the disappearing use value of their neighborhood's housing'. Working with local Puerto Rican and other Latino residents in Southside (or Los Sures as it was commonly known), the activists were successful in occupying and restoring a number of individual apartments – and later buildings – in the neighbourhood. To do so, they first identified landlord-abandoned buildings that were without basic services (electricity, heat and water). Prospective 'occupiers' were then encouraged to pool resources otherwise used to pay rent in order to secure and pay for these services. Where buildings required significant repairs, tenants where moved in, though they were not required to pay into the service fund until initial renovations had been completed. The adoption of self-help strategies proved a success in Los Sures, and local community organisers were able to convince the city and the HPD to hand over *in rem* properties to them and other grassroots housing groups as part of what became known as the Community Management Programme. Funds were also released to help support the rehabilitation of properties.[29]

Hundreds of buildings across New York were salvaged in this way, though thousands more remained empty. By the 1980s, the federal homesteading programme was shelved, though the Community Management Programme continued until 1994. Officials in New York were, in turn, increasingly reluctant to hand over buildings as property values in the city were surging. While the abandonment of buildings continued, it was neighbourhood gentrification which became an equally potent source of displacement in the 1980s. And yet, these were not competing forms of urban dispossession: abandonment on the one hand; gentrification on the other. Rather they spoke, as Peter Marcuse argued at the time, to the relationship between the commodification of urban space and the neoliberal remaking of government policy.[30] As a 'political project', neoliberalism was closely connected, after all, to a renewed understanding of the city as profitable terrain for 'capital surplus production and absorption'.[31]

It is against this backdrop that a new generation of activists continued to occupy buildings in Chelsea, Harlem, the Bronx and especially the Lower East Side (or Loisaida as it was also known). A mixed group of local tenants, activists and artists, they adopted a more radical approach to homesteading. Some still saw themselves as homesteaders who turned to self-help and DIY practices to create liveable homes in the hope that the city would pass the title on to them. Many others self-identified as squatters who were unwilling to be co-opted by the housing market.

The former approach was adopted by ACORN, which commandeered twenty-five properties in the East New York district of Brooklyn between June and August 1985 after facing years of official government intransigence. As one of the group's organisers proclaimed, 'we're entitled to decent housing and we're going to have decent housing even if we have to take it'. The city initially responded by arguing that the buildings had been sealed and were unsafe and uninhabitable. Eighteen squatters and their supporters were arrested. A temporary restraining order was taken out on ACORN calling on the organisation to cease and desist in its efforts to squat buildings. Officials later backtracked as the scale of support for ACORN became clear.[32] The city granted the squatters access to fifty-eight buildings and a revolving loan fund of $2.7 million. They also received additional technical assistance as part of a new programme called 'mutual housing', a form of 'sweat-equity-earned co-op ownership'. According to the terms of the programme, the apartments could not be sold on for a profit.[33]

Another group of would-be homesteaders in the Lower East Side squatted six buildings in the mid-1980s on East 13th Street between Avenues A and B with a view to forming 'some sort of co-operative economy'.[34] As the city was unwilling to negotiate with the squatters, they formed their own not-for-profit group and were able to secure funds to start the Lower East Side's first recycling programme as well as a neighbourhood credit union. Infighting between members meant, however, that the group was unable to convert their occupations into legal homesteads. A vibrant community sprang up nevertheless around the 13th Street squats which became part of the city's underground art scene.[35]

Other Lower East Side squatters took a more combative and militant approach in the face of acute social service cutbacks and deepening gentrification. 'Increasing numbers of elderly and Latinos were,' according to former *Village Voice* journalist Sarah Ferguson, 'driven from their rent-controlled units [in the neighbourhood] through a combination of illegal buyouts, harassment and denial of services as landlords emptied buildings in order to drive up their resale value. Whole buildings were warehoused vacant while the streets became flooded with homeless people.'[36] By the early 1980s, the HPD had also begun to exploit the 200 *in rem* buildings in the Lower East Side to help kick-start and leverage the regeneration process. In August 1981, sixteen properties were chosen as part of an Artist Homeownership Programme and as a 'stimulus for overall neighbourhood revitalisation'.[37] As Rosalyn Deutsche and Cara Ryan concluded, 'the site of this brave new art scene' has become the 'strategic urban arena where the city, financed by big capital, wages its war of position against an impoverished and increasingly isolated local population'.[38]

The response of many Eastside artists was ambivalent. Some were undoubtedly complicit in the gentrification of the neighbourhood. Others actively challenged it.[39] Most local squatters, in turn, responded to these developments with outright antagonism. A new 'corridor of squats' was opened on East 8th Street between Avenues B and C drawing inspiration from tactics first adopted by European squatters, some of whom were now living on the Lower East Side. 'We were the anarchist squatters', recalled one of the activists who occupied 327–9 East 8th Street

in the autumn of 1984. 'We had no intention of going legal ...
We'd been squatting in Europe, where you just didn't consider
that.' For Frank Morales, one of the movement's more important interlocutors, '327 was a mothership on the block ... Eighth
Street became the initial jumping-off point, and little by little,
we moved out to [other squats] in the neighbourhood'. Over the
next few years, a number of squats were set up across the Lower
East Side. An ad even went out in the *Village Voice* ('Need a
Home, Squat ... ').[40]

The new movement reached its peak in 1988/1989 when there
were at least two dozen squats in the Lower East Side and an
equal number in East Harlem, Washington Heights and the South
Bronx. While uptown squats were closely rooted to longstanding
tenant struggles and supported by local communities of colour,
houses on the Lower East Side were brazenly confrontational and
part of a 'more militant, youthful and openly contentious squatting movement'. The newcomers saw squatting 'as the antidote
to forced removal, a means of community self-defence as well as
a means, through use of abandoned spaces, to meet the necessity
of a home, and build solidarity and power on the grass roots'.[41]
An older generation of housing activists remained suspicious
of the squatters' intentions and criticised their unwillingness to
cooperate with the wide coalition of community groups that
were active in the neighbourhood, including the Lower East Side
Joint Planning Council, an umbrella organisation that brought
together over thirty different groups.[42] Others were equally scep-
tical of the squatters' complex and often ambivalent relationship
to property and ownership.[43]

And yet, unlike many older homesteaders, the Lower East
Side squatters moved in and occupied the spaces they worked
on from the very beginning. They rejected government funding
and relied on recycled materials (studs, drywall, flooring, insu-
lation, etc.) and their own building skills and experiences which
were passed on from house to house. As the squatters themselves
pointed out, 'by recycling materials, [we] restore buildings at a
fraction of the regular costs. We are constantly improving our

environment – by making our buildings safe, by helping clean up our blocks, by establishing community gardens and recycling centres'. 'Squatters rights don't exist on paper,' added Morales, 'but in the concrete action of opening up empty buildings, working on them and creating homes.'[44]

If the Lower East Side squatting movement lacked any central organising structure, it nevertheless adopted tactics popularised by its European antecedents as a way of constructing a sense of community. As one squatter noted at the time, 'it's not about creating institutions but creating convergences of people'. 'There was a level of self-organisation in the beginning,' recalled another, 'a kind of organic connection. We weren't just inhabiting space, we were actually changing [it].'[45] The squatters set up an 'eviction watch', a phone tree that was used to fend off eviction efforts by the police, as well as attacks by local drug dealers. The watch quickly became an important solidarity-building tool within the squats as well as the neighbourhood at large. Squatters also converted the ground floor of 537 East 13th Street into a community kitchen which served the neighbourhood using food that had been skipped or donated by local restaurants.[46] Many of the squats were also closely connected to a wider underground arts and music scene hosting exhibitions and staging hardcore punk gigs and other concerts. There were close ties to ABC No Rio, a building on 156 Rivington Street which was occupied in 1980 as an 'art-making centre', while another squat at 292 East 3rd Street housed the 'Bullet Space' gallery on its ground floor in an apartment block owned, ironically enough, by Shapolsky et al. Manhattan Real Estate Holdings whose properties featured in Hans Haacke's cancelled 1971 exhibition at the Guggenheim.[47] The Bullet Space gallery was a 'vital node in the art squat network' in the Lower East Side, and was included in Martha Rosler's series of groundbreaking exhibitions on homelessness in New York City, 'If You Lived Here', that ran between 1987 and 1989.[48]

Despite ongoing evictions, fires and demolitions, something of a radical infrastructure – experimental, makeshift and subversive

– was therefore created on the Lower East Side. In the words of Ash Thayer, a photographer and former squatter whose recent collection of images represents a key visual record of the period, 'we worked on our buildings during the day and partied at night. There were group construction projects, community room potlucks, and notorious concerts in the basement.'[49] The intensity of engagement described and documented by Thayer and many others left a mark on buildings whose rehabilitation went far beyond the aesthetic, or for that matter the purely pragmatic, 'both producing and reflecting a historical narrative in which anti-capitalist forces [grew] in the spaces left vacant by creative destruction'.[50]

This is admittedly a narrative shaped as much by the very objects and materials that went into the remaking of squatted spaces as it is a story of the people who brought them back to life. As *Survival Without Rent*, a 1986 how-to guide published by Lower East Side squatters, made clear, this is a story of crowbars, piss buckets, kerosene heaters and woodstoves. It is also equally a story of mending and repair; of hanging new doors, replacing floors and joists, patching roofs and framing out walls, installing new plumbing, BX cable and wiring.[51] According to Fly, a long-time neighbourhood squatter, 'a new squat can be really raw'. 'Being involved in this whole process,' she added, 'learning the steps of building a habitable space, really makes you appreciate and respect your surroundings ... The knowledge of how to build and maintain my own living space gave me a sense of calm in the midst of chaos.'[52]

Squatters in the Lower East Side were, of course, acutely aware that both the spaces they assembled and the subcultures that they cultivated were set against a wider ecology of despair. For many, the Lower East Side remained a dangerous place in the 1980s and draconian policing efforts only succeeded, for the most part, in driving the local drug economy further underground. The squatters also understood that their efforts to rehabilitate the neighbourhood came at a price as the tenements they occupied quickly became valuable real estate.

They thus faced something of a double bind. On the one hand, activists located their actions within a decades-old struggle against what they described as the 'spatial deconcentration' of inner-city neighbourhoods and the calculated displacement of low-income residents from city centres to outlying suburbs.[53] On the other hand, their very endurance and survival stemmed, in no small part, from the cultural capital they conferred on an increasingly neoliberal city. Squatters, in other words, 'made troubled neighbourhoods appeal to punks and creative types for the subcultural richness, which in turn appealed to wealthier artists, which in turn made the neighbourhood appear safer for the white middle class'.[54] It was only a matter of time before developers and the city attempted to 'capture' and 'neutralise' these energies and clear out the squatters who now stood in the way of large profit-making opportunities.

It was a riot on the edge of Tompkins Park in August 1988 that, in the end, marked a major turning point in the recent history of housing activism in New York. The park had become a hangout for the homeless as well as drug dealers, punks and other so-called 'undesirables' in the eyes of a city seeking to tame and domesticate the neighbourhood. The riot erupted when the police enforced a 1:00 am curfew in the park on the pretext of clearing out its various occupants. While a diverse mix of activists, artists, punks, squatters, park inhabitants and community residents resisted the police, this was first and foremost, as Neil Smith has argued, a *police* riot. It was riot cops with their badges concealed that entered the park just before midnight forcibly evicting everyone. They were backed up by thirty mounted police on horseback, sharpshooters on neighbouring rooftops as well as a 'mobile command unit'. In order to clear the crowd, the police mounted a series of baton charges and fanned out over the neighbourhood attacking demonstrators and lashing out at local residents, many of whom had never gone near the park. The police were forced, however, to strike an 'ignominious retreat', and by 4:00 am the demonstrators had reoccupied the park. Fifty-three people were injured including fourteen police officers. There were thirty-one arrests and 121 complaints of police brutality and the use of excessive force.[55]

The police operation only succeeded in radicalising the wider Lower East Side neighbourhood. Some of the more militant squatters chose to occupy the park as both an encampment for the homeless and as a 'firewall' of sorts that would protect and immunise the neighbourhood against further gentrification east of Avenue A. Evictees soon returned and, by the summer of 1989, there were over 300 people sleeping in the park on any given night, many of whom had in fact been referred to the park by the city itself. It soon became clear that the city was using the park and its residents as an excuse to move in on the wider squatting scene. The squats on East 8th Street were the first to go as several buildings were cleared in 1989. The occupants of 316 East 8th Street were evicted in April 1989. The building had been condemned after a city bulldozer 'accidentally' ran into the front façade as it cleared the remains of the neighbouring tenement.[56] Number 319 followed a month later. In this case it was a small fire that was used as a pretext for eviction. According to Chris Flash, editor of the local underground newspaper, *The Shadow*, many squatters believed that the 'not-so-mysterious fires at various squats that took place in the months following the [Tompkins] riot were due to the city and NYPD desiring to remove a major element of opposition to the city's plan to change the demographics of the Lower East Side. In most cases, fire fighters stood by doing nothing as squats continued burning.'[57]

As squats were cleared and demolished, the police also moved in on Tompkins Park. Raids in July and December 1989 destroyed the tents and belongings of the park's residents, though many of the evictees returned to the park and erected semi-permanent structures. The city finally took action in June 1991. It closed the park and evicted everyone. It also erected an eight-foot-high chain-link fence that enclosed the park, while a team of fifty police officers were assigned to guard the park permanently as it underwent a two-year renovation. For the evictees, no alternative housing was arranged. Some moved into local squats.

Another group set up two makeshift encampments on vacant lots east of the park. Each of these – the number grew to ten – became known as 'Dinkinsville' after Mayor David Dinkins and in a sardonic nod to the numerous 'Hoovervilles' that sprang up across the city during the Depression.[58] Others still rejoined existing homeless communities under the Brooklyn, Manhattan and Williamsburg Bridges. Fire tore through the Manhattan Bridge encampment in 1992 killing one resident. The long-standing shantytown, known for its eighteen-foot teepee which 'towered over wood and tar paper shacks' was finally bulldozed in August 1993.[59]

The protracted struggle over Tompkins Park reignited tensions within the Lower East Side as an older generation of housing advocates accused many of the squatters of political grand-standing and that their actions jeopardised the neighbourhood's ability to secure low-income housing. Many of the squatters were unwilling, however, to negotiate with the city and believed that in doing so they would only fuel the further gentrification of the neighbourhood. The deadlock between squatters and the city was finally broken in July 1994 when the city announced plans to convert five squats on East 13th Street into low-income housing. The plan, led by recently elected City Councillor Antonio Pagan, was predicated on the use of tax credits to sub-sidise the renovation of the buildings. The new housing would, in turn, be managed by a non-profit housing association run by Pagan himself.[60]

In response, the squatters formed the East 13th Street Homesteaders Coalition and took the city to court. They sought a temporary restraining order against eviction while a case for adverse possession could be made. In October 1994, Supreme Court Justice Elliot Wilk granted the restraining order which was upheld on 2 November of the same year. A few months later, in April 1995, the Department of Buildings for the City of New York issued a peremptory 'vacate order' for two buildings on East 13th Street – 541 and 545 – as well as the first floor of 539, claiming that 'there is imminent danger to the safety and life of the occupants'.[61] Two other squats on the same street were unaffected. The order was based on two walk-through inspections that took place on 22 November 1994 and 12 April 1995, and highlighted a series of problems including 'deteriorated joists, buckling walls, sagging floors, and disintegrating window lintels'.[62]

These claims were refuted by experts called in by the squatters in a subhearing set up to assess the legitimacy of the vacate order. According to Stanley Cohen, a lawyer for the squatters, the court found that there was, in fact, no danger of collapse or need to vacate the buildings and that 'the [vacate] orders were a subterfuge to get around litigation, and the city's witnesses were untruthful'.[63] In April 1995, Judge Wilk ordered that the city make the necessary repairs and that the residents need not be removed. The city appealed the ruling on 25 May 1995, which effectively suspended Judge Wilk's decision. According to New York State law, an automatic freeze is put on any adverse ruling that the city has challenged. The appeal paved the way for the eviction of the three houses, which finally arrived on 30 May 1995 in the form of a heavily militarised multi-million-dollar operation involving riot police, SWAT teams, snipers, helicopters and even an armoured tank from the Korean War that had been repurposed by the city.[64]

As their expulsion approached, the squatters erected a series of intricate defences which took many hours to clear.[65] At the end of the day, however, the five buildings targeted by the city were behind police lines. Three of them were now empty. Despite the palpable sense of loss, many activists were more resolved than ever to hold on to the remaining occupied houses in the Lower East Side. 'This was,' according to poet and former squatter, Peter Spagnuolo, 'a wake-up call for everyone to take organizing seriously. You couldn't be an "a-political" squatter: the radical essence of squatting could no longer be denied by anyone, and slacking on the politics could be fatal to any given house.'[66] A group of squatters briefly retook two of the houses on East 13th Street in June 1995, escaping before the police could arrest them. The police responded by closing the entire block between Avenues A and B with checkpoints on either end. In October of the same year, Judge Wilk issued a preliminary injunction ruling that the occupants of the two remaining squats on East 13th Street could stay put while he decided on whether they had the right to remain in the buildings.[67] Judge Wilk's injunction was overturned in August 1996 by the Appellate Division of the State Supreme Court as it was deemed that the squatters had not demonstrated continuous occupancy as per the terms of the state's adverse possession statute. The squatters were evicted a few days later in another large police operation.[68]

It was the evacuation and demolition of the 5th Street squat in February 1997 that effectively brought an end to the squatter movement's defiance. The building was demolished in a police action after a minor fire in the building damaged part of the interior on three separate floors.[69] The action was ordered before any official investigation into the fire could be conducted and despite two court injunctions. One squatter, as Fly recalls, was able to stall the eviction for a couple of hours 'by climbing back into the building and escaping police detection for a few hours. When it became clear that they would continue to demolish the building even though they couldn't find him he emerged from his hiding place in fear for his life'.[70]

The mounting pressure took its toll on the squatters. In the face of a rapidly neoliberalising and conspicuously 'revanchist' city, a group of squatters finally opened negotiations with municipal authorities through the Urban Homesteading Assistance Board (UHAB), a non-profit organisation set up in New York in 1973 to provide support for urban homesteaders.[71] In 2002, a deal was announced in which eleven of the twelve remaining squats in the Lower East Side were to be sold to the UHAB for $1 each. The UHAB would take out loans on behalf of the squatters to bring the buildings up to code at which point title would be transferred to the occupants. The buildings would, in the process, become low-income, limited-equity co-operatives. By 2015, only half of the buildings had finished the process.

While some squatters believed that the deal was the only way to secure genuine low-income housing for the Lower East Side, others saw it as a cop out representing a complete betrayal of the movement's guiding ethos. Most were ambivalent. Legalisation may have bought them some breathing space. It also foreclosed other possibilities.[72]

It is these very possibilities that transformed the struggle for low-income affordable housing in the Lower East Side into a movement that was unique in the United States in terms of its scale, organisation, culture and durability. According to Jerry Wade ('the Peddler'), another well-known Lower East Side activist, squatters in the neighbourhood 'held more land, longer, than any other leftist group anywhere in the United States'.[73]

There were of course other squatting 'scenes' across the country that encompassed a 'rich tradition of communitarian living' and drew on experiments across a range of metropolitan and rural settings.[74] While New York was both exemplary and exceptional, squatting movements also emerged during the same period in Detroit, Seattle, St Louis and most notably in Philadelphia, where ACORN were active in the 1980s. A number of homeless organisations turned to squatting as a tactical response to deinstitutionalisation, privatisation and widespread cuts in welfare and social service budgets. These included the Kensington Welfare Rights Union in Philadelphia, Mad Houses in Atlanta and Chicago and Homes Not Jails in San Francisco.[75] Homes Not Jails were especially successful during the 1990s in commandeering houses to shelter the city's growing homeless community. The group combined 'political squats' that drew symbolic attention to their demands with 'survival squats' that were covertly occupied and used to 'house people for as long as possible'.[76]

Deprivation-based forms of squatting carried out by the homeless continued throughout the 1980s and 1990s as well, and gained, if anything, a new urgency in the wake of the 2008 financial crisis which led to a surge of foreclosures and an exponential rise in the number of abandoned properties across the country. These developments exacerbated existing geographical fault lines as cities, already devastated by decades of deindustrialisation and capital flight, were soon reeling from rising rates of foreclosure and a surge in the rent burden taken on by low-income households. As Matthew Desmond and Gretchen Purser have recently shown, evictions have become routine events throughout the country, upturning the lives of millions and leaving a geography of distressed neighbourhoods, trailer parks, homeless shelters and abandoned houses.[77] Other forms of disaster capitalism have emerged, and in the case of post-Katrina New Orleans the magnitude of the hurricane's destruction was such that by 2011 there were at least 6,000 squatters living in a city with approximately 43,000 abandoned structures.[78]

In New York, the last twenty years have been characterised by an ever-worsening housing crisis. Throughout the Giuliani and Bloomberg years, rents soared while the number of subsidised and rent-stabilised apartments shrank. Despite a brief recessional slowdown in the early 1990s, state-led gentrification soon returned. New 'urban frontiers' were opened up as luxury development and other large-scale projects spread into traditional working-class neighbourhoods, displacing residents into increasingly crammed spaces on the urban margins.[79] For migrants and other low-income residents, including longstanding communities of colour, the city had become 'ever more precarious'.[80]

These dynamics have accelerated the 'spatial deconcentration' of poor inner-city neighbourhoods, though they have also spawned a new wave of struggles in New York against urban renewal, corporate property speculation and forced displacement. Tenant unions as well as a range of grassroots community organisations turned once again to longstanding practices and tools developed by the city's various housing movements. Rent strikes were organised, evictions were blocked and demonstrations were held in support of fair rent, public housing and security of tenure. Other groups including the Harlem-based Movement for Justice in El Barrio (MJB) adopted a wider transnational approach. They drew inspiration from the Zapatistas as well as the Miami-based Take Back the Land Movement, whose actions – inspired by the Landless Workers' Movement in Brazil and the struggles of shack dwellers in South Africa – focused on eviction resistance and the rehousing of homeless people in foreclosed homes. While rooted in the local neighbourhood, MJB connected their own fight for decent housing to a much wider network of struggle against the forces of 'neoliberal displacement'.[81]

In New York, the loss of over 200,000 units of affordable housing for low- and moderate-income families has, in recent years, been accompanied by the rise of luxury condominiums in traditional working-class neighbourhoods and the prospect of a new wave of gentrification. The global financial crisis and the recession that followed in its wake has meant, however, that many of these condos remain empty or unsold. Others remain half-built or have entered foreclosure. As the New York Chapter of the Right to the City Alliance concluded in a 2010 report, the city is 'left with thousands of units of vacant housing at a time when low-income New Yorkers are facing a serious housing shortage'. It is filled, they added, 'with people without homes and homes without people'.[82]

While squatters in New York have a long history of occupying the city's 'ghost housing', the 'neoliberal city' pointed to a more circumscribed field of action.[83] The UHAB sales heralded a form of legalisation and institutionalisation that, in many ways, marked the end of squatting in the Lower East Side. In the South Bronx and East Harlem, the Inner City Press Homesteaders, a grassroots group of mainly Latino families, were still squatting buildings during the early 2000s, though the eviction of Casa del Sol, a well-established squat and community centre on 136th Street in the South Bronx in 2004 was a major blow to housing activists in the neighbourhood. Held on grounds of adverse possession since 1985, the deeds of the house were transferred to ACORN who had purchased the building with a view to converting it into low-income housing. A few hours after the eviction, over half of the building was consumed in a suspicious fire.[84]

If squatting receded from the public eye in the years that followed, the salience of squatting and other occupation-based practices was revived as part of a broader Occupy movement in 2011. It was again New York and the Occupy Wall Street (OWS) encampment at Zucotti Park in Lower Manhattan that became a key site within a larger struggle against the wave of austerity measures rolled out by Western governments in the wake of the global financial crisis. The camp was itself short-lived, occupying the park for two months in 2011. The camp's forced eviction in November 2011 prompted members of the OWS Direct Action Committee to join forces with young housing activists that were part of a local group, Organising for Occupation (O4O). The group was supported by former Lower East Side squatter and activist, Frank Morales. They occupied homes foreclosed by the global financial crisis and refurbished them for families made homeless by the crisis. Many occupiers also came together to form Occupy Sandy to support New York area communities devastated by the storm in October 2012. Neighbourhood distribution centres sprang up as activists created a base for identifying and addressing acute housing needs. In so doing, they also extended Occupy's work of 'creating and maintaining spaces that enable people to care for each other's needs while challenging the scarcity logics of capitalism'.[85]

The Occupy movement for housing is no longer active. It nevertheless drew attention to the importance of urban squatting – however fragile and precarious – as a form of direct action that remained first and foremost a struggle over the right to be in the city and against the commodification of land and housing. The history of squatting in New York was, in other words, part of a longstanding struggle for a more radical and socially just urbanism. This is history that has its origins in distant struggles over the meaning of land and property in the nineteenth century and whose repertoire of contention can, in turn, be traced back to the first tenant mobilisations of the early twentieth century. The tenant movement and its various offshoots spoke 'unabashedly' for a different New York and, in the process, imagined and assembled an alternative to the home ownership model that shaped post-war American society. As a movement, it also helped to create and sustain other realities: from multi-racial neighbourhoods to women's political empowerment; from collective ownership to new subcultural formations.[86]

Many of the sites and spaces that are central to this history have admittedly disappeared or have, in recent years, assumed a new shape and form in the face of relentless redevelopment and displacement. It is only through an attentiveness to what squatters said and did – to *the act of squatting itself* – that we are, in some way, able to reconstruct and reanimate these spaces. While it is often difficult to gather together and make sense of the fragments and remnants of earlier activist histories and do justice to their emotional investments and undercurrents, squatters have always been active documentarians. It is still possible, therefore, amid the flyers, brochures, photographs and other marginalia collected by activists in New York, to catch a glimpse or outline of an alternative vision of collective city life, whether it be the scribbled minutes of a house meeting or a modest handwritten flowchart documenting and tracing the various occupants of squatted houses on East 13th Street in the Lower East Side. One might even detect, in the case of the latter, a radical analogue to the kind of kinship diagrams and other schematics used by anthropologists to create a snapshot of a community with its various arrangements, interactions and reciprocities.[87]

A former squatter, Peter Spagnuolo, captures this problem of documentation and commemoration in one of his most poignant poems, 'The Squatters Midden'. Spagnuolo describes how squatters 'carved homes out of tenements from the top down, always deferring the work of removal for another time, leaving a ground-floor mound we now excavated a decade later'. What Spagnuolo describes as an 'act of reclamation' was, however, 'lost with the eviction that came later – bulldozed, I suspect, in a Jersey landfill'. And yet, as Spagnuolo concludes, other forms of historical recovery do still exist: 'I rebuild this all here from memory, where I've kept it safe.'

In New York, housing activists have always kept the memories of their actions safe. In 2015, the Interference Archive in Brooklyn held an exhibition entitled 'We Won't Move: Tenants Organise in New York City'. The exhibition focused on the rich history of tenant struggle and neighbourhood resistance in New York. It highlighted 'the diverse array of tactics adopted by tenant organisers' while situating the 'fight for affordable housing within racial and economic justice struggles'.[88] Across the city, in the Lower East Side, C-Squat, one of the eleven UHAB buildings currently under renovation, has been transformed into MoRUS, the Museum of Reclaimed Urban Space. The museum retraces the history of community gardening, homesteading and squatting in the Lower East Side. In both cases, the very act of documentation served as much more than simply a reminder that cities have always been places full of radical possibilities. If anything, they point to the enduring need for 'housing alternatives and a new collective, sustainable approach to urban housing models'.[89] There is, after all, still much to be learned from squatting.

Afterword

From Survival to Hospitality: Reimagining the Squatted City

Somebody's gotta tell them, that we are not ghosts, that we are in this city and we are alive!

jessica Care moore, Detroit-based poet[1]

Cuando vivir es un lujo, okupar es un derecho. (When life has become a luxury, to squat is a right.)

Popular Spanish squatting slogan[2]

It is perhaps unsurprising that the final word in the recent history of squatting in Europe and North America begins with another occupation. This is, however, a different kind of occupation. On 26 May 2016, the American Pavilion at the Venice Architecture Biennale was digitally 'squatted' by an activist collective based in Detroit. The collective, Detroit Resists, installed its own virtual exhibition on the pavilion site which was accessible through the LAYAR augmented reality smartphone app.

The occupation superimposed images of protest and resistance over the existing exhibition. These are images that have been routinely omitted from recent architectural visions of a 'resilient' regenerating Detroit. 'This is resistance,' as the organisers of the occupation argued, 'to mass water shutoffs, mass foreclosures, mass evictions, unconstrained gentrification and other examples of spatial racism.'[3] It includes the words and images of many city residents such as the late activist and feminist Grace Lee Boggs, the poet and writer Tawana Petty, the hip hop collective Raiz Up and the grassroots coalition Detroit Eviction Defense.

Detroit Resists were responding and, in turn, refunctioning the official Biennale show. Entitled 'The Architectural Imagination', the exhibition encompasses a series of 'speculative architectural projects' that have been designed for four different sites across Detroit: the abandoned Packard Automobile Plant; the Dequindre Cut greenway; an empty lot in the city's Mexicantown; and the derelict 1960 Riverfront Post Office. The curators of the exhibition selected twelve 'visionary' American architects who were tasked with designing new work that responded to the challenges that a conspicuously post-industrial city faced in 'finding its way to the future'. In their own words, 'it is possible to imagine new scenarios for the city through architecture ... architecture has the possibility to catalyse change'.[4]

'The Architectural Imagination' draws, in this way, on Detroit's long history as a source of architectural inventiveness. The final designs grew out of a series of conversations between the architects, city officials and local community groups. They point, on the one hand, to the role of architecture as a potential regenerative force in Detroit, a city now synonymous with loss – be it population, property values, jobs, infrastructure, investment, security or a sense of 'cityness' itself.[5] On the other hand, these are projects – from a vertical garden to a recycling centre, a wood skyscraper to an automated manufacturing hub – that have also been designed to serve as models for other post-industrial cities. At stake here is an architectural vision that transforms the challenges of austerity, endurance and resilience into new forms of living and working.

For the Detroit Resists Collective, however, the exhibition does little ultimately to address the 'urban catastrophe that many of Detroit's residents are currently attempting to survive'. This is an exhibition that testifies, in their eyes, to architecture's 'political indifference' to an austerity urbanism that has left countless city residents without water and many others searching for an affordable home while thousands of 'blighted' houses are demolished or remain empty, their former occupants evicted in the wake of the largest municipal tax foreclosure in US history.[6]

And this is to say nothing of the mass dispossession of Detroit's predominantly African American population that is itself the culmination of a long history of racialised discrimination, political marginalisation and financial mismanagement. This is, after all, a city that, between 2000 and 2010, lost over 25 per cent of its population. By 2013, up to forty of the city's 139 square miles were largely abandoned or empty. Over 90,000 properties were vacant. Detroit averaged 90,000 fires in 2008 – twice the number of New York, a city eleven times more populous. At the time that the city declared bankruptcy in July 2013, it took the police department an average of fifty-eight minutes to respond to emergency calls.[7]

Detroit's 'zone of abandonment' – a roughly twenty-mile arc around the city's commercial core – has often been depicted as a derelict space of 'social death and feral emptiness' characterised by 'hulking industrial ruins, panoramic urban prairies, and dramatically burned-out or overgrown homes'.[8] It is not, however, empty. Families and neighbourhoods continue to exist there, and it is estimated that over 88,000 people live in the city's high-vacancy zone.[9] As public infrastructure services and networks disappear or are decommissioned, many have turned to squatting. Some continue to live in their homes after foreclosing on them. Others occupy abandoned houses and other vacant buildings scheduled for demolition.[10]

In the case of Detroit, it would be tempting to see in the city a place that has seemingly fallen out of the property regimes and profit-making activities that we have come to associate with contemporary late capitalism. And yet, while the problems of vacancy and abandonment are often associated with the absence of capital, in Detroit the opposite holds true. In recent years, the city has become a key site for new forms of exploitation that have simply 'widened the avenues of extractive and predatory speculation'.[11] Beginning in the late 1990s, a series of bills drafted by the Hudson Institute, a private free market think tank, were introduced in the Michigan Legislature including Public Act 123 (PA 123). The act devolved responsibility for tax-foreclosed properties from state to local government. Land auctions were mandated and the entire process was shortened to three years. PA 123 was paired with an Urban Homesteading Act which was intended to facilitate the transfer of vacant public housing into private ownership, and in so doing provide support for low-income residents in the state.[12]

In Detroit, the provision of housing for the city's poor was never implemented. In its place, a small group of speculators used the auction of tax-foreclosed properties as a vehicle for volume acquisition, predatory investment, widespread tax avoidance and property dumping. The most dilapidated properties were never auctioned and the city was left to manage the 'spatial residues' of the state's 'market-based experimentation' – abandoned valueless buildings, deserted vacant lots and poorly serviced neighbourhoods.[13]

It is ultimately these residues that have come to characterise the deep urban crisis that has forced many of Detroit's inhabitants to develop new skills of endurance and survival, an array of makeshift objects, practices, techniques and collectives that have tended to exist outside the logics of capitalist accumulation. As the members of Detroit Resists as well as other local activists and citizens know all too well, squatting and other forms of urban informality have played an important role in sustaining an alternative and deeply fragile city in the face of intense inequality.[14]

For the bankers, developers and boosters supporting the Detroit Future City Plan – an ambitious large-scale reimagining and 'right-sizing' of Detroit – these are, in fact, creative 'pioneering' practices that provide a template for the city's large-scale redevelopment. The plan itself calls for the regeneration of the city's vacant industrial spaces as 'live-make' neighbourhoods. Abandoned zones with little 'market value' are to be repurposed, in turn, as ecologically sustainable communities supporting a new 'blue and green infrastructure' made up of retention ponds, carbon forests, urban farms and greenways.[15] Traditional public services (public transportation, water, sanitation and street lights) will be withdrawn from these zones as a way of 'encouraging' their residents to leave.

The plan's settler colonial rhetoric with its urban 'pioneers', 'wastelands' and 'frontiers' has not been lost on its many critics for whom it has come to represent 'a pernicious reworking of the logic of ethical environmentalism, enabling and justifying otherwise controversial dispossessions'.[16] The repurposing of the sometimes inventive, sometimes experimental strategies adopted by many Detroit residents were, in this way, 'captured' and placed in the service of a market-oriented programme of greening, austerity and gentrification.[17]

However, more often than not these were practices and strategies that emerged out of a desperate search to meet the most basic of needs – shelter – amid deep material inequality. As the geographers Don Mitchell and Nik Heynen remind us, the very question of how it is still possible – or practically impossible – for many people to inhabit and make a life in cities, the question of the 'social and structural constraints on accessing even the most basic materials for human survival', was a central preoccupation of one of Detroit's most prescient interlocutors, the radical (and radically eccentric) geographer Bill Bunge.[18] In the late 1960s, Bunge, a professor at Wayne State University in Detroit, collaborated with local black activists to set up the Detroit Geographical Expedition and Institute (DGEI) which drew critical attention to the effects of racism, inequality and disinvestment on the city's African American population.[19] The DGEI offered free college extension courses for local inner-city residents and participated in a number of grassroots initiatives which culminated in the publication of *Fitzgerald*, a radical people's geography of the eponymous Detroit neighbourhood.[20]

It was Bunge who first talked of a 'geography of survival' as a way of describing the different spaces and spatial relations that shape how *and increasingly if* people are able to live in cities.[21] For squatters in Detroit as well as elsewhere in North America and Europe, this is a geography that has assumed a certain urgency in recent years. The history of urban squatting has always been closely connected to housing insecurity and the efforts of ordinary people to secure their own right to housing and the basic fundamentals of survival. The global financial crisis has, if anything, created a situation where even more people are without adequate housing across the Global North. This has led to the re-emergence of radical housing movements in Berlin, London, New York and Paris and, in particular, in cities across Southern Europe (Greece, Italy and Spain) where the elementary brutalities of the crisis have forced thousands of people out of their homes.[22]

In Spain, the housing crisis has been especially acute. Since 2008, foreclosures have skyrocketed. Between 2008 and 2012, over 400,000 evictions took place. By some estimates, somewhere between 5 and 6 million housing units sit empty across the country, roughly 20 per cent of the country's housing stock.[23] Spanish mortgage laws require debtors to repay their loans in full even after they have declared bankruptcy and their homes have been repossessed.

While there has been a squatting movement (*movimiento okupa*) in Spain for many decades, recent years have seen a resurgence of squatting and other forms of occupation that have carved out a broad geography of survival that 'speaks to the reproduction of precarious communities, to a new strategy of people simply and straightforwardly seizing what they need to survive while simultaneously attacking the system that ensures their precarity'.[24] This includes the actions of a number of evicted families living in and around the city of Seville who joined forces with activists who had emerged out of the neighbourhood assemblies of the 15-M Movement (15th of May Movement). In 2012, they occupied a number of empty apartment buildings and began to fill them with people who were in need of shelter as part of a process of '*realojo*' ('rehousing').[25] The occupations known as '*corralas*' – after the seventeenth-century residential structures – proved popular and led to the formation of a network of previously vacant properties.[26]

What has been described as the 'two faces of occupation in an age of austerity' – responding to people's basic needs and constituting an autonomous political force – have also played an important role in the emergence of one of the largest radical housing movements in Europe, the Plataforma de Afectados por la Hipoteca (PAH, or Platform for Mortgage Victims).[27] Set up by local activists in Barcelona in February 2009, one of whom, Ada Colau, would later become mayor of the city, the PAH is a grassroots movement to protect the rights of citizens across Spain who are facing expulsion from their homes.

The work of the PAH focuses on eviction resistance, the settlement of mortgage debts (known as '*Dación en pago*' or 'handing back the keys') and the transformation of vacant housing held by financial institutions into affordable social housing (the Obra Social campaign).[28] The PAH has adopted a wide range of direct action techniques that include the squatting of buildings to house homeless families. Their actions have proved so popular and successful that by 2015 there were 226 separate PAH chapters across Spain, seventy-two of them in Catalonia.[29]

The crisis in Spain and the various movements (PAH, 15-M Movement) that emerged to challenge the neoliberal policies adopted by successive Spanish governments also brought new life to a well-established squatters' scene in cities such as Madrid and Barcelona. Many squatter activists detected a close affinity between the new self-managed camps and the longstanding social centres that they were connected to (this included spaces such as Patio Maravillas, Casablanca and Tabacalera in Madrid and La Rimaia, Can Masdeu and Barrilonia in Barcelona).[30] They gave material support and advice to the open-air occupations which they saw as an ersatz form of squatting that was, in turn, responsible for the production of a 'temporary self-made city'.[31]

It is against this backdrop that squatting was quickly adopted by a new generation of activists in the 15-M Movement for whom the right to affordable housing had become the key source of their struggles. This led to a large wave of occupations in the summer of 2011 as many local residents in cities such as Madrid turned to undetected forms of stealth squatting as a means to meet immediate housing needs. They were often supported by former squatters as well as 15-M activists. At the same time, other public and collective squats were established, though many have since been evicted. Most acted as community social centres, others served exclusively as dwellings. Some combined the two.[32]

While the 15-M Movement helped to rejuvenate the squatter movement in Spain, it also extended another front in a wider geography of survival, in this case the ongoing refugee crisis in Europe which has transformed its cities into spaces of containment, exclusion and policing, on the one hand, as well as sites of care, refuge and hospitality on the other.

Refugee and migrant solidarity has long played an important role within various squatter movements across Europe that have traditionally been anti-racist, anti-fascist and anti-imperialist and that have, as such, criticised the violent and increasingly militarised border regimes set up by their governments. The interactions and connections between squatters and migrants have, in this context, assumed a number of different forms though they have, if anything, intensified in recent years.[33]

In Spain, particularly in cities such as Barcelona and Madrid, the recent crisis has fostered a new commitment to the development of practices that seek to resist the forms of 'precarious living' increasingly shared by migrants and local residents alike.[34] Autonomous social centres and other squatted spaces have played an important organising role in a number of campaigns around the legal status of undocumented migrants, their right to live and work, and the growing and often illegitimate use of detention and deportation centres. As the housing crisis intensified, it was often migrants who were most affected. Many joined the PAH movement and were active in the Obra Social campaign to occupy and 'liberate' abandoned buildings. There were also earlier instances of squats autonomously established by migrants such as the Cuarteles de San Andreu in Barcelona (2002–4) or the Palacete okupado in Madrid (2008).[35]

In the end, it is not only in Spain that squatting has come to offer an urgent and necessary alternative to dominant anti-immigrant policies that seek to deny asylum seekers and refugees the 'agency to shape the city' on their own fragile terms.[36] Elsewhere across Europe, a number of squats have been set up as spaces of refuge and hospitality for forced migrants who often find themselves in political limbo or unable to access local social services. In Athens, there are currently seven separate squats housing over 1,500 refugees.[37] A number of squatted spaces have, in turn, been established across Italy in Bologna, Milan, Naples, Rome and in Turin where the Ex Moi occupation (the former 2006 Olympic Village) houses over 1,000 squatters from thirty different countries.[38] Similar efforts are also taking place in France and Germany, where refugees have set up their own protest camps and squats to defend their right to work and education while seeking access to decent affordable accommodation and emergency health care.[39]

The various occupations undertaken by squatters, housing activists, refugees and other migrants point, in this way, to the articulation of an alternative right to the city. This is a right, as Henri Lefebvre reminds us, to 'habitat and to inhabit' (*'a l'habitat et à l'habiter'*). It is in other words, a right to a place to make a life ('habitat') as well as a right to make that place one's own ('to inhabit') and express a basic right *to be* and persist in that place and participate in the production of a different kind of city.[40]

The recent actions of squatters therefore point to forms of care, generosity and dwelling whose history is unthinkable outside the precarious conditions that they emerged out of. And yet, the autonomous city charted in these pages was more than a simple matter of survival. It encompassed an expansive and enduring set of political demands; demands that still speak to how we might come to know and live the city differently. For squatters, the right to the city has always been a right to remake the city and transform it through hope, resistance and solidarity.[41]

Acknowledgments

This is a book that has taken many years to complete and it would not have been possible without the support of my editor at Verso, Leo Hollis. I am indebted to him for his advice, guidance (and patience) throughout the writing process.

As a book on the dreams and practices of squatters, it's genesis and development has always been a collective endeavour – thank you so very very much to all the activists and squatters who shared their stories with me. This is, moreover, a project that is the culmination of countless conversations, debates (and disagreements) with friends and colleagues over the past few years. A big thank you to Josh Akers, Alex Andrews, Alex Baker, Azozomox, David Bell, Emily Bennett, Milo Bettocchi, Bethan Bowett, Katherine Brickell, Sophie Cee, Petra Davis, Matthew Farish, Melissa Fernandez, Mara Ferreri, Rosa Gilbert, Cat Gold, Dan Hancox, Lani Hanna, Dorte Ellesøe Hansen, Alex Jeffrey, Tariq Jazeel, Ask Katzeff, Michele Lancione, Audrea Lim, David Madden, Alfredo Mazzamauro, Colin McFarlane, Pietro Piana, Rachel Rosenfelt, Amy Starecheski, Bart van der Steen, Marie Thompson, Andy Wolff and Christine Ziegler.

This is, in turn, a book that is the product of the kindness and generosity of the many archivists with whom I worked across Europe and North America. In so many cases, they are the custodians of collections whose survival means a great deal to me and whose materials provide us with a glimpse into what a radically different city might still come to look like. A heartfelt thanks go to the following archives and libraries: Infoshop 56a in London, the Staatsarchief at the Institute of Social History in Amsterdam, the Arbejdermuseet Archive in Copenhagen, the Rigsarkivet in Copenhagen, the Hamburg Institute of Social History Archive, the Central Archive of the Technical University Berlin, Papiertiger Archiv in Berlin, the Robert Havemann Gesellschaft Archiv in Berlin, the APO-Archiv at the Free University in Berlin, the Archivio Primo Moroni in Milan, the Istituto Gramsci in Turin, the Archivio Storico della Nuova Sinistra 'Marco Pezzi' in Bologna, the Istituto Parri in Bologna, the Interference Archive in New York, the Squatters' Rights Collection at the Tamiment Library at NYU, the City of Vancouver Archives, the North Vancouver Museum & Archives and Special Collections at the University of British Columbia, Vancouver.

Closer to home, I owe a great deal of thanks to the School of Geography at the University of Nottingham and, in particular, to Stephen Daniels, Isla Forsyth, Shaun French, Mike Heffernan, Jake Hodder, Stephen Legg and Charles Watkins.

A special thanks to my parents for their unwavering love and support and for reminding me that the struggle for a more equal and just world really does matter. To Christine and David McFarlane as well as Doug McFarlane and Daisy Mallabar who have supported me through my book-writing adventure and have always made feel at home. And finally to Megan whose love means absolutely everything and without whom I could not have written this book.

Chapter 5 builds on and extends arguments recently outlined in *Metropolitan Preoccupations: The Spatial Politics of Squatting in Berlin*.

Notes

Introduction

1. Michel Foucault, 'Lives of Infamous Men', in Michel Foucault, *Power Truth, Strategy* (Sydney: Feral Publications, 1979), pp. 76–91, p. 80; Michel Foucault, *The Courage of Truth: The Government of Self and Others, 1983–1984* (Basingstoke: Palgrave Macmillan, 2011), p. 340.
2. Stine Krøijer, *Figurations of the Future: Forms and Temporalities of Left Radical Politics in Northern Europe* (New York: Berghahn Books, 2015), p. 83.
3. 'Militæret hjalp ved rydningen af Ungdomshuset' (politiken.dk); for a parliamentary discussion of military involvement in the Ungdomshuset eviction, see answer to Spørgsmål nr. S 3850 (question nr. 3850) from Member of Parliament Line Barfod (EL) (ft.dk).
4. René Vázquez Díaz, 'Un laboratoire policier sous le regard des pays européens? Répression pour l'exemple à Copenhague'. *Le Monde Diplomatique* (April 2007), p. 3; see also Andreas Karker, *Jagtvej 69. Historien om et hus* (Copenhagen: Lindhardt og Ringhof, 2007).
5. 'Kronologi over urolighederne i København' (dr.dk).
6. Díaz, 'Un laboratoire policier'.
7. 'Politiet brugte livsfarlig tåregas' (politiken.dk).
8. Díaz, 'Un laboratoire policier'.
9. Ibid.
10. Ibid.
11. Karker, *Jagtvej 69*, p. 10, 20.
12. Quoted in Krøijer, *Figurations of the Future*, p. 69.
13. Ibid., p. 92.
14. Karker, *Jagtvej 69*, p. 114.
15. See René Karpantschof and Flemming Mikkelsen, 'Youth, Space and Autonomy in Copenhagen: The Squatters' and Autonomous Movement, 1962–2012', in Bart van der Steen, Ask Katzeff and Leendert van Hoogenhuijze (eds), *The City is Ours: Squatting and Autonomous Movements in Europe from the 1970s to the Present* (San Francisco: PM Press, 2014), pp. 178–205, p. 195.

16. Dan Nemser, 'The Other Occupy Movement' (thenewinquiry.com).
17. 'La nouvelle loi pour lutter contre les squatteurs votée à l'unanimité' (leparisien.fr).
18. Michigan Legislature, 'House Bill 5070' (legislature.mi.gov); Nevada Legislature, 'AB386 Overview' (leg.state.nv.us).
19. David Madden and Peter Marcuse, *In Defense of Housing* (London: Verso, 2016), p. 1.
20. Friedrich Engels, *The Housing Question* (London: Lawrence and Wishart, 1936 [1872]), p. 17.
21. Madden and Marcuse, *In Defense of Housing*, p. 10.
22. Hans Pruijt, 'The Logic of Urban Squatting'. *International Journal of Urban and Regional Research* 37 (2013), pp. 19–45, p. 19.
23. Colin Ward, *Cotters and Squatters: Housing's Hidden History* (Nottingham: Five Leaves Books, 2002).
24. Robert Neuwirth, *Shadow Cities: A Billion Squatters, A New Urban World* (London and New York: Routledge, 2006), p. 311.
25. See Mike Davis, *Planet of Slums* (London: Verso, 2006); Anna-Maria Makhulu, *Making Freedom: Apartheid, Squatter Politics and the Struggle for Home* (Durham, NC: Duke University Press, 2015); Edgar Pieterse, *City Futures: Confronting the Crisis of Urban Development* (London: SAGE, 2008); Richard Pithouse, 'Thinking Resistance in the Shanty Town' (metamute.org); AbdouMaliq Simone, *City Life from Jakarta to Dakar* (London and New York: Routledge, 2010). Elsewhere, I have argued for the need to develop a 'global geography of squatting'. See Alexander Vasudevan, 'The Makeshift City: Towards a Global Geography of Squatting'. *Progress in Human Geography* 39 (2015), pp. 338–59, p. 353.
26. A notable exception are the important efforts made in recent years by the Squatting Europe Kollective (SqEK).
27. John F.C. Turner, *Housing by People: Towards Autonomy in Building Environments* (London: Marion Boyars, 1976), p. 17.
28. Ward quoted in ibid., p. 5, emphasis in original.
29. John F.C. Turner, Robert Fichter and Peter Grenell, 'The Meaning of Autonomy', in John F.C. Turner and Robert Fichter (eds), *Freedom to Build: Dweller Control of the Housing Process* (New York: Macmillan, 1972), pp. 241–54, p. 241.
30. Miguel A. Martínez López, 'The Squatters' Movement in Europe: A Durable Struggle for Social Autonomy in Urban Politics'. *Antipode* 45 (2013), pp. 866–87, p. 867; see SqEK (ed.), *The Squatters' Movement in Europe: Commons and Autonomy as Alternatives to Capitalism* (London: Pluto Press, 2014).
31. Krøijer, *Figurations of the Future*, p. 92.
32. See van der Steen, Katzeff and van Hoogenhuijze (eds), *The City is Ours*; Knud Andresen and Bart van der Steen (eds), *A European*

Youth Revolt: European Perspectives on Youth Protest and Social Movements in the 1980s (Basingstoke: Palgrave Macmillan, 2016).

33. Geoff Eley, 'Politics and the City: A Badly Bifurcated Left' (h-net. org).
34. Ibid.; Claudio Cattaneo and Miguel A. Martínez López, 'Squatting as an Alternative to Capitalism', in SqEK (ed.), *The Squatters' Movement in Europe*, pp. 1–25, p. 5.
35. Geoff Eley, 'Politics and the City'.
36. David Harvey, 'The Right to the City'. *New Left Review* 53 (2008), pp. 23–40, p. 24.
37. Margit Mayer, 'Preface', in SqEK (eds), *Squatting in Europe: Radical Spaces, Urban Struggles* (London: Minor Compositions), pp. 1–9, p. 3.
38. See Ward, *Cotters and Squatters*.

1. Squatter Sovereignty

1. *New York Times* (hereafter *NYT*), 11 July 1880.
2. Langston Hughes, *Langston Hughes Reader* (New York: George Braziller, Inc., 1958), p. 101.
3. Cynthia A. Young, *Soul Power: Culture, Radicalism and the Making of a U.S. Third World Left* (Durham, NC: Duke University Press, 2006), pp. 101, 121; Jonas Mekas, *Movie Journal: The Rise of the New American Cinema, 1959–1971* (New York: Macmillan, 1971), p. 305.
4. 'Poor Families Taking Over Condemned Buildings', *NYT*, 24 April 1970; Rose Muzio, 'The Struggle Against "Urban Renewal" in Manhattan's Upper West Side and the Emergence of El Comité'. *Centro Journal* 21 (2009), pp. 109–41, p. 122.
5. Roberta Gold, *When Tenants Claimed the City: The Struggle for Citizenship in New York City Housing* (Urbana: University of Illinois Press, 2014), p. 191.
6. Quoted in Young, *Soul Power*, p. 140.
7. Muzio, 'The Struggle Against "Urban Renewal"', pp. 121–122.
8. Young, *Soul Power*, p. 139.
9. David Madden and Peter Marcuse, *In Defense of Housing: The Politics of Crisis* (London: Verso, 2016), p. 147.
10. Gold, *When Tenants Claimed the City*, p. 3.
11. Hannah Dobbz, *Nine-Tenths of the Law: Property and Resistance in the United States* (Oakland, CA: AK Press, 2012), p. 33.
12. Dobbz, *Nine-Tenths of the Law*, pp. 35, 51; see Eduardo Moisés Peñalver and Sonia K. Latyal, *Property Outlaws: How Squatters, Pirates and Protesters Improve the Law of Ownership* (New Haven,

CT: Yale University Press, 2010); and Neil Smith, *The New Urban Frontier: Gentrification and the Revanchist City* (London and New York: Routledge, 1996), p. 232.

13. For a definitive history of the Anti-Rent movement in New York, see Charles W. McCurdy, *The Anti-Rent Era in New York Law and Politics, 1839–1865* (Chapel Hill: University of North Carolina Press, 2001).

14. Christopher Mele, *Selling the Lower East Side: Culture, Real Estate and Resistance in New York City* (Minneapolis: University of Minnesota Press, 2000), pp. 38, 40–41.

15. Jared N. Day, *Urban Castles: Tenement Housing and Landlord Activism in New York City, 1890–1943* (New York: Columbia University Press, 1999), p. 14.

16. The statistics are quoted in Richard Plunz, *A History of Housing in New York City: Dwelling Type and Social Change in the American Metropolis* (New York: Columbia University Press, 1990); *Report of the Council of Hygiene and Public Health of the Citizens' Association of New York Upon the Sanitary Condition of the City* (New York: Appleton, 1867), p. lxxiii.

17. See Seneca Village Project (mcah.columbia.edu).

18. 'Our Squatter Population', *NYT*, 15 July 1867.

19. See Joseph Alexiou, *Gowanus: Brooklyn's Curious Canal* (New York: NYU Press, 2015).

20. Lisa Goff, *Shantytown, USA: Forgotten Landscapes of the Working Poor* (Cambridge, MA: Harvard University Press, 2016), pp. 86, 87; Robert Neuwirth, *Shadow Cities: A Billion Squatters, A New Urban World* (London: Routledge, 2006), p. 212.

21. 'Ten Thousand Squatters', *NYT*, 20 April 1880.

22. 'Backgrounds of Civilisation', *New York Illustrated News*, 11 February 1860.

23. Lisa Goff, *Shantytown, USA*, p. 85.

24. 'Female Pugnacity', *Brooklyn Daily Eagle*, 27 June 1851.

25. Goff, *Shantytown, USA*, p. 103.

26. 'Our Squatter Population', *NYT*.

27. See Goff, *Shantytown, USA*, pp. 119–41.

28. Day, *Urban Castles*, pp. 18, 19.

29. Day, *Urban Castles*, p. 21.

30. See Jacob A. Riis, *How the Other Half Lives: Studies among the Tenements of New York* (New York: C. Scribner's and Soris, 1903).

31. Jenna Weissman Joselit, 'The Landlord as Czar: Pre-World War I Tenant Activity', in Ronald Lawson and Mark Nelson (eds), *The Tenant Movement in New York City, 1904–1984* (New Brunswick, NJ: Rutgers University Press, 1986), pp. 39–50; pp. 41–42; Day, *Urban Castles*, p. 75.

32. Joselit, 'The Landlord as Czar', p. 43.
33. *New York World* (hereafter *NYW*), 30 December 1907.
34. See Victor Rousseau, 'Low Rent or No Rent: The Tenement Dweller's Rebellion in New York', *Harper's Weekly*, 25 January 1908, pp. 148–52; *NYW*, 27 and 29 December 1907.
35. Joselit, 'The Landlord as Czar', p. 46.
36. Madden and Marcuse, *In Defense of Housing*, pp. 156–7.
37. Gold, *When Tenants Claimed the City*, p. 13; see Robert M. Fogelson *The Great Rent Wars: New York, 1917–1929* (New Haven, CT: Yale University Press, 2013).
38. Madden and Marcuse, *In Defense of Housing*, p. 159.
39. Erik S. McDuffie, *Sojourning for Freedom: Black Women, American Communism, and the Making of Black Left Feminism* (Durham, NC: Duke University Press, 2011), p. 45; Mark Naison, 'From Eviction Resistance to Rent Control: Tenant Activism in the Great Depression', in Ronald Lawson and Mark Naison (eds), *The Tenant Movement in New York City*, pp. 94–133, p. 98.
40. 'Hardluck-on-River: New Town for Idle'. *NYT*, 3 August 1932.
41. See Goff, *Shantytown, USA*, pp. 221–5.
42. *The Daily Worker*, 19 May and 3 June 1933.
43. Gold, *When Tenants Claimed the City*, p. 18.
44. Naison, 'From Eviction Resistance to Rent Control', p. 125; Gold, *When Tenants Claimed the City*, p. 18.
45. Gold, *When Tenants Claimed the City*, pp. 20, 21. On suburbanisation, see Kenneth T. Jackson, *The Crabgrass Frontier: The Suburbanisation of the United States* (Oxford: Oxford University Press, 1985).
46. Gold, *When Tenants Claimed the City*, p. 10.
47. 'OPA Dies Saturday', *NYT*, 27 May 1947.
48. 'Text of Emergency New State Emergency Rent Measure', *NYT*, 30 March 1950.
49. NYCHA, *Development Data Book* (New York: NYCHA, 1950), p. 10.
50. 'The Housing Act of 1949' (Public Law 81-171), US Statues at Large, Vol. 63, Part I, p. 413.
51. Gold, *When Tenants Claimed the City*, p. 39; Rose Muzio, 'The Struggle Against "Urban Renewal"', p. 118.
52. 'East Side "Suburb in a City" to House 30,000 after War', *NYT*, 19 April 1943.
53. Samuel Zipp, *Manhattan Projects: The Rise and Fall of Urban Renewal in Cold War New York* (Oxford: Oxford University Press, 2010), pp. 121–2.
54. Gold, *When Tenants Claimed the City*, p. 53.
55. Frances Goldin quoted in ibid., p. 55.
56. Ibid., p. 54–55.

57. Norman I. Fainstein and Susan S. Fainstein, 'The Politics of Urban Development: New York since 1945'. *City Almanac* 17 (April 1984), pp. 1–22, pp. 2–3.

58. Gold, *When Tenants Claimed the City*, p. 97; Tamiment Library, New York University (hereafter TL), Minutes, April–June 1959, Metropolitan Council of Housing Collection, Box 4, Folder 6.

59. See Joshua B. Freeman, *Working-Class New York: Life and Labour since World War II* (New York: The New Press, 2000).

60. Gold, *When Tenants Claimed the City*, p. 116; Harlem Youth Opportunities Unlimited, Inc., *Youth in the Ghetto: A Study of the Consequences of Powerlessness and a Blueprint for Change* (New York: HARYOU, 1964), n.p.

61. Gold, *When Tenants Claimed the City*, p. 113.

62. 'Angry Tenants', *New York Amsterdam News* (hereafter *NYAN*), 4 July 1959; 'Harlem Volunteers Inspect Tenements', *NYT*, 9 April 1961; 'Live Rat Disrupts Housing Hearing', *NYT*, 20 October 1961.

63. See Mandi Isaacs Jackson, 'Harlem's Rent Strike and Rat War: Representation, Housing Access and Tenant Resistant in New York, 1958–1964'. *American Studies* 47 (2006), pp. 53–79; Joel Schwartz, 'The New York City Rent Strikes of 1963–1964'. *Social Service Review* 57.4 (1983), pp. 545–64.

64. Jackson, 'Harlem's Rent Strike', p. 61; 'Harlem Slum Fighter Jesse Gray', *NYT*, 31 December 1963.

65. *Newsweek*, 13 January 1964; see also Jackson, 'Harlem's Rent Strike', pp. 53–4.

66. 'Slum Rent Strike Upheld by Judge', *NYT*, 31 December 1963.

67. 'Court Halts Rent for Unfit Slums', *NYT*, 9 January 1964.

68. A chapter was also set up in Brooklyn. See Donna Jean Murch, *Living for the City: Migration, Education, and the Rise of the Black Panther Party in Oakland, California* (Chapel Hill: University of North Carolina Press, 2010), p. 174; Alondra Nelson, *Body and Soul: The Black Panther Party and the Fight against Medical Discrimination* (Minneapolis: University of Minnesota Press, 2011), pp. 90, 92.

69. 'A Rally Urges Seizure', *NYT*, 4 May 1969.

70. 'Poor Families Taking Over Condemned Buildings', *NYT*, 24 April 1970.

71. 'A Large Family of Squatters Finds Risks Worth Taking', *NYT*, 11 October 1970.

72. Muzio, 'The Struggle Against "Urban Renewal"', pp. 120–1.

73. Gold, *When Tenants Claimed the City*, p. 192.

74. 'Squatter Movement Grows as Housing Protest Tactic', *NYT*, 22 July 1970; '150 Police Evict Squatter Group', *NYT*, 3 August 1970.

75. Gold, *When Tenants Claimed the City*, p. 192.

76. Ibid., p. 171.

77. Ibid., p. 193.
78. 'Squatters Occupy Flats on West Side', *NYT*, 26 July 1970.
79. Muzio, 'The Struggle Against "Urban Renewal"', p. 111.
80. Ibid., p. 125.
81. Ibid., p. 124.
82. 'Squatters Score Nearby Wrecking', *NYT*, 1 August 1970; TL, trial flyers, n.d., Metropolitan Council of Housing Collection, Box 30, Folder 2. See also Gold, *When Tenants Claimed the City*, p. 205.
83. 'Mock Trial', *The New Yorker*, 9 January 1971, p. 22; Gold, *When Tenants Claimed the City*, pp. 204, 205.
84. Muzio, 'The Struggle Against "Urban Renewal"', p. 125.
85. 'Squatters Asked to Pay City Rents', *NYT*, 14 June 1971.
86. Richard Sennett, *The Uses of Disorder: Personal Identity and City Life* (London: Penguin Books, 1970), pp. 11, 72.
87. Joel Schwartz, 'Tenant Power in the Liberal City, 1943–1971', in Lawson and Naison (eds), *The Tenant Movement in New York City*, pp. 134–208, p. 197.
88. Madden and Marcuse, *In Defense of Housing*, p. 173.

2. 'Who are the Squatters?'

1. *The Poems of Shelley*, vol. 3, edited by Jack Donovan et al. (London: Routledge, 2014), p. 53.
2. Quoted in Nick Wates and Christian Wolmar (eds), *Squatting: The Real Story* (London: Bay Leaf Books, 1980), p. 77.
3. 'Hidden Histories: Common Land and Squatting in Hackney' (alphabetthreat.co.uk).
4. Russell Parton, 'Tom Hunter on Squatting in Hackney during the 90s: "It Gave My Art a Meaning and a Purpose"' (eastendreview.co.uk).
5. Ibid.
6. Russell Parton, 'Tom Hunter on Squatting in Hackney'.
7. Bart van der Steen, 'A Gilded Crowbar for the Bailiff', History Workshop Online (historyworkshop.org.uk). The long-abandoned double decker bus was recently discovered alongside a road in Central France (bbc.co.uk).
8. John Levin, 'Radical Hackney After World War One' (anterotesis.com)
9. Even the recent *A People's History of London* only devotes a brief paragraph to the history of squatting in the city. See John Rees and Lindsey German, *A People's History of London* (London: Verso, 2012). On the legal history of squatting in London and elsewhere in the UK, see Lucy Finchett-Maddock, 'Squatting in London: Squatters' Rights and Legal Movement(s)', in Bart van der Steen, Ask

Katzeff and Leendert van Hoogenhuijze (eds), *The City is Ours: Squatting and Autonomous Movements in Europe from the 1970s to the Present* (Oakland, CA: PM Press, 2014), pp. 207–31.

10. See madepossiblebysquatting.co.uk.

11. Ann Cvetkovich, *An Archive of Feelings: Trauma, Sexuality and Lesbian Public Cultures* (Durham, NC: Duke University Press, 2003), p. 166.

12. Amy Starecheski, 'Squatting History: The Power of Oral History as a History-Making Practice'. *Oral History Review* 41 (2014), pp. 187–216, p. 214.

13. x-Chris, 'Partisan Notes towards a History of UK Squatting (1980 to the Present)', in Alan Moore and Alan Smart (eds), *Making Room: Cultural Production in Occupied Spaces* (Barcelona: Other Forms, 2015), pp. 116–21, pp. 116–17; a few other articles were published in the late 1970s and 1980s by Kevin C. Kearns. See Kearns, 'Intra-urban Squatting in London'. *Annals of the Association of American Geographers* 69 (1979), pp. 589–98; 'Urban Squatting: Social Activism in the Housing Sector'. *Social Policy* 11 (1980), pp. 21–9; 'Urban Squatter Strategies: Social Adaptation to Housing Stress in London'. *Urban Life* 10 (1981), p. 123.

14. Ron Bailey, *The Squatters* (London: Penguin, 1973), p. 21; see Colin Ward, *Cotters and Squatters: Housing's Hidden History* (Nottingham: Five Leaves, 2002).

15. Ward, *Cotters and Squatters*, pp. 156, 158; see Dennis Hardy and Colin Ward, *Arcadia for All: The Legacy of a Makeshift Landscape* (London: Mansell Publishing, 1984); Colin Ward, 'The Hidden History of Housing' (historyandpolicy.org).

16. Bailey, *The Squatters*, p. 21.

17. *Time*, 23 July 1945.

18. Bailey, *The Squatters*, p. 22; see Andrew Friend, 'The Post War Squatters', in Wates and Wolmar (eds), *Squatting*, pp. 110–19.

19. James Hinton, 'Self-Help and Socialism: The Squatters' Movement of 1946'. *History Workshop Journal* 25 (1988), pp. 100–26, p. 111; see Noreen Branson (ed.), *Our History: London Squatters 1946, Proceedings of a Conference held by the Communist Part History Group, May 1984* (London: Communist Party History Group, 1989); *Daily Worker*, 25 September 1945.

20. Diana Murray Hill, 'Who are the Squatters'. *Pilot Papers* 1 (November 1946), pp. 11–27, pp. 24–5.

21. It was the *Daily Mail*, in particular, which came to champion the cause of the squatters.

22. Hinton, 'Self-Help and Socialism', pp. 111–12; in at least two instances, horse charges were used to disperse protests in support of the squatters (see *Daily Herald*, 13 September 1946; *Daily Telegraph*, 13 September 1946).

23. Hinton, 'Self-Help and Socialism', p. 115; *Daily Herald*, 18 September 1946.
24. Hinton, 'Self-Help and Socialism', p. 115.
25. Bailey, *The Squatters*, p. 31.
26. Friend, 'The Post War Squatters', p. 119.
27. Nicolas Walter, 'The New Squatters'. *Anarchy* 102 (1969), pp. 225–30, p. 226; see earlier 1963 issue of *Anarchy* dedicated to the question of housing and squatting.
28. Jim Radford, 'The Squatting Campaign: Homes for Families', *The Guardian*, 11 February 2004.
29. Steve Platt, 'Setting the Stage', in Wates and Wolmar (eds), *Squatting*, pp. 14–29, p. 15.
30. Bailey, *The Squatters*, p. 34.
31. Ibid., pp. 46–7.
32. Platt, 'Setting the Stage', p. 18.
33. Quoted in Bailey, 'The Squatters and the Law'. *Anarchy* 102 (1969), pp. 230–9, p. 235; Bailey, *The Squatters*, pp. 59–60.
34. Bailey, 'The Squatters and the Law', p. 235.
35. Platt, 'Setting the Stage', p. 18.
36. According to a pamphlet produced by Solidarity, the bailiffs were from a private security firm that had close links to Oswald Mosley as well as the National Front. See pamphlet, 'The Squatters: Ilford – A Report and Critique' (libcom.org).
37. Affidavit signed by Mrs Mary Fleming and quoted in Bailey, 'The Squatters and the Law', p. 239.
38. Bailey, *The Squatters*, p. 100.
39. Platt, 'Setting the Stage', p. 21.
40. Bailey, *The Squatters*, p. 113. In the United Kingdom, a licence entitles an occupant to live in a property though they are afforded less security than other types of tenure. Short-life licences were often guaranteed by local authorities for at least six months. In many cases they were renewed or the occupants were offered another licensed property.
41. Bailey, *The Squatters*, pp. 123, 134.
42. Platt, 'Setting the Stage', pp. 26–7.
43. Ibid., p. 29.
44. 'Derry' was common slang for derelict house. See 'The Dilly Dossers and the London Street Commune' (wussu.com).
45. Phil Cohen, *Reading Room Only: Memoir of a Radical Bibliophile* (Nottingham: Five Leaves, 2013), p. 116; I would like to thank Ross Bradshaw for drawing this to my attention.
46. Infoshop 56A, Leaflet, South East London Squatters, n.d.
47. Quoted in Platt, 'Setting the Stage', p. 23.
48. Ibid., p. 25 and Platt, 'Mounting Opposition' in Wates and Wolmar (eds), *Squatting*, pp. 48–63, p. 59.

49. Kesia Reeve, 'Criminalising the Poor: Squatting, Homelessness and Social Welfare', in Lorna Fox O'Mahoney, David O'Mahoney and Robin Hickey (eds), *Vulnerable Demons? Moral Rhetoric and the Criminalisation of Squatting* (London: Routledge, 2014), pp. 133–54, p. 148.

50. Steve Platt, 'Here, There and Everywhere', in Wates and Wolmar (eds), *Squatting*, pp. 30–47, p. 33.

51. Infoshop 56A, Unpublished ms., David Morris, 'A Look Back at Brougham Road, E8: 1974–1980', n.d., Boxfile Squatting London (Hackney, Haringey, Camden, etc.), Folder (Islington).

52. *The Villain*, produced by the squatters on Villa Road, is one of the more important examples from the period.

53. See Ann Pettitt, 'Better than the Telly Any Day', in Wates and Wolmar (eds), *Squatting*, pp. 122–9; Mark Kauri, '62 Fieldgate Street: Yesterday, Today and Tomorrow'. *The Occupied Times* 25 (2014), p. 7.

54. 'David Hoffmann at Fieldgate Mansions' (spitalfieldslife.com).

55. Nick Wates, 'The Tolmers Village Squatters'. *New Society* 33 (1975), pp. 364–6, pp. 364, 365.

56. See Nick Wates, *The Battle for Tolmers Square* (London: Routledge, 2012, [1976]).

57. Wates, 'The Tolmers Village Squatters', p. 365.

58. Ibid.; see also Sacha Craddock, 'Tolmers United', in Astrid Proll (ed.), *Goodbye to London: Radical Art and Politics in the 70s* (Ostfildern: Hatje Cantz, 2010), pp. 34–9.

59. Steve Bythesa, 'For Me – Villa Road', *The Villain*, 21 December 1976.

60. Bishopsgate Institute (hereafter BI), brochure, Self-Help Housing Research Library, 'Squatters – Myth & Fact', June 1977, Advisor Service for Squatters Archive, Folder 17.

61. See Chris Whitehouse, 'Squatters in Central Twickenham (A Survey)' (wussu.com); see also Patrick J. Day's personal report on squatting as a medical doctor in the *British Medical Journal*. Day, 'Personal View'. *British Medical Journal* (November 1974), p. 340.

62. Mayday Rooms Archive (hereafter MRA), typed manuscript, 'Thinking Autonomy', n.d., Boxfile East London Big Flame (ELBF/All).

63. MRA, Pamphlet, 'People's Food Co-op, Lincoln Estate, Bow', n.d., Boxfile ELBF/ALL.

64. MRA, flyer, 'A Home is Everyone's Right', n.d., Boxfile ELBF/All.

65. MRA, typed page, 'Mass Squatting in Tower Hamlets', n.d., Boxfile ELBF/All; MRA, typed manuscript, 'BHAG and Stephen and Matilda', n.d., Boxfile ELBF/All. The BHAG was closely linked, in turn, with the Race Today Collective that was set up after the dissolution of the British Black Panthers in the early 1970s. BHAG

held a double meaning as the word *bhag* means tiger in Bengali. See Geoff Dench, Kate Gavron and Michael Young, *The New East End: Kinship, Race and Conflict* (London: Profile Books, 2006), p. 46.

66. See Alexandra M. Kokoli, *The Feminist Uncanny in Theory and Art Practice* (London: Bloomsbury, 2016), especially chapter 4 ('Squats and Evictions: The Uncanny as Unhomely').

67. Matt Cook, '"Gay Times": Identity, Locality, Memory, and the Brixton Squats in 1970s London'. *Twentieth Century British History* 24 (2013), pp. 84–109, p. 87.

68. As Matt Cook has argued, within a wider queer community in the 1970s, there was still a practice of separatism. There were lesbian squats at Radnor Terrace in Vauxhall as well as on Bellefields Road in Brixton though little cross-over with the squats on Railton Road. See Cook, '"Gay Times"', p. 97; see also Peter Cross, 'Revolting Queers: A Memory of South London Gay Liberation', in Proll (ed.), *Goodbye to London*, pp. 76–83, p. 76.

69. Ibid., p. 90.

70. Mark Urban, 'The Brixton Fairies and the South London Gay Community Centre, Brixton 1974–76' (urban75.org).

71. Cook, '"Gay Times"', p. 109; Gavin Brown, 'Mutinous Eruptions: Autonomous Spaces of Radical Queer Activism'. *Environment and Planning A* 29 (2007), pp. 2685–99, pp. 2686, 2696.

72. Lambeth Council Archives (hereafter LCA), 'Interview with Jennifer Lewis', Oliver Morris Collection IV/279/2/29/1a,1b,2a.

73. See Colin A. Beckles, 'We Shall not be Terrorised Out of Existence: The Political Legacy of England's Black Bookshops'. *Journal of Black Studies* 29 (1998), pp. 51–72; LCA, 'Interview with Sandra Hurst', Olive Morris Collection IV/279/2/4/1–5.

74. 'Bengali Squat in the East End'. *Race Today* (September 1974), pp. 144–5.

75. On intersectionality, one of the key texts remains Kimberle Crenshaw, 'Mapping the Margins: Intersectionality, Identity Politics, and Violence against Women of Colour'. *Stanford Law Review*, 43 (1991), pp. 1242–300.

76. Steve Platt, 'Fighting Back', in Wates and Wolmar (eds), *Squatting*, pp. 64–71, pp. 69–71. This also includes the efforts of the London Squatters.

77. See Finchett-Maddock, 'Squatting in London', p. 215.

78. David Watkinson, 'The Erosion of Squatters Rights', in Wates and Wolmar (eds), *Squatting*, pp. 158–63, p. 161. The Homeless Persons Act was introduced in December 1977. While it made local authorities responsible for securing accommodation for the homeless, it excluded the majority of homeless people (singles and couples

without children). See personal collection, brochure, The Kensington Empty Property Group, *What Housing?!?* (London: The Bleinheim Project, 1979), pp. 7–8.

79. See John Davis and Juliane Fürst, 'Drop-Outs', in Robert Gildea, James Mark and Anette Warring (eds), *Europe's 1968: Voices of Revolution* (Oxford: Oxford University Press, 2013), pp. 193–210; Nick Anning and Jill Simpson, 'Victoria Villa', in Wates and Wolmar (eds), *Squatting*, pp. 142–49, p. 149.

80. Steve Platt, 'A Whole New Ball Game', in Wates and Wolmar (eds), *Squatting*, p. 89.

81. Ibid., p. 93; for more info on Frestonia, see frestonia.org.

82. Valerie Hirsch, 'Just a Roof Over My Head'. *The Leveller* (28 May–10 June 1982), pp. 22–3, p. 23.

83. Infoshop 56a, no author, typed manuscript, 'Local Tradition and Trajectories at 56a Infoshop, South London', n.d.

84. x-Chris, 'Partisan Notes towards a History of UK Squatting', p. 117.

85. See Hirsch, 'Just a Roof Over My Head'.

86. 'Live Series 2 and London Ambulance Station' (crab.wordpress .com).

87. Infoshop 56a, flyer, 'Notes for New Squatters', n.d., Boxfile Squatting South London.

88. Infoshop 56a, newsheet, 'Homes For All', October 1984, Boxfile Squatting South London.

89. Infoshop 56a, 'Local Traditions and Trajectories at 56a Infoshop'.

90. Infoshop 56a, typed manuscript, Hackney Housing Action Group, 'The Eviction of Stamford Hill Eviction', March 1988, Boxfile Squatting North London, Folder Hackney.

91. x-Chris, 'Partisan Notes towards a History of UK Squatting', p. 118.

92. Tim Malyon, 'Tossed in the Fire and they Never Got Burned: The Exodus Collective', in George McKay (ed.), *DIY Culture: Party and Protest in Nineties Britain* (London: Verso, 1998), pp. 187–207.

93. 'Criminal Justice and Public Order Act 1994' (legislation.gov.uk).

94. x-Chris, 'Partisan Notes towards a History of UK Squatting', p. 119.

95. Michael Segalov, 'Grow Heathrow: Celebrating Six Years and Counting', (huckmagazine.com).

96. See Finchett-Maddock, 'Squatting in London', p. 214.

97. Alexander Vasudevan 'Criminalising Squatting would Threaten Our Rights', *The Guardian*, 22 June 2011.

98. See Danny Dorling, *All That is Solid: The Great Housing Disaster* (London: Allen Lane, 2014).

99. Paul Watt and Anna Minton, 'London's Housing Crisis and its Activisms'. *City* 20 (2016), pp. 204–21, p. 206.

100. Ben Campkin, *Remaking London: Decline and Regeneration in Urban Culture* (London: I.B. Tauris, 2013); Danny Dorling, *All That is Solid*; Loretta Lees, 'The Urban Injustices of New Labour's "New Urban Renewal": The Case of the Aylesbury Estate'. *Antipode* 46 (2014), pp. 921–47.

101. Paul Watt, 'A Nomadic War Machine in the Metropolis: En/countering London's 21st-century Housing Crisis with Focus E15'. *City* 20 (2016), pp. 297–320; Jade Jakeman, 'Twenty-Four Hours inside Sisters Uncut's East London Occupation' (huckmagazine.com).

102. David Rosenberg, *Rebel Footprints: A Guide to Uncovering London's Radical History* (London: Pluto Press, 2015).

103. Kesia Reeve, *Squatting: A Homelessness Issue, An Evidence Review* (London: Crisis, 2011).

104. Tracy McVeigh and Chris Hunter, 'The Father who Froze to Death in a Kent Village', *The Guardian*, 14 April 2013.

3. From Squatting to Squatters' Movement

1. Quoted in Justus Uitermark, 'Framing Urban Injustices: The Case of the Amsterdam Squatter Movement'. *Space and Polity* 8 (2004), pp. 227–44, p. 232.

2. Janice Perlman and Hans Spiegel, 'Copenhagen's Black Quadrant: The Façade and Reality of Participation', in Lawrence Susskind and Michael Elliott (eds), *Paternalism, Conflict and Coproduction: Learning from Citizen Action and Citizen Participation in Western Europe* (New York: Plenum Press, 1983), pp. 35–65, pp. 54–7; René Karpantschof and Flemming Mikkelsen, 'Youth, Space and Autonomy in Copenhagen: The Squatters' and Autonomous Movement, 1962–2012', in Bart van der Steen, Ask Katzeff and Leendert van Hoogenhuijze (eds), *The City is Ours: Squatting and Autonomous Movements in Europe from the 1970s to the Present* (San Francisco: PM Press, 2014), pp. 178–205.

3. Tom Heinemann, *Uro 25 års gadekamp* (Copenhagen: Tiderne Skifter, 1995), p. 38; see Bolette Chrstensen, *Fortællinger fra Indre Nørrebro: Solidaritet og handlekraft I det lokale* (Copenhagen: Jurist – of Økonomforbundets Forlag, 2000).

4. Heinemann, *Uro 25 års gadekamp*, p. 39.

5. Quoted in Perlman and Spiegel, 'Copenhagen's Black Quadrant', p. 57.

6. Karpantschof and Mikkelsen, 'Youth, Space and Autonomy in Copenhagen', p. 184.

7. Lynn Owens, *Cracking Under Pressure: Narrating the Decline of the*

Amsterdam Squatters' Movement (Amsterdam: Amsterdam University Press, 2009), pp. 81, 67.

8. Eric Duivenvoorden, *Een voet tusse de deur: Geschiedenis van de kraakbeweging, 1964–1999* (Amsterdam: Arbeiderspers, 2000); an online version is available on the Staatsarchief (the squatters' movement) website (iisg.nl) which is hosted by the International Institute of Social History (hereafter IISH). All citations are from the online version.

9. Joshua Clover, *Riot. Strike. Riot: The New Era of Uprisings* (London: Verso, 2016); see also Alain Badiou, *The Rebirth of History: Times of Riots and Uprisings* (London: Verso, 2012); Eric Hobsbawm and George Rude, *Captain Swing: A Social History of the Great English Agricultural Uprising of 1830* (New York: W.W. Norton, 1968); E.P. Thompson, 'The Moral Economy of the English Crowd'. *Past and Present* 50 (1971), pp. 76–136.

10. Owens, *Cracking Under Pressure*, p. 31, emphasis added.

11. Stine Krøijer, *Figurations of the Future: Forms and Temporalities of Left Radical Politics* (New York: Berghahn Books, 2015), p. 25.

12. I am drawing here on arguments made by Deborah Gould, *Moving Politics: Emotion and ACT UP's Fight Against Aids* (Chicago: The University of Chicago Press, 2009), p. 441.

13. Charles Tilly, *Regimes and Repertoires* (Chicago: The University of Chicago Press, 2006), pp. 182–3; see also Doug McAdam, Sidney Tarrow and Charles Tilly, *Dynamics of Contention* (Cambridge: Cambridge University Press, 2001).

14. René Karpantschof, 'Bargaining and Barricades: The Political Struggle over the Freetown Christiania, 1971–2011' in Håkan Thörn, Cathrin Wasshede and Tomas Nilson (eds), *Space for Urban Alternatives? Christiania, 1971–2011* (Gothenburg: Gidlunds Förlag, 2011), pp. 38–67, p. 38.

15. Karpantschof and Mikkelsen, 'Youth, Space and Autonomy in Copenhagen', p. 181.

16. Ibid., pp. 181–182.

17. Karpantschof, 'Bargaining and Barricades', p. 39.

18. Garbi Schmidt, *Nørrebros indvandringshistorie, 1885–2010* (Copenhagen: Museum Tusculanum Press, 2015), p. 247.

19. See especially Karpantschof and Mikkelsen, 'Youth, Space and Autonomy in Copenhagen'.

20. *Hovedbladet*, 2–3 October 1971.

21. Karpantschof, 'Bargaining and Barricades', pp. 39–40.

22. Quoted in Håkan Thörn, 'Governing Freedom: Debating the Freetown in the Danish Parliament', in Håkan Thörn, Cathrin Wasshede and Tomas Nilson (eds), *Space for Urban Alternatives?*, pp. 68–97, p. 69.

23. Christiania, 'Christianias Målsætning/Manifest – 13.11.1971' (christiania.org); translation modified by author.

24. Karpantschof, 'Bargaining and Barricades', p. 41; Jordan Zinovich, 'Christiania: How They Do It and for How Long', in Alan Moore and Alan Smart (eds), *Making Room: Cultural Production in Occupied Spaces* (Barcelona: Los Malditos, 2015), pp. 84–94, p. 87.

25. Rasmus Mariager and Regin Schmidt, *PET's overvågning af protestbevægelser, 1945–1989: Fra atomkampagnen til BZ-brigaden* (Albertslund: Schulz Distribution, 1999), pp. 389–92, 392.

26. Perlman and Spiegel, 'Copenhagen's Black Quadrant', p. 38; Krøijer, *Figurations of the Future*, p. 8.

27. Rigsarkivet (Danish National Archive, hereafter RA), pamphlet, Nørrebro Beboeraktion, 'Sanering og byfornylese', n.d., Private Institutioner, Norrebros Beboeraktion 1974-ca.1990, Arkivnr. 10.874.

28. Perlman and Spiegel, 'Copenhagen's Black Quadrant', p. 46.

29. RA, pamphlet, Nørrebro Beboeraktion, no title, May 1979, Private Institutioner, Norrebros Beboeraktion 1974-ca.1990, Arkivnr. 10.874.

30. RA, pamphlet, Nørrebro Beboeraktion, 'Brand skiring', June 1976, Private Institutioner, Norrebros Beboeraktion 1974-ca.1990, Arkivnr. 10.874.

31. Karpantschof and Mikkelsen, 'Youth, Space and Autonomy in Copenhagen', p. 183.

32. In 1976, the NB had split into two separate neighbourhood groups. There was the NBB (Nørrebro Beboeraktion Blagardsgade) which was focused on developing grassroots community participation and a mass base of potential activists. It's rival, the NBT (Nørrebro Beboeraktion Tomrergade), preferred a small cadre of leaders who would direct the group in small actions rather than widespread organising.

33. Heinemann, *Uro 25 års gadekamp*, p. 46; Karpantschof and Mikkelsen, 'Youth, Space and Autonomy in Copenhagen', p. 184.

34. Heinemann, *Uro 25 års gadekamp*, p. 47; René Karpantschof, 'Kopenhagen, Jagtvej 69: Ein Jugendzentrum zwischen Besetzungen, Politik und Polizei (1981–2007)', in Peter Birke and Chris Holmsted Larsen (eds), *Besetze deine Stadt! Bz din by! Häuserkämpfe und Stadtentwicklung in Kopenhagen* (Berlin: Assoziation A, 2007), pp. 53–78, p. 56.

35. Karpantschof and Mikkelsen, 'Youth, Space and Autonomy in Copenhagen', p. 185.

36. Mariager and Schmidt, *PET's overvågning af protestbevægelser, 1945–1989*, p. 407.

37. Dorte Ellesøe Hansen, ''Den gamle kasse' og 'Ungeren' – Da Jagtvej 69 var på plakaten'. *Årbog* (2007), pp. 36–51, p. 43. In 1910, Clara Zetkin launched International Women's Day at a meeting at the Folkets Hus.

38. Karpantschof, 'Kopenhagen, Jagtvej 69', p. 60.

39. No author, 'Ryesgade 58: Et nyt bzat hus'. *Fingeren* 1 (1983), p. 8.

40. No author, 'Gyldenløvesgade – hva sker der!' *Fingeren* 4 (1983), pp. 16–17; No author, 'Sidste nyt fra Vesterbro'. *Fingeren* 18 (1987), p. 18.

41. I am indebted to Nazima Kadir for this point. See Kadir, *The Autonomous Life: Paradoxes of Hierarchy and Authority in the Squatters Movement in Amsterdam* (Manchester: Manchester University Press, 2016), p. 3.

42. René Karpantschof and Flemming Mikkelsen, 'Fra slumstormerne til de autonome: Husbesættelse, ungdom og social protest i Danmark 1965–2001', in Flemming Mikkelsen (ed.), *Bevægelser i demokrati: Foreninger og kollektive aktioner i Danmark* (Aarhus: Aarhus Universitetsforlag, 2002), pp. 99–129, p. 113.

43. See De Autonome, *De Autonome – en bog af den autonome bevægelse* (Copenhagen: Autonomt Forlag, 1994), p. 133.

44. Quoted in Heinemann, *Uro 25 års gadekamp*, p. 133.

45. Karpantschof and Mikkelsen, 'Youth, Space and Autonomy in Copenhagen', pp. 192–3.

46. Håkan Thörn, Cathrin Wasshed and Tomas Nilson, 'Introduction: From "Social Experiment" to "Urban Alternative": 40 Years of Research on the Freetown', in Thörn, Wasshede and Nilson (eds), *Space for Urban Alternatives*, pp. 7–37, pp. 7–8.

47. David Goldblatt, 'Christiania: A Small Community With Big Hearts' (theguardian.com).

48. Karpantschof and Mikkelsen, 'Youth, Space and Autonomy in Copenhagen', p. 194.

49. Ibid., p. 195.

50. See Eric Duivenvoorden, *Een Voet Tussen De Deur*; Virginie Mamadouh, *De Stad in Eigen Hand: Provo's, Kabouters En Krakers Als Stedelijke Sociale Beweging* (Amsterdam: Sua, 1992).

51. Owens, *Cracking Under Pressure*, p. 47.

52. Ibid., p. 48.

53. Duivenvoorden, *Een voet tusse de deur*; see *De Waarheid*, 6 and 7 January 1965.

54. Owens, *Cracking Under Pressure*, pp. 54–5.

55. On this point, see especially Kadir, *The Autonomous Life*.

56. Owens, *Cracking Under Pressure*, p. 47.

57. IISH, flyer, 'Het witte huizen plan', n.d., Provo Files, SAVRZ 005, DOOS 1, MAP 1.4.

58. The other two groups were the Woningsburo de Koevoet (The Crowbar Housing Agency) and de Commune (The Commune). See Kadir, *The Autonomous Life*, p. 11.

59. Owens, *Cracking Under Pressure*, p. 48; see Duivenvoorden, *Een voet tusse de deur*.

60. ADILKNO, *Cracking the Movement: Squatting Beyond The Media* (New York: Autonomia, 1994), online version (thing.desk.nl).
61. Duivenvoorden, *Een voet tusse de deur*.
62. Ibid.; Alan Smart, 'Rules for Breaking In: Squatter Handbooks as Radical Specifications' (arpajournal.net).
63. Smart, 'Rules for Breaking In'.
64. Kadir, *The Autonomous Life?*, p. 12.
65. Owens, *Cracking Under Pressure*, p. 49.
66. Kadir, *The Autonomous Life?*, p. 13.
67. Kadir is right to point out the absence of any substantive literature in this context, though there is archival material available at the IISH.
68. IISH, letter, 'Open brief ann: De politieke partijen in Amsterdam', 28 October 1974, pamphlets, Universiteitsbibliotheek Amsterdam afd. Sociale Dokumentatie (UB), UB 16.1.
69. IISH, flyer, 'Demo for 11.6.1974', June 1974, pamphlets, Universiteitsbibliotheek Amsterdam afd. Sociale Dokumentatie (UB).
70. Duivenvoorden, *Een voet tusse de deur*; Smart, 'Rules for Breaking In'.
71. Owens, *Cracking Under Pressure*, p. 52.
72. Smart, 'Rules for Breaking In'.
73. Owens, *Cracking Under Pressure*, p. 52; Duivenvoorden, *Een voet tusse de deur*.
74. See Kadir, *The Autonomous Life?*, on this point.
75. Owens, *Cracking Under Pressure*, p. 63; ADILKNO, *Cracking the Movement*.
76. Nazima Kadir, 'Myth and Reality in the Amsterdam Squatters' Movement, 1975–2012', in van der Steen, Katzeff and van Hoogenhuijze (eds), *The City is Ours*, pp. 21–61, p. 33; Owens, *Cracking Under Pressure*, p. 66; see also IISH, pamphlet, 'Over de Groote Keyser', September 1979, Groote Keyser files, SAVR2001, DOOS3, MAP1.5.
77. IISH, flyer, 'Tanks en barrikades in Amsterdam', 9 March 1980, Vondelstraat Files, SAVR015, DOOS1, MAP 4; press release, 'Persverklaring', n.d. Vondelstraat Files, SAVR015, DOOS1, MAP 4.
78. IISH, flyer, 'Weg met de militaire terreur van Polak', Vondelstraat Files, SAVR015, DOOS1, MAP 4.
79. Owens, *Cracking Under Pressure*, p. 68.
80. Kadir, 'Myth and Reality in the Amsterdam Squatters' Movement', p. 35.
81. Quoted in 'De stad was van ons', dir. Joost Seelen, 105 min.
82. Duivenvoorden, *Een voet tusse de deur*.
83. Ibid., see also 'De stad was van ons'.
84. Justus Uitermark, 'An Actually Existing Just City? The Fight for the Right to the City in Amsterdam', in Neil Brenner, Peter Marcuse and Margit Mayer (eds), *Cities for People, Not for Profit: Theory/*

Practice (Oxford: Blackwell, 2011), pp. 197–214, p. 202; see also Virginie Mamadouh, *De stad in eigen hand*; Hans Pruijt, 'Cityvorming gekraakt'. *Agora* 1 (1985), pp. 9–11.

85. Uitermark, 'An Actually Existing Just City?', p. 203.

86. Neil Smith, *The New Urban Frontier: Gentrification and the Revanchist City* (London: Routledge, 1996), p. 168.

87. On *anti-kraak*, see Tino Bucholz, 'Creativity and the Capitalist City', in Moore and Smart (eds), *Making Room*, pp. 42–50. Anti-squatting as a commercial enterprise has expanded to other European countries including the UK under the guise of property guardians. See Gloria Dawson, Mara Ferreri and Alexander Vasudevan, 'Living Precariously: Property Guardianship and the Flexible City'. *Transactions of the Institute of British Geographers*, forthcoming; Property Guardian Research Collective, 'The Temporary Home: Live-in Guardians in the Neoliberal City' (newleftproject.org).

88. See Geert Lovink and Jojo van der Spek, 'Buikdansen op de barricade'. *Marge* 10 (1986), pp. 22–9.

89. Kadir, 'Myth and Reality in the Amsterdam Squatters' Movement', p. 40.

90. Duivenvoorden, *Een voet tusse de deur*; Kadir, *The Autonomous Life?*, p. 8.

4. 'The Struggle Over Housing Continues'

1. Refrain from a well-known song by the German band Ton Steine Scherben; the title of this chapter, 'The Struggle Over Housing Continues' ['*Der Häuserkämpfe geht weiter*'] is a slight reworking of the title of a song by the same band.

2. Cover of German radical Left magazine, *Wir wollen alles* (Nr. 13/14, 1974) documenting struggles over housing in Frankfurt.

3. Hamburg Institüt für Sozialforschung (hereafter HIS), flyer, 'Hausbesetzung Info: Ekhofstraße 39', n.d., Boxfile SBe 600. (Hausbesetzungen/Häuserkämpfe); HIS, flyer, Initiativegruppe Graumansweg 13, 'Untitled', n.d., Boxfile SBe 600 (Hausbesetzungen/Häuserkämpfe); Geronimo, *Fire and Flames: A History of the German Autonomist Movement* (Oakland, CA: PM Press, 2012 [1995]), pp. 55–6.

4. HIS, flyer, 'Haus besetzt', n.d., Boxfile SBe 600 (Hausbesetzungen/Häuserkämpfe).

5. Karl-Heinz Dellwo, 'Ekhofstraße 39 und die frühen Jahre', in Baer and Dellwo (eds), *Häuserkampf II: Wir wollen alles – Hausbesetzungen in Hamburg* (Hamburg: Laika-Verlag, 2012), pp. 43–58, p. 49.

6. HIS, flyer, 'Besetztes Haus, Ekhofstraße 39: War wir gemacht haben, was wir machen werden', n.d., Boxfile SBe 600 (Hausbesetzungen/ Häuserkämpfe).

7. Geronimo, *Fire and Flames*, pp. 55–6.

8. Schutzpolizeiamt Hamburg, 'Hausräumung Ekhofstraße (23.5.1973)' (youtube.com).

9. HIS, flyer, 'Grosse Demonstration', n.d., Boxfile SBe 600 (Hausbesetzungen/Häuserkämpfe).

10. Dellwo, 'Ekhofstraße 39 und die frühen Jahre', pp. 52–3.

11. Ibid., p. 55.

12. See David Harvey, 'The Right to the City'. *New Left Review* 53 (2008), pp. 23–40; David Harvey, *Rebel Cities: From the Right to the City to the Urban Revolution* (London: Verso, 2012).

13. See Saskia Sassen, *Expulsion: Brutality and Complexity in the Global Economy* (Cambridge, MA: Harvard University Press).

14. For a useful discussion of violence and counter-violence, see Étienne Balibar, *Violence and Civility: On the Limits of Political Philosophy* (New York: Columbia University Press, 2015).

15. Timothy Brown, *West Germany and the Global Sixties: The Anti-authoritarian Revolt, 1962–1978* (Cambridge: Cambridge University Press, 2013), p. 275.

16. Timothy Brown, 'Music as a Weapon? Ton Steine Scherben and the Politics of Rock in Cold War Berlin'. *German Studies Review* 32 (2009), pp. 1–22, pp. 6, 7.

17. Jan-Ove Arps, *Frühschicht: Linke Fabrikinterventionen in den 70er Jahren* (Berlin: Assoziation A, 2011).

18. Michael Hardt, 'Laboratory Italy', in Michael Hardt and Paulo Virno (eds), *Radical Thought in Italy: A Potential Politics* (Minneapolis: University of Minnesota Press, 1996), pp. 1–10, p. 2; see also Vasudevan, *Metropolitan Preoccupations: The Spatial Politics of Squatting in Berlin* (Oxford: Wiley Blackwell, 2015), pp. 91–2.

19. See Serhat Karakayali, 'Across Bockenheimer Landstraße'. *Diskus* 2 (2000) (copyriot.com); Serhat Karakayali, 'Lotta Continua in Frankfurt, Türken Terror in Köln: Migrantische Kämpfe in der Geschichte der Bundesrepublik'. *Grundrisse* 14 (2005), (grundrisse. net); Manuela Bojadžijev, *Die windige Internationale: Rassismus und Kämpfe der Migration* (Münster: Westfälisches Dampfboot, 2008).

20. Brown, *West Germany and the Global Sixties*, p. 274; see Arps, *Frühschicht* as well.

21. Amantine, *Gender und Häuserkampf* (Münster: Unrast Verlag, 2011), p. 12.

22. Brown, 'Music as a Weapon', p. 7.

23. Pamphlet from occupation, quoted in Volkhard Brandes and Bernhard Schön (eds), *Wer sind die Instandbesetzer? Selbstzeugnisse,*

Dokumente, Analysen. Ein Lesebuch (Bensheim: Päd. Extra Buch-verlag), 1981, p. 41. See also Reiner Schmidt, Anne Schulz and Piu von Schwind (eds), *Die Stadt, das Land, die Welt verändern! Die 70er/80er Jahre in Köln – alternative, links, radikal, autonom* (Köln: KiWi, 2014).

24. This topic was made famous by the journalist Ulrike Meinhof whose television movie *Bambule: Fürsorge – Sorge für wen?* documented the Eichenhof girls' home in Berlin-Reinickendorf and was pulled from the schedule after Meinhof took part in the breakout of Andreas Baader from the reading room of the Social Studies Institute of West Berlin's Free University (Freie Universität), an event which led to the formation of the Red Army Faction (Rote Armee Faktion or RAF). See Ulrike-Marie Meinhof, 'Bambule: Fürsorge – Sorge für wen?' *Rotbuch* 24 (1971).

25. See Andrew Goffey, 'Guattari and Transversality: Institutions, Analysis and Experimentation'. *Radical Philosophy* 195 (2016), pp. 38–47.

26. Brown, *West Germany and the Global Sixties*, p. 270.

27. Egon Schewe, *Selbstverwalte Jugendzentren. Entwicklung, Konzept und Bedeutung der Jugendzentrumsbewegung* (Bielefeld: Pfeffer, 1980).

28. Anon, *Manifest, Aktion 507* (Berlin: Eigenverlag, 1968); Sven Reichardt, *Authentizität und Gemeinschaft: Linksalternatives Leben in den siebziger und frühen achtziger Jahren* (Frankfurt: Suhrkamp Verlag, 2014), p. 506. Aktion 507 was a group of young architects, planners and students that was formed at the TU-Berlin in 1968 and in response to the poverty of modern urban planning and design in West Berlin and the close relationship between city planners, developers and politicians (see Chapter 5). Ironically, former members of the group would later play an important role in the 'renewal' of Berlin in the 1980s and 1990s. For a detailed discussion of the Häuserkampf in Frankfurt, see Häuserrat Frankfurt, *Wohnungskampf in Frankfurt* (München: Trikont Verlag, 1974).

29. Häuserrat Frankfurt, *Wohnungskampf in Frankfurt*, p. 23. Of the neighbourhood's 40,000 residents, only 28,000 remained by the late 1960s. See Karakayali, 'Across Bockenheimer Landstraße'.

30. *Frankfurter Allegemeine Zeitung*, 18 August 1970.

31. Margret Stehen, 'Das "Café Marx" und ein 'Fünf-Finger-Plan'. Das Westend', in Jürgen Engelhardt (ed.), *Frankfurt zu Fuß. 20 Rundgänge durch Geschichte und Gegenwart* (Hamburg: VSA-Verlag, 1987), pp. 171–183.

32. Quoted in Rudolf Heinrich Apel, *Heißer Boden: Stadtentwicklung und Wohnprobleme* (Frankfurt/M: Presse- und Informationsamt der Stadt Frankfurt, 1974), p. 40.

33. Til Schulz, 'Zum Beispiel Eppsteiner Straße 47: Wohnungskampf,

Hausbesetzung, Wohnkollektiv'. *Kursbuch* 27 (1972), pp. 85–97, p. 89.

34. See also Serhat Karakayali, 'Across Bockenheimer Landstraße'; Karakayali, 'Lotta Continua in Frankfurt'; Bojadžijev, *Die windige Internationale*.
35. Reichardt, *Authentizität und Gemeinschaft*, p. 510.
36. 'Der Häuserkampf geht weiter'. *Wir wollen alles* 4 (May 1973), pp. 2–3, p. 3; also quoted in Geronimo, *Fire and Flames*, p. 53.
37. For an account of the Grüneburgweg eviction, see Heinz J. Franz, *Hausbesetzungen: Aktionen gegen Mietwucher und Spekulationen* (Ulm: Süddeutsche Verlagsanstalt, 1974), pp. 19–21.
38. Reichardt, *Authentizität und Gemeinschaft*, p. 511.
39. Quoted in Amantine, *Gender und Häuserkampf*, p. 15.
40. Christoph Kremer, 'Mietstreik und Vermieterjustiz'. *Kritische Justiz* 7 (1974), pp. 96–109.
41. See also Serhat Karakayali, 'Across Bockenheimer Landstraße'; Karakayali, 'Lotta Continua in Frankfurt'.
42. Berliner Redaktionskollektiv, 'Gewalt'. *Konkret* 6 (1968), pp. 24–8, p. 27.
43. Brown, *West Germany and the Global Sixties*, p. 335.
44. See, for example, Wolfgang Kraushaar, 'Rudi Dutschke und der bewaffnete Kampf', in Wolfgang Kraushaar und Jan Philipp Reemtsma, *Rudi Dutschke, Andreas Baader und die RAF* (Hamburg: Hamburger Edition, 2005), pp. 13–51.
45. Brown, *West Germany and the Global Sixties*, p.333.
46. 'Die Gewalt der heutigen Gesellschaft'. *Graswurzelrevolution* (1973).
47. HIS, brochure, no title, produced by Unione Inquilini on housing struggles in Frankfurt, n.d., Boxfile SBe 600 (Hausbesetzungen/ Häuserkämpfe).
48. Häuserrat Frankfurt, *Wohnungskampf in Frankfurt*, pp. 61–3.
49. HIS, brochure, Häuserrat Frankfurt and AstA, Goethe University Frankfurt, 'Kettenhofweg 51: Wohungskämpfe in Frankfurt', n.d. Boxfile SBe 600 (Hausbesetzungen/Häuserkämpfe), p. 8.
50. Ibid.
51. *Frankfurter Allegemeine Zeitung*, 20 March 1973; *Abendpost*, 20 March 1973.
52. Rudi Dutschke quoted in Quinn Slobodian, *Foreign Front: Third World Politics in Sixties West Germany* (Durham, NC: Duke University Press, 2012), p. 73.
53. Häuserrat Frankfurt and AstA, 'Kettenhofweg 51: Wohungskämpfe in Frankfurt', p. 9.
54. Tim Brown has suggested that the term *Putzgruppe* appears to stem from the phrase '*Pig ist Pig und Pig musst put*' ('A pig is a pig and a pig must be destroyed'), though it may also be an acronym for

Proletarische Union für Terror und Zerstörung. See Brown, *West Germany and the Global Sixties*, p. 276.

55. Häuserrat Frankfurt and AstA, 'Kettenhofweg 51. Wohungskämpfe in Frankfurt', pp. 8–10.

56. Ibid., p. 18; see also Anon, 'Die Räumung'. *Wir Wollen Alles* (April 1973), p. 7.

57. Reichardt, *Authentizität und Gemeinschaft*, p. 512.

58. See discussion in Häuserrat Frankfurt, *Wohnungskampf in Frankfurt*, pp. 124–6.

59. Gerd Koenen, *Das rote Jahrzehnt* (Köln: Kiepenheuer & Witsch, 2001), pp. 343–4.

60. Geronimo, *Fire and Flames*, p. 55.

61. See for example Andrew Tompkins, 'Grassroots Transnationalism: Franco-German Opposition to Nuclear Energy in the 1970s'. *Contemporary European History* 25 (2016), pp. 117–42; Willi Baer and Karl-Heinz Dellwo (eds) *Lieber besser aktiv als radioaktiv I* (Hamburg: Laika Verlag, 2011).

62. Franz, *Hausbesetzungen*, pp. 28–30.

63. Häuserrat Frankfurt, 'Unsere Gewalt und ihre'. *Wir wollen alles* (February/March 1974), pp. 4–5, p. 4.

64. Cohn-Bendit quoted in 'Häuserkampf-Tribunal', in Thomas Atzert et al. (eds), *Küss den Boden der Freiheit* (Berlin: Edition ID-Verlag, 1992), p. 295.

65. Jeremy Varon, *Bringing the War Home: The Weather Underground, the Red Army Faction, and Revolutionary Violence in the Sixties and Seventies* (Berkeley: University of California Press, 2004).

66. See Reichardt, *Authentizität und Gemeinschaft*.

67. Geronimo, *Fire and Flames*, p. 141; Hella Küllmer, 'Zusammen leben, zusammen kämpfen', in Willi Baer and Karl-Heinz Dellwo (eds), *Häuserkampf II: Wir wollen alles – Hausbesetzungen in Hamburg* (Hamburg: Laika-Verlag, 2012), pp. 75–89, p. 75.

68. Küllmer, 'Zusammen leben, zusammen kämpfen', p. 75.

69. 'Offener Brief an Senator Lange', in Initiativkreis für den Erhalt der Hafenstraße, *Hafenstraße: Chronologie eines Kampfes*, Papier Tiger Archiv (hereafter PTA), n.d., Boxfile Häuserkampf, Widerstand BRD, Hamburg-Hafenstraße (1981–8).

70. *TAZ*, 20 July 1982.

71. Küllmer, 'Zusammen leben, zusammen kämpfen', p. 78.

72. The repairs were undertaken to help stabilise a block of houses at Bernhard-Nocht-Straße 16 and Hafenstraße 126 whose foundations were cited by the city as grounds for the houses' imminent demolition. See Erdmann Prömmel, 'Nicht all Köpfe rollen erst nach 500 Jahren – Störtebeker in der Hafenstraße', in Baer and Dellwo (eds), *Häuserkampf II*, pp. 157–61, p. 159–160.

73. Geronimo, *Fire and Flames*, pp. 141–2.
74. Erdmann Prömmel, '"Hamburgs größtes Problem" oder wer war Hermann Nyenkerken?' in Baer and Dellwo (eds), *Häuserkampf II*, pp. 189–207, p. 195.
75. PTA, *Hafenstraße: Chronologie eines Kampfes*.
76. *TAZ*, 16 October 1985; Prömmel, '"Hamburgs größtes Problem" oder wer war Hermann Nyenkerken?', p. 196.
77. Prömmel, '"Hamburgs größtes Problem" oder wer war Hermann Nyenkerken?', p. 196.
78. PTA, *Hafenstraße: Chronologie eines Kampfes*.
79. Geronimo, *Fire and Flames*, p. 144.
80. PTA, *Hafenstraße: Chronologie eines Kampfes*.
81. Ibid.
82. Ibid.
83. Nina Fraser, 'Gängeviertel, Hamburg', in Alan Moore and Alan Smart (eds), *Making Room: Cultural Production in Occupied Spaces* (Barcelona: Los Malditos Impresores), pp. 172–7, pp. 173, 174.
84. Quoted in Amantine, *Gender und Häuserkampf* (Münster: Unrast Verlag, 2011), p. 112.
85. Azozomox, 'Squatting and Diversity: Gender and Patriarchy in Berlin, Madrid and Barcelona', in SqEK (eds), *The Squatters' Movement in Europe: Commons and Autonomy as Alternative to Capitalism* (London: Pluto Books, 2014), pp. 189–210, p. 192; I strongly disagree with a recent commentary by the German autonomist activist Geronimo on the negative effect that feminist politics has played within the squatting scene in Germany. See Geronimo, 'Foreword', in Bart van der Steen, Ask Katzeff and Leendert van Hoogenhuijze (eds), *The City is Ours: Squatting and Autonomous Movements in Europe from the 1970s to the Present* (Oakland, CA: PM Press, 2014), pp. xii–xix.
86. Quoted in Amantine, *Gender und Häuserkampf*, p. 112.
87. *TAZ*, 9 June 1984, 26 April 1989.
88. See Amantine, *Gender und Häuserkampf*, pp. 128–34 for a lengthy discussion of the assault.

5. Reassembling the City

1. Freiburg squatters quoted in Michael Haller, *Aussteigen oder rebellieren: Jugendliche gegen Staat und Gesellschaft* (Hamburg: Rowohlt, 1981), p. 11.
2. Ermittlungsausschuss im Mehringhof, *Dokumentation: Dezember Berlin, 1980* (Berlin: Mehringhof, 1981), p. 6.

3. *Berliner Zeitung*, 30 June 2012; *The Guardian*, 20 July 2012; *TAZ*, 29 June 2012.

4. Jacob Fezer et al., *Wohnungsfrage: Stille Straße 10 + Assemble* (Leipzig: Spector Books, 2015), p. 36.

5. Ibid., p. 52.

6. See assemblestudio.co.uk. On Assemble, see Owen Hatherley, 'The Cult of Self-Build and Do-It-Yourself Won't Solve the Housing Crisis' (dezeen.com).

7. Fezer at al., *Wohnungsfrage: Still Straße 10 + Assemble*, p. 38.

8. Ibid., p. 42.

9. Ibid., pp. 84–92.

10. See Alexander Vasudevan, *Metropolitan Preoccupations: The Spatial Politics of Squatting in Berlin*, RGS-IBG Book Series (Oxford: Wiley-Blackwell, 2015); see brochure, 'Kämpfende Hütten: Urbane Proteste in Berlin von 1872 bis heute', 2016 exhibition catalogue, Theater-SpielRaum, Bethanien (1–18 October 2015).

11. Tim Brown, *West Germany and the Global Sixties: The Antiauthoritarian Revolt, 1962–1978* (Cambridge: Cambridge University Press, 2013), p. 36; see Florian Havemann, '68er Ost'. *UTOPIE kreativ* 164 (2004), pp. 544–56.

12. Emily Pugh, *Architecture, Politics and Identity in Divided Berlin* (Pittsburgh: University of Pittsburgh Press, 2014), p. 27.

13. Vittorio Magnago Lampugnani, 'From Large Housing Estates on the Outskirts to Rebuilding the Inner City: Urban Development Debates in Germany 1960–1980', in Josef Paul Kleinhues et al. (eds), *Josef Paul Kleinhues: The Art of Urban Architecture* (Berlin: Nicolai, 2003), pp. 67–80, p. 69.

14. Florian Urban, 'The Hut on the Garden Plot: Informal Architecture in Twentieth-Century Berlin'. *Journal of the Society of Architectural Historians* 72 (2013), pp. 221–49, p. 241.

15. Mathias Heyden and Ines Schaber, 'Here is the Rose, Here is the Dance!', in Stephanie Strathaus and Florian Wüst (eds), *Who Says Concrete Doesn't Burn, Have you Tried? West Berlin Film in the '80s* (Berlin: b_books, 2008), pp. 132–48, p. 140.

16. Mary Fulbrook, *The People's State: East German Society from Hitler to Honecker* (New Haven: Yale University Press, 2005), p. 50.

17. Paul Betts, *Within Walls: Private Life in the German Democratic Republic* (Oxford: Oxford University Press, 2010), p. 120.

18. H.F. Buck, *Mit hohem Anspruch gescheitert: Die Wohnungspolitik der DDR* (Münster: Lit Verlag, 2004).

19. Alexander Vasudevan, 'Schwarzwohnen: The Spatial Politics of Squatting in East Berlin' (opendemocracy.net); Udo Grashoff, *Leben in Abriss: Schwarzwohnen in Halle an der Saale* (Halle: Hasenverlag, 2011); Udo Grashoff, *Schwarzwohnen: Die Unterwanderung*

der staatlichen Wohnraumlenkung in der DDR (Göttingen: V & R unipress, 2011).

20. Quinn Slobodian, *Foreign Front: Third World Politics in Sixties West Germany* (Durham, NC: Duke University Press, 2012), p. 16; Ulrich Enzensberger, *Die Jahre der Kommune I: Berlin, 1967–1979* (Cologne: Kiepenheuer & Witsch, 2004); Peter Schneider, *Rebellion und Wahn: Mein '68* (Cologne: Kiepenheuer & Witsch, 2010).

21. Rudi Dutschke quoted in Ulrich Chaussy, *Die drei Leben des Rudi Dutschke: Eine Biographie* (Zürich: Pendo Verlag, 1999), p. 160.

22. Enzensberger, *Die Jahre der Kommune I*, pp. 96–7.

23. See Rainer Langhans and Fritz Teufel, *Klau mich* (Berlin: Edition Verlag, 1968); see Nick Thomas, *Protest Movements in 1960s West Germany: A Social History of Dissent and Democracy* (Oxford and New York: Berg, 2003).

24. Peter Schneider, *Rebellion und Wahn*, p. 134.

25. Ulrike Kätzel, *Die 68erinnen: Porträt einer rebellischen Frauengeneration* (Hamburg: Rowohlt), p. 208.

26. See especially Aribert Reimann, *Dieter Kunzelmann: Avantgardist, Protestler, Radikaler* (Göttingen: Vandenhoeck and Ruprecht, 2009).

27. See P. Knorr, 'Bei Kommunarden in Berlin und Hamburg'. *Pardon* 5 (1969), pp. 26–40.

28. Brown, *West Germany and the Global Sixties*, p. 36. One of the few attempts to engage with the history of Kommune I-Ost can be found in Peter Mitchell, 'Contested Space: The History of Squatting in Divided Berlin, c. 1970–c. 1990', PhD Dissertation, University of Edinburgh, 2015.

29. The Stasi Records Agency (hereafter BStU), MfS, BV Berlin akg 771, fol. 1, 2.

30. Brown, *West Germany and the Global Sixties*, p. 37.

31. G. Kirchknopf, 'Vom elastischen Familienverband zur Kommune'. *Kursbuch* 14 (1968), pp. 110–15, p. 113.

32. Heide Brendt, 'Kommune und Familie'. *Kursbuch* 17 (1969), pp. 129–46, p. 144.

33. See for example Heide Berndt, *Das Gesellschaftsbild bei Stadtplanern* (Stuttgart: Karl Krämer Verlag, 1968).

34. Ingrid Krau, 'Die Zeit Der Diagnose'. *Stadtbauwelt* 80 (1983), pp. 340–5, p. 343; Aktion 507 emerged out of a wider demand by architectural students and professionals to transform their curriculum radically. See Technische Universität Berlin, Universitätsarchiv (hereafter TU-Archiv), typed manuscript, G. Friedmann, 'Zur Geschichte der Studentenbewegung an der Fakultät für Architektur der TU Berlin', December 1970, Akz 2015/8, Abtleilung 1, Ordner I.2.

35. Brochure, Aktion 507, 'Manifest. Austellung: Diagnose zur Bauen in West-Berlin', 1968, author's own collection.

36. The emergence of the Basisgruppen can be linked, in turn, to the work of radical students that were part of the *Rotz Bau* (*Rote Zelle Bau*).

37. See Jan-Ole Arps, *Frühschicht: Linke Fabrikinterventionen in den 70er Jahren* (Berlin: Assoziation A, 2011); Johannes Brunner et al., *Aufbruch zum Proletariat: Dokumente der Basisgruppen* (Berlin: Taifun-Verlag, 1988).

38. Timothy Brown, 'Music as a Weapon? Ton Steine Scherben and the Politics of Rock in Cold War Berlin'. *German Studies Review* 32 (2009), pp. 1–22, p. 7.

39. Agnes Hüfner, *Straßentheater* (Frankfurt: Suhrkamp, 1968), p. 12; see Dorothea Krauss, *Theater-Protest: Zur Politisierung von Straße und Bühne in den 1960er Jahren* (Frankfurt: Campus Verlag, 2007).

40. Helga Reidemeister and her partner Andreas Reidemeister as well as a number of activists including Rudi Dutschke were briefly involved in plans to design a commune in 1966 in West Berlin. Reidemeister worked as a social worker in the Märkisches Viertel before turning her attention to filmmaking. See Katja Reichard, 'Uffdecken der janz kleenen persönliche Scheisse: Operative Medienpraxis, Projektarbeit und kollektive Organisierung im Märkischen Viertel der 70er Jahren' (transform.eipcp.net).

41. Marc Silberman, 'Interview with Helga Reidemeister' (ejumpcut. org). See also Helga Reidemeister, 'Schöner Wohnen: Protokoll aus dem Märkischen Vietel, Berlin 1971/1972'. *Kursbuch* 27 (1972), pp. 1–11.

42. Brown, *West Germany and the Global Sixties*, p. 172.

43. Hamburger Institüt für Sozialforschung (hereafter HIS), *Rote Presse Korrespondenz*, 'Polizeiterror in Märkisches Viertel', 2, 64 (1970), p. 11.

44. HIS, 'Polizeiterror in Märkisches Viertel', p. 11.

45. See J. Beck et al. (eds), *Wohnste sozial, haste die Qual: Mühsamer Weg zur Solidarisierung* (Hamburg: Rowholt, 1975).

46. The Märkisches Viertel remained an important point of reference for Meinhof and appeared in many of the communiqués published by the Red Army Faction including the group's first statement in the radical journal *Agit 883* on 5 June 1970.

47. Peter Möbius, 'Kinderkultur'. *Kursbuch* 34 (1973), pp. 25–48.

48. See Brown, 'Music as a Weapon?', pp. 1–22.

49. Azozomox, n.d., 'Squatting in Berlin, 1970–2014', working paper.

50. R. Schön, 'Besetzung leerstehende Häuser – Hausfriedensbruch?' *Neue Juristische Wochenschrift* 35 (1982), pp. 1126–9. See *Der Spiegel*, 19 April 1982. As jurists and legal scholars have shown, challenges to §123 of the German Criminal Code (Trespass or

Hausfriedensbruch) were contingent on an argument that showed how abandoned homes and properties no longer satisfied the legal conditions necessary as a dwelling or 'pacified estate' (*befriedeten Besitztums*). The origins of the legal terms of reference date back to Prussian times and the late eighteenth century in the first instance. See Christina Rampf, *Hausfriedensbruch: §123 StGB* (Berlin: Berliner-Wissenschafts-Verlag, 2009).

51. Brown, *West Germany and the Global Sixties*, p. 271.

52. Kreuzberg Museum (hereafter KM), untitled pamphlet, Ordner Hausbesetzungen.

53. Brown, 'Music as a Weapon?', p. 11.

54. *BZ*, 9 December 1971.

55. Azozomox, 'Squatting in Berlin, 1970–2014'; Reichardt, *Authentizität und Gemeinschaft*, p. 519.

56. Reichardt, *Authentizität und Gemeinschaft*, p. 500.

57. Bernd Laurisch, *Kein Abriß unter dieser Nummer* (Berlin: Anabas Verlag, 1981), p. 34.

58. Kuno Haberbusch quoted in Sabine Rosenbladt, 'Die "Legalos" von Kreuzberg', in Stefan Aust and Sabine Rosenbladt (eds), *Hausbesetzer: Wofür sie kämpfen, wie sie leben und wie sie leben wollen* (Hamburg: Hoffmann und Campe, 1981), pp. 28–51, p. 36; J. Klein and S. Porn, 'Instandbesetzen' in Inga Müller-Münch et al. (eds), *Besetzung – weil das Wünschen nicht geholfen hat* (Hamburg: Rowohlt, 1981), pp. 108–25, p. 112, emphasis added.

59. Carla MacDougall, 'Cold War Capital: Contested Urbanity in West Berlin, 1963–1989', PhD dissertation, Rutgers University, 2011, p. 89.

60. KM, flyer, n.d., Ordner Hausbesetzungen.

61. *Südost Express*, December 1979.

62. Papier Tiger Archiv (hereafter PTA), Besetzerrat, 'Presserklärung', 16 January 1981, Ordner Häuserkampf, 1/1981.

63. PTA, 'Pressemitteilung Nr. 2 des Senators für Inneres – Pressreferent', 27 January 1981, Ordner Häuserkampf, 1/1981.

64. Benny Härlin, 'Vom Haus zu Haus – Berliner Bewegeungsstudien'. *Kursbuch 65*, pp. 1–28, p. 6.

65. Härlin, 'Vom Haus zu Haus', p. 8, English in original.

66. MacDougall, 'Cold War Capital', p. 148.

67. Härlin, 'Vom Haus zu Haus', p. 8.

68. Laurisch, *Kein Abriß unter dieser Nummer*, pp. 68, 103, 106.

69. PTA, 'Hauskonzept – Manteuffelstraße 40/41', 10 October 1981, Ordner Häuserkämpfe, 10/1981.

70. PTA, flyer, 'Nachrichten für Handwerk-kollektiv', January 1981, Ordner Häuserkämpfe, 1/1981.

71. PTA, *Instand-Besetzer-Post*, volumes 1–5 especially. See for example,

'Strom: Einiges zur Elektrik', 11 March 1981, p. 6; 'Neues vom Bauhof: Wo findet man Strom', 17 March 1981, pp. 10–11; 'Wasser', 25 March 1981, pp. 16–17; 'Sein wir schlau am Bad', 1 April 1981, p. 16; 'Sein wir schlau: irgendwo musse's raus – der Abfluss', 5 April 1981, p. 18; 'Kohlebadeofen: under Liebster', 9 April 1981, p. 18.

72. Härlin, 'Vom Haus zu Haus', p. 18, emphasis added.

73. PTA, uncatalogued brochure, 'Blockrevue, Operation Picobello, Block 101/103', p. 11.

74. Dougal Sheridan, 'The Space of Subculture in the City: Getting Specific about Berlin's Indeterminate Territories'. *Field Journal* 1 (2007), pp. 97–119, p. 115.

75. PTA, pamphlet, 'Hauskonzept – Manteuffelstraße 40/41', 10 October 1981, Ordner Häuserkämpfe, 10/1981.

76. Reichardt, *Authentizität und Gemeinschaft*, pp. 546–57. Café Krantscho was located in a squat at Willibald-Alexis-Straße, Lokal Lummerland at Winterfeldstraße 38, the Besetzereck at Oranienstraße 45, the Bobby Sands Pub at Bülowstraße 89 and Café Knüppel at Knobelsdorffstraße 40.

77. Kerngehäuse Cuvrystraße, *Gewerbehof Cuvrystraße 20/23: Leben und arbeiten in SO 36* (Berlin: Initiative 'Kerngehäuse Cuvrystraße', 1980), p. 4.

78. Regenbogenfabrik Block 109 e.v. *Festschrift zum 25. Jubiläum der Regenbogenfabrik* (Berlin: Kreuzberg Museum, 2006), pp. 10, 19.

79. Reichardt, *Authentizität und Gemeinschaft*, pp. 528–32; see also Holm and Kuhn, 'Squatting and Urban Renewal: The Interaction of Squatter Movements and Strategies of Urban Restructuring'. *International Journal of Urban and Regional Research* 35 (2011), pp. 644–58.

80. Holm and Kuhn, 'Squatting and Urban Renewal', p. 648.

81. Manfred Ackermann, 'Architektur und Bauwesen in der Diskussion'. *Deutschland Archiv* 6 (1981).

82. See Grashoff, *Leben in Abriss*.

83. Grashoff, *Schwarzwohnen*, p. 19.

84. Interview with J.L. (July 2013).

85. Quoted in Moldt, *Der mOaning star 1985–1989: eine Ostberliner Untergrundpublikation* (Berlin: Robert-Havemann-Gesellschaft, 2005), p. 7.

86. Quoted in Grashoff, *Schwarzwohnen*, p. 11.

87. Interview with J.L. (July 2013); see Peter Mitchell, 'Socialism's Contested Urban Space: A Study of East German Squatters', unpublished ms., p. 5.

88. Robert-Havemann-Gesellschaft (hereafter RHG), *Umweltblätter*, 1987, Nr. 7, p. 2f; see also Grashoff, *Schwarzwohnen*, p. 152.

89. Andreas Glaeser, *Political Epistemics: The Secret Police, The Opposition and the End of East German Socialism* (Chicago: University of Chicago Press, 2011), 345–6.

90. RHG, 'Behörden erneut gegen instandbesetzte Lychener 61'. *Umweltblätter* 4 (1988), p. 2.

91. RHG, 'Lychener Straße 61'. *Umweltblätter* 10 (1988), p. 2f.

92. See PTA, *Interim*, 11 January 1990; HIS, 'Über die Hausbesetzerbewegung in Ost-Berlin, Teil 1'. *Telegraph* 9 (1995), pp. 37–48, pp. 38–40.

93. Holm and Kuhn, 'Squatting and Urban Renewal', p. 650. See Ralf Brand and Sara Fregonese, *The Radicals' City: Urban Environment, Polarisation, Cohesion* (London: Ashgate, 2013).

94. HIS, 'Über die Hausbesetzerbewegung in Ost-Berlin, Teil 3'. *Telegraph* 11/12 (1995), pp. 36–47, p. 37. See Susan Arndt et al., *Berliner Mainzer Straße. Wohnen ist wichtiger als das Gesetz* (Berlin: Basisdruck, 1992); Holm and Kuhn, 'Squatting and Urban Renewal'.

95. Ibid., p. 37. See Arndt et al., *Berliner Mainzer Straße*, pp. 43–55. An earlier version of the 'Tuntenhaus' had been set up in West Berlin in 1981.

96. See two films on the Tuntenhaus made by Juliet Bashore (*The Battle of Tuntenhaus*, video, 25 mins, and *The Battle of Tuntenhaus*, update, video, 20 mins).

97. Holm and Kuhn, 'Squatting and Urban Renewal', p. 651.

98. PTA, brochure, *Hausbesetzer, Selbstdarstellung von 16 Projekten*, n.d., Ordner Häuserkämpfe O-Berlin.

99. Ibid.

100. See Ursula Maria Berzborn and Steffi Weismann (eds), *KuLe: Kunst and Leben: Ein Haus in Berlin-Mitte seit 1990* (Berlin, Revolver, 2016).

101. PTA, *Hausbesetzer, Selbstdarstellung von 16 Projekten*.

102. See bandito.blogsport.de/uber-uns.

103. PTA, *Hausbesetzer, Selbstdarstellung von 16 Projekten*.

104. See Matthias Heyden, 'Evolving Participatory Design: A Report from Berlin, Reaching Beyond'. *Field Journal* 2 (2008), pp. 31–46.

105. See Heyden, 'Evolving Participatory Design'.

106. Claire Colomb, 'Pushing the Urban Frontier: Temporary Uses of Space, City Marketing, and the Creative City Discourse in 2000s Berlin'. *Journal of Urban Affairs* 34 (2012), pp. 131–52, p. 132; see Johannes Novy and Claire Colomb, 'Struggling for the Right to the (Creative) City in Berlin and Hamburg: New Urban Social Movements, New "Spaces of Hope"?' *International Journal of Urban and Regional Research* 37 (2013), pp. 1816–38; Margit Mayer, 'First World Urban Activism'. *City* 17 (2013), pp. 5–19.

107. Margit Mayer, 'Preface', in SqEK (eds), *Squatting in Europe: Radical*

Spaces, Urban Struggles (London: Minor Compositions, 2013), pp. 1–9, p. 5.

108. See Azozomox, 'Besetzen im 21. Jahrhundert. Die Häuser denen, die drin wohnen', in Andrej Holm (ed.), *Reclaim Berlin: Soziale Kämpfe in der neoliberalen Stadt* (Berlin: Assoziation A, 2014), pp. 273–304.

109. 'The Uncertain Future of Berlin's Squat Houses' (citylab.com). As this book goes to press, it has become clear that the attempt to criminalise the occupants of Rigaer Straße 94 has not been successful. A Berlin court ruled that the police operation to clear part of the house in June 2016 was illegal. See *TAZ*, 2 and 14 July 2016.

110. The Kotti & Co protest camp is often described as a '*gecekondu*' in reference to the squatter dwelling that remains a common feature of Turkish cities. See brochure, 'Kämpfende Hütten'; Kotti & Co (eds), *und deswegen sind wir hier* (Leipzig: Spektor Books, 2015).

111. Keller Easterling, *Extrastatecraft: The Power of Infrastructure Space* (London: Verso, 2014).

6. We Want to Occupy Everything

1. Antonio Negri, 'Multitude and Metropolis' (generation-online.org) (2002).

2. '"Andiamo e capire che succede": il prof porta gli studenti a vedere lo sgombero' (bologna.repubblica.it); 'Sgomberato l'ex Dima: era stato occupato da 150 persone' (corrieredibologna.corriere.it).

3. '"Andiamo e capire che succede"'.

4. 'Occupy Turin: Refugees Find a Home in Italy's Abandoned Olympic Village' (theguardian.com).

5. Jason E. Smith, 'The Politics of Incivility: Autonomia and Tiqqun'. *The Minnesota Review* 32 (2010), pp. 119–32, p. 120, emphasis in original.

6. Sylvère Lotringer and Christian Marazzi, 'The Return of Politics', in Lotringer and Marazzi (eds), *Autonomia: Post-political Politics* (Los Angeles, CA: Semiotext(e), 2007), pp. 8–21, p. 10.

7. Steve Wright, *Storming Heaven: Class Composition and Struggle in Italian Autonomist Marxism* (London: Pluto Press, 2002), pp. 6–7.

8. Robert Lumley, *States of Emergency: Cultures of Revolt in Italy from 1968 to 1978* (London: Verso, 1990), p. 14; Nanni Balestrini and Primo Moroni, *L'orda d'oro, 1968–1977: La grande ondata rivoluzionaria e creativa, politica ed esistenziale* (Milan: Feltrinelli, 2011 [1988]), p. 16.

9. Balestrini and Moroni, *L'orda d'oro*, p. 17; Wright, *Storming Heaven*, p. 11.

10. Lumley, *States of Emergency*, p. 27.

11. David Forgacs, *Italy's Margins: Social Exclusion and Nation Formation since 1861* (Cambridge: Cambridge University Press, 2014), pp. 29, 30.

12. Pierpaolo Mudu, 'Housing and Homelessness in Contemporary Rome', in Isabella Clough Marinaro and Bjørn Thomassen (eds), *Global Rome: Changing Faces of the Eternal City* (Bloomington: Indiana University Press, 2014), pp. 62–78, p. 65.

13. Lila Leontidou, *The Mediterranean City in Transition: Social Change and Urban Development* (Cambridge: Cambridge University Press, 2006), p. 252; see also Franco Ferrarotti, *Vite di baraccati: Contributo alla sociologia della marginalità* (Naples: Liguori, 1974). The Pasolini quote is taken from Pier Paolo Pasolini, *Tutte le poesie*, vol. 1 (Milan: Mondadori, 2003), pp. 925–6.

14. John Foot, 'Revisiting the *Coree*: Self-Construction, Memory and Immigration on the Milanese Periphery, 1950–2000', in Robert Lumley and John Foot (eds), *Italian Cityscapes: Culture and Change in Italy from the 1950s to the Present* (Exeter: University of Exeter Press, 2004), pp. 46–60, pp. 46, 48; Forgacs, *Italy's Margins*, p. 32.

15. Foot, 'Revisiting the Coree', pp. 50, 47, 53.

16. Paul Ginsburg, *A History of Contemporary Italy: Society and Politics, 1943–1988* (Basingstoke: Palgrave Macmillan, 2003), p. 225.

17. 'Operai Lavoratori', supplement from *Lotta Continua*, 13 April 1973, p. 42.

18. Nicola Pizzolato, *Challenging Global Capitalism: Labour Migration, Radical Struggle and Urban Change in Detroit and Turin* (Basingstoke: Palgrave Macmillan, 2013), p. 78.

19. 'Operai Lavoratori', p. 14; Andreina Daolio, *Le lotte per la casa in Italia: Milano, Torino, Roma, Napoli* (Milan: Feltrinelli, 1974), p. 17.

20. Nicola Pizzolato, 'Transnational Radicals: Labour Dissent and Political Activism in Detroit and Turin (1950–1970)'. *International Institut voor Sociale Geschidenis* 56 (2011), pp. 1–30, p. 12.

21. Danilo Montaldi, *Bisogna sognare: Scritti 1952–1975* (Milan: Cooperativa Co libri, 1994), p. 501.

22. Wright, *Storming Heaven*, p. 32.

23. Pizzolato, 'Transnational Radicals', pp. 15, 16. See Emiliana Armano, Devi Sacchetto and Steve Wright, 'Coresearch and Counter-Research: Romano Alquati's Itinerary Within and Beyond Italian Radical Political Thought' (viewpointmag.com); Romano Alquati, *Cultura formazione e ricerca* (Torino: Velleità Alternative, 1994), p. 37. Two key texts by Alquati during this period were 'Relazione sulle "forze

nuove": Convegno del Psi sulla Fiat (gennaio 1961)', pp. 215–39. *Quaderni Rossi* 1 (September 1961) and 'Documenti sulla lotta di classe alla Fiat'. *Quaderni Rossi* 1 (September 1961), pp. 198–214.

24. Gigi Roggero, 'Organised Spontaneity: Class Struggle, Workers Autonomy and Soviets in Italy' (libcom.org).

25. Antonio Negri, *Pipeline: Letters from Prison* (Cambridge: Polity, 2015), p. 89.

26. Michael Hardt, 'Laboratory Italy', in Michael Hardt and Paolo Virno (eds), *Radical Thought in Italy: A Potential Politics* (Minneapolis, MN: University of Minnesota Press, 1996), pp. 1–10, p. 2; Mario Tronti, 'The Strategy of Refusal' (libcom.org).

27. Negri, *Pipeline*, p. 95, emphasis added.

28. Smith, 'The Politics of Incivility', p. 119.

29. 'Take Over the City' ('*Prendiamoci la città*'), a series of sections from the journal *Lotta Continua* that were translated from Italian and republished in Radical America 7 (1973); quoted in Mitchell, 'Contested Space', p. 78.

30. Smith, 'The Politics of Incivility', p. 120.

31. Wright, *Storming Heaven*, p. 89.

32. Lumley, *States of Emergency*, pp. 63, 64.

33. Anon, *Libro bianco sulla Facoltà di Archittettura di Milano* (Milan: Facoltà di Archittettura di Milano, 1967), pp. 1, 2; Wright, *Storming Heaven*, p. 89.

34. Quoted in Balestrini and Moroni, *L'orda d'oro*, p. 203.

35. 'Tesi di Sapienza', in *Università: l'ipotesi rivoluzionaria* (Padua: Marsilio, 1968), pp. 176–7.

36. Lumley, *States of Emergency*, pp. 66–7.

37. Ibid., p. 90.

38. Wright, *Storming Heaven*, p. 119; Pizzolato, 'Transnational Radicals', p. 21.

39. Wright, *Storming Heaven*, p. 120; Nanni Balestrini, *Vogliamo tutto: The Novel of Italy's Hot Autumn* (Melbourne: Telephone Publishing, 2014 [1969]), p. 116.

40. Balestrini, *Vogliamo tutto*, p. 132.

41. Ibid., pp. 168, 161, 163, emphasis added.

42. Negri, *Pipeline*, pp. 121, 122.

43. Mario Tronti, 'Factory and Society', (operaismoinenglish.wordpress.com).

44. Bifo, 'Anatomy of Autonomy', in Sylvère Lotringer and Christian Marazzi (eds), *Autonomia: Post-political Politics* (Los Angeles, CA: Semiotext(e), 2008 [1981]), pp. 148–72, p. 150.

45. Steve Wright, 'Mapping Pathways with Italian Autonomist Marxism: A Preliminary Survey'. *Historical Materialism* 16 (2008), pp. 111–40, p. 118; Giorgio Bocca, *Il caso 7. Aprile* (Milan: Feltrinelli, 1980), p. 87.

46. 'Non paghiamo più l'affitto'. *Lotta Continua* 1 (November 1969), pp. 3–5.

47. On role of PCI, see Pierpaolo Mudu, 'Ogni Sfrati Sarà Una Barricata: Squatting for Housing and Social Conflict in Rome', in SqEK (eds), *The Squatters' Movement in Europe: Commons and Autonomy as Alternatives to Capitalism* (London: Pluto Press, 2014), pp. 136–63, p. 138.

48. John Foot, *The Man Who Closed the Asylums: Franco Basaglia and the Revolution in Mental Health Care* (London: Verso, 2015), p. 188.

49. Pizzolato, *Challenging Global Capitalism*, pp. 198, 199.

50. 'Take Over the City'.

51. Ibid.

52. Eddy Cherki and Michel Wieviorka, 'Autoreduction Movements in Turin', in Sylvère Lotringer and Christian Marazzi (eds), *Autonomia*, pp. 72–8, p. 73.

53. See Comitati autonomi operai di Roma, eds, *Autonomia Operaia* (Milan: Savelli, 1976).

54. Cherki and Wieviorka, 'Autoreduction Movements in Turin', p. 76.

55. Daolio, *Le lotte per la casa*, p. 19.

56. Peter Schneider, 'Die Häuserbesetzung in der Via Tibaldi'. *Kursbuch* 26 (1972), pp. 109–111.

57. *Il Manifesto*, 2 June 1971.

58. *Il Manifesto*, 9 June 1971.

59. 'Take Over the City'.

60. Mudu, 'Ogni Sfrati Sarà Una Barricata', p. 139.

61. Wright, *Storming Heaven*, p. 150.

62. 'Piccolo gruppo in moltiplicazione'. *A/traverso* (May 1975), p. 171.

63. Balestrini and Moroni, *L'orda d'oro*, p. 436; Smith, 'The Politics of Incivility', pp. 102, 126, 127.

64. Nanni Balestrini, 'Cattivi maestri', in Sergio Bianchi and Lanfranco Caminiti (eds), *Settantasette: La rivoluzione che viene*, 2nd edition (Rome: Derive Approdi, 2004), pp. 325–7, p. 326.

65. Bifo quoted in Patrick Gun Cunninghame, 'Autonomia: A Movement of Refusal – Social Movements and Social Conflict in Italy in the 1970s', PhD dissertation, Middlesex University, 2002, p. 1.

66. 'Piccolo gruppo in moltiplicazione', p. 171.

67. Cunninghame, 'Autonomia: A Movement of Refusal', p. 123.

68. See Lumley, *States of Emergency*; see also Antonio Negri, *Revolution Retrieved: Writings on Marx, Keynes, Capitalist Crisis and New Social Subjects, 1967–1983* (London: Red Notes, 1988), p. 272.

69. Negri quoted in Kathi Weeks, *The Problem with Work: Feminism, Marxism, Antiwork Politics and Postwork Imaginaries* (Durham, NC: Duke University Press, 2011), p. 255.

70. Balestrini and Moroni, *L'orda d'oro*, p. 488.

71. Perry Wilson, *Women in Twentieth Century Italy* (London: Palgrave Macmillan, 2010), p. 153; Maud Anne Bracke, *Women and the Reinvention of the Political: Feminism in Italy, 1968–1983* (London: Routledge, 2014), p. 68.

72. Anna Rita Calabrò and Laura Grasso, *Dal movimento femminista al femminismo diffuso: Storie e percorsi a Milano dagli anni '60 agli anni '80*, 2nd edition (Milano: FrancoAngeli, 2004), p. 78

73. Elena Vacchelli, 'Geographies of Subjectivity: Locating Feminist Political Subjects in Milan'. *Gender, Place & Culture* 18 (2011), pp. 768–85, pp. 769, 774.

74. Various authors, 'Lavoro domestico e salario'. *Rosso* 11 (June 1974), pp. 33–4, p. 33, emphasis added.

75. Sergio Bologna, 'Composizione di classe e sistema politico', in R. Lauricella et al. (eds), *Crisi delle politiche e politiche nella crisi* (Naples: Libreria L'Ateneo di G. Pronti, 1980), p. 28–9, emphasis added.

76. Geoff Eley, 'Politics and the City: A Badly Bifurcated Left' (h-net. org).

77. *Sarà un risotto che vi seppellirà – materiali dei circoli proletari giovanili di Milano* (Milan: Squilibri Edizioni, 1977), p. 39.

78. Balestrini and Moroni, *L'orda d'oro*, p. 445.

79. John N. Morton and Primo Moroni, *La luna sotto casa: Milano tra rivolta esistenziale e movimenti politici* (Milan: Shake Edizioni, 2007), p. 175.

80. Con Consorzio Aaster et al. *Centri sociali: geografie del desiderio* (Milan: Shake Edizioni Underground, 1996), p. 108; see also Cox 18 et al. *Storia di un'autogestione* (Milan: Edizione Colibri, 2010); Morton and Moroni, *La luna sotto casa*.

81. Mudu, 'Resisting and Challenging Neoliberalism', p. 66.

82. *Re Nudo* 21, 1973.

83. See Egeria Di Nallo, *Indiani in città* (Bologna: Cappelli, 1977); Pablo Echaurren, *Il movimento del '77 e gli indiani metropolitani* (Milan: Postmedia Books, 2016).

84. 'Memoirs of a Metropolitan Indian' (libcom.org).

85. Lumley, *States of Emergency*, p. 301.

86. The adoption of the 'American Indian' as a figure of playful resistance drew as much from a politics of radical empathy and anti-colonial solidarity than it did from an older criminal tradition in Rome where 'Indian' code names were widely used. See Donald R. Katz, 'Italian Youth Movement Turns to Violence for Cultural Change', *Rolling Stone*, 17 November 1977

87. Sebastian Haumann, '"*Stadtindianer*" and "*Indiani Metropolitani*": Recontextualising an Italian Protest Movement in West Germany', in Martin Klimke et al. (eds) *Between Prague Spring and French May: Opposition and Revolt in Europe, 1960–1980* (New York: Berghahn,

2013), pp. 141–53, pp. 147, 148; the 1 March 1977 manifesto of the *indiani* unsurprisingly called for the squatting of all empty buildings.

88. Lumley, *States of Emergency*, p. 295.
89. 'Memoirs of a Metropolitan Indian'.
90. Ibid.
91. No author, 'Nelle assemblee di massa dell'Università emerge il nuovo soggetto proletario'. *A/Traverso*, February 1977.
92. 'Memoirs of a Metropolitan Indian'.
93. Ibid.; Lumley, *States of Emergency*, p. 295; see Claudio Del Bello (ed.), *Una sparatoria tranquilla: Per una storia orale del '77* (Milan: Odradek, 2005); Luca Pastore, *La vetrina infranta. La violenza politica a Bologna negli anni del terrorismo rosso, 1969–1974* (Bologna: Instituto Parri, 2013).
94. 'Memoirs of a Metropolitan Indian'; Red Notes Pamphlet, 'Italy, 1977–78: "Living with an Earthquake"' (London: Red Notes), n.p.
95. See especially Franco 'Bifo' Beradi and Gomma, *Alice è il diavolo. Storia di una radio sovversiva* (Milan: Shake Editions, 2006).
96. Bifo, 'Anatomy of Autonomy', p. 158, 159.
97. Balestrini and Moroni, *L'ordo d'oro*, p. 577.
98. See Maurizio Torealta, 'Painted Politics', in Sylvère Lotringer and Christian Marazzi (eds), *Autonomia*, pp. 102–6.
99. 'Lotte, attacco, organizzazione: Construiamo la milizia operaia e proletari per il potere comunista', in Sergio Bianchi and Lanfranco Caminiti (eds), *Gli autonomi: Le storie, le lotte, le teorie* (Rome: Derive Approdi, 2007), pp. 271–8, p. 278.
100. Lumley, *States of Emergency*, pp. 281–2.
101. Negri, *Revolution Retrieved*, p. 246; Timothy S. Murphy, 'Editor's Introduction', in Antonio Negri, *Books for Burning: Between Civil War and Democracy in 1970s Italy* (London: Verso, 2005), pp. ix–xxii, pp. xi, xx, xxi.
102. Alessandro Portelli, 'Oral Testimony, the Law and the Making of History: The "April 7" Murder Trial'. *History Workshop Journal* 20 (1985), pp. 5–35, p. 6.
103. Félix Guattari and Sylvère Lotringer, 'A New Alliance is Possible', in Félix Guattari, *Soft Subversions: Texts and Interviews, 1977–1985*, pp. 113–27, p. 119.
104. Mudu, 'Resisting and Challenging Neoliberalism', pp. 76, 73.
105. Miguel Angel Martínez López, 'The Squatters' Movement in Europe: A Durable Struggle for Social autonomy in Urban Politics'. *Antipode* 45 (2013), pp. 866–87, p. 875.
106. Mudu, 'Resisting and Challenging Neo-liberalism', p. 80.
107. Mudu, 'Ogni Sfrati Sarà Una Barricata', pp. 139, 141.
108. Ibid., pp. 142–7.

109. Darren Patrick, 'Bologna's Latest Eviction Threatens to Whitewash the "Red" City's Political Legacy' (theguardian.com).

110. Wu ming, '"Prima i poveri!" La resistenza dell' #ExTelecom e la gestione del potere a #Bologna' (wumingfoundation.com); 'Sgombero in via Irnerio, occupanti sul tetto' (zic.it). The final housing occupation in Bologna was, in fact, cleared as this book went to press. See 'Last Remaining Housing Occupation in Bologna Has Been Evicted' (strugglesinitaly.wordpress.com).

111. Patrick, 'Bologna's Latest Eviction'.

112. I am indebted to Bethan Bowett for reminding me of this. See 'Taking Back Naples' (jacobinmag.com); 'Il regalo di De Magistris ai centri sociali: gli immobili occupati diventano "bene commune"' (napoli.fanpage.it).

7. Mudflats Living and the Makeshift City

1. Malcolm Lowry, 'Lament in the Pacific Northwest', in Malcolm Lowry, *The Voyage That Never Ends: Fictions, Poems, Fragments, Letters* (New York: NYRB, 2007), p. 266.

2. A Poem by Bud Osborn, 'Raise Shit' (societyandspace.com).

3. Victor Doyen, 'From Innocent Story to Charon's Boat: Reading the "October Ferry" Manuscripts', in Sherrill E. Grace (ed.), *Swinging the Maelstrom: New Perspectives on Malcolm Lowry* (Montreal: MQUP, 1992), pp. 162–208, p. 166.

4. Stephen Osbourne, 'Evictions' (geist.com).

5. Doyen, 'From Innocent Story to Charon's Boat', p. 167.

6. *Selected Letters of Malcolm Lowry* (New York: J.P. Lippincott, 1965), p. 339.

7. Malcolm Lowry, *October Ferry to Gabriola* (Harmondsworth: Penguin, 1971), p. 73.

8. Doyen, 'From Innocent Story to Charon's Boat', pp. 163–6; D.T. Max, 'Day of the Dead', *The New Yorker* (newyorker.com).

9. Brochure, 'from shangri-la to shangri-la', January 2010, Vancouver, Site Gallery.

10. *Vancouver Sun*, 4 September 2010.

11. See *Intertidal: Vancouver Art and Artists* (Antwerp, Museum van Hedendaagse Kunst and Vancouver Belkin Art Gallery, 2005).

12. Robert MacDonald, *The Making of Vancouver: Class, Status, and Social Boundaries, 1863–1913* (Vancouver: UBC Press, 1996).

13. Raymond Frogner, 'The Enormous Condescension of Cartography: Squatters Rights, Prairie Settlement and the Archival Meridian of William Pearce'. Unpublished ms, p. 7.

14. Ibid., p. 10.
15. Paige Raibmon, 'Unmaking Native Space: A Genealogy of Indian Policy, Settler Practice, and the Microtechniques of Dispossession', in Alexandra Harmon (ed.), *The Power of Promises: Re-thinking Indian Treaties in the Pacific Northwest* (Vancouver: UBC Press, 2008), pp. 56–85, p. 64.
16. Ibid., p. 63.
17. Cole Harris, *The Resettlement of British Columbia: Essays on Colonialism and Geographical Change* (Vancouver: UBC Press, 1996), p. xi.
18. Raibmon, 'Unmaking Native Space', p. 58.
19. Cole Harris, *Making Native Space: Colonialism, Resistance, and Reserves in British Columbia* (Vancouver: UBC Press, 2002), p. xvii.
20. Jean Barman, 'Erasing Indigenous Indigeneity in Vancouver'. *BC Studies* 155 (2007), pp. 3–30, p. 7.
21. Malcolm Lowry, 'The Forest Path to the Spring', in Lowry, *The Voyage That Never Ends*, pp. 158–241, p. 171.
22. Stephen Osbourne, 'Evictions'.
23. Nicholas Blomley, *Unsettling the City: Urban Land and the Politics of Property* (London and New York: Routledge, 2004), p. 112.
24. Harris, *The Resettlement of British Columbia*, p. 102.
25. Renisa Mawani, *Colonial Proximities: Crossracial Encounters and Juridical Truths in British Columbia, 1871–1921* (Vancouver: UBC Press, 2009), p. 5.
26. Blomley, *Unsettling the City*, p. 114.
27. Jean Barman, *Stanley Park's Secret: The Forgotten Families of Whoi Whoi, Kanaka Ranch, and Brockton Point* (Madeira Park: Harbour Publishing, 2005), p. 13; Mawani, 'Genealogies of the Land', p. 325.
28. Renisa Mawani, 'Genealogies of the Land: Aboriginality, Law, and Territory in Vancouver's Stanley Park'. *Social and Legal Studies* 14 (2005), pp. 315–39, pp. 323, 324.
29. Quoted in Mawani, 'Genealogies of the Land', p. 324 and Barman, *Stanley Park's Secret*, p. 39.
30. Quoted in Barman, *Stanley Park's Secret*, p. 55.
31. Mawani, 'Genealogies of the Land', p. 325.
32. Ibid., p. 326.
33. Sean Kheraj, *Inventing Stanley Park: An Environmental History* (Vancouver: UBC Press, 2009), p. 88.
34. Quoted in Mawani, 'Genealogies of the Land', p. 327, emphasis added.
35. Barman, *Stanley Park's Secret*, pp. 227–8.
36. Mawani, 'Genealogies of the Land', p. 327.
37. Mawani, *Colonial Proximities*, p. 8.
38. MacDonald, *Making Vancouver*, p. 86.

39. See Rolf Knight, *Along the No. 20 Line: Reminiscences of the Vancouver Waterfront* (Vancouver: New Star Books, 1980).

40. Jill Wade, *Houses for All: The Struggle for Social Housing in Vancouver, 1919–1950* (Vancouver: UBC Press, 1994), p. 19.

41. J.D. Hulchanski, 'The 1935 Dominion Housing Act: Setting the Stage for a Permanent Federal Presence in Canada's Housing Sector'. *Urban History Review* 15 (1986), pp. 19–39, p. 25; see also Wade, *Houses for All*.

42. See Wade, *Houses for All*.

43. MacDonald, *Making Vancouver*.

44. Jill Wade, '"A Palace for the Public": Housing Reform and the 1946 Occupation of the Hotel Vancouver'. *BC Studies*, 69–70 (1986), pp. 288–310.

45. City of Vancouver Archive (hereafter CVA), City of Vancouver, minutes, 'Special Committee re: Fraser River Shacks', 16 May 1939, Box 27-D-7, Folder 28; City of Vancouver, Health Department, 'Survey, Fraser River North Arm Foreshacks, Etc', 3 November 1938, Box 27-D-7, Folder 28.

46. CVA, City of Vancouver, 'Draft Recommendation', 14 November 1956, Box 9-B-1, Folder 3, City Clerk's Office.

47. Jeff Sommers and Nicholas Blomley, '"The Worst Block in Vancouver"', in Stan Douglas, *Every Building on 100 West Hastings*, pp. 18–58, p. 36.

48. 'Summer of Yippie' (pasttensevancouver.wordpress.com); *Vancouver Sun*, 27 June 1970.

49. *Vancouver Sun*, 29 May 1971.

50. Donald Gutstein, *Vancouver Ltd* (Toronto: Lorimer, 1975), p. 187; 'All Season's Park Lives On', *The Tower*, 5 December 1971.

51. Tom Burrows, 'I Moved to the Mudflats', unpublished ms.

52. Ibid.

53. Scott Watson, 'Urban Renewal: Ghost Traps, Collage, Condos, and Squats – Vancouver Art in the Sixties', in *Intertidal: Vancouver Art and Artists* (Antwerp, Museum van Hedendaagse Kunst and Vancouver Belkin Art Gallery, 2005), pp. 31–48, p. 41.

54. Ibid., p. 41.

55. Ibid., p. 42.

56. Andrea Karin Anderson, '"A Sculpture of Concrete, Sculpture of Dreams": Looking for the Utopian in the Everyday', MA dissertation, University of British Columbia, p. 112.

57. Tom Burrows, 'Only Take for Granted the Things That You Can Touch'. *artscanada* 164/5 (February/March, 1972), pp. 126–7, p. 126.

58. Burrows, 'Only Take for Granted the Things That You Can Touch', p. 126.

59. 'Tom Burrows, Bio' (tomburrows.wordpress.com).

60. 'Dialogue on the Squatters' Movement – Assembled and Edited by Tom Burrows', unpublished ms; 'Composite Dialogue on Third World Housing', unpublished ms. I am indebted to Tom Burrows for providing me with a copy of these texts.

61. The original *Skwat Doc* is part of the collection at the Morris and Helen Belkin Art Gallery at the University of British Columbia in Vancouver.

62. Watson, 'Urban Renewal', p. 43.

63. Burrows, 'I Moved to the Mudflats'.

64. Watson, 'Urban Renewal', p. 43.

65. Bart de Baere and Dieter Roelstraete, 'Introducing Intertidal', in *Intertidal: Vancouver Art and Artists* (Antwerp, Museum van Hedendaagse Kunst and Vancouver Belkin Art Gallery, 2005), pp. 7–15, p. 11.

66. Ibid., p. 13.

67. Neil Smith, *The New Urban Frontier: Gentrification and the Revanchist City* (London and New York: Routledge, 1996), p. 16.

68. Sommers and Blomley, 'The Worst Block in Vancouver', p. 45.

69. Blomley, *Unsettling the City*, pp. 38–9.

70. 'Lessons Learned'. *Open Road* (Summer 1986), n.p.

71. 'Press Statement from Squatters' Alliance Vancouver East', in Sheila Baxter (ed.), *Under the Viaduct: Homeless in Beautiful B.C.* (Vancouver: New Star Books, 1991), pp. 79–80, p. 79.

72. Keith Chu, 'The Frances Street Squats', in Sheila Baxter, *Under the Viaduct*, pp. 80–8, pp. 82, 84.

73. Graham Cameron, 'Squatters' Future Left Hanging'. *The Ubyssey* 73 (1990), p. 3.

74. Flyer, Squatters' Alliance of Vancouver East, June 1993 (vanarchive. wordpress.com).

75. CVA, Office of the Mayor, 2 January 1991, Box 244-F-2, Folder 9.

76. *Flour Power* ('Zine of Anarchist Politics and Punk Music from Vancouver and Victoria), 3 (August 1993), n.p.

77. Blomley, *Unsettling the City*, pp. 39–42.

78. Ivan Drury, 'The First Two Evictions of the Woodwards Squat'. *West Coast Line* 41 (Fall/Winter, 2004), pp. 51–7, pp. 54, 56. The whole issue of *West Coast Line* was focused on 'Woodsquat'.

79. 'The Six Demands of the Coalition of Woodwards Squatters and Supporters'. *West Coast Line* 41 (Fall/Winter, 2004), pp. 42–3.

80. Trevor M., 'Woodsquat'. *West Coast Line* 41 (Fall/Winter, 2004), pp. 107–17, p. 116; 'Third Woodsquat Memo'. *West Coast Line* 41 (Fall/Winter, 2004), pp. 169–72. On the PHS, see Jesse Proudfoot, 'The Derelict, The Deserving Poor and the *Lumpen*: A History of the Politics of Representation in the Downtown Eastside', in Stan Douglas, *Abbot and Cordova, 7 August 1971* (Vancouver: Arsenal Pulp Press, 2011), pp. 88–105.

81. Trevor M., 'Woodsquat', p. 116.
82. See 'Inside Woodward's, a Still-Contentious Social Housing Experiment' (thetyee.ca).
83. See Stan Douglas, *Abbot and Cordova, 7 August 1971*.

8. Reclaiming New York

1. Tamiment Library and Robert F. Wagner Archives, NYU (hereafter TL), TAM 336 (Squatters Rights Collection), notebook, n.d., Peter Spagnuolo Papers, Box 3, Folder 3.
2. TL, TAM 335 (Squatters Rights Collection), flyer, 'The Squatters are Your Neighbours', Kurt Reynertson Papers, Box 1, Folder 1.
3. 'The Night New York Saved Itself from Bankruptcy', *The New Yorker*, 16 October 2015; David Harvey, 'Neoliberalism and the City'. *Studies in Social Justice* 1 (2007), pp. 1–12, p. 6.
4. Ibid.
5. Quoted in 'The Night New York Saved Itself from Bankruptcy', *The New Yorker*.
6. Kim Moody, *From Welfare State to Real Estate: Regime Change in New York City, 1974 to the Present* (New York: The New Press, 2007), p. 61.
7. Kim Phillips-Fein, 'Lessons from the Great Default Crisis of 1975' (thenation.com).
8. David Madden and Peter Marcuse, *In Defense of Housing: The Politics of Crisis* (London: Verso, 2016), p. 173; see David Harvey, *Rebel Cities: From the Right to the City to the Urban Revolution* (London: Verso, 2012); Roberta Gold, *When Tenants Claimed the City: The Struggle for Citizenship in New York City Housing* (Urbana: University of Illinois Press, 2014), especially chapters 7–8.
9. Jamie Peck, 'Austerity Urbanism'. *City* 16 (2012), pp. 626–55; Harvey, *Rebel Cities*, p. 32.
10. Harvey, *Rebel Cities*, pp. 50–1, p. 11.
11. See Moody, *From Welfare State to Real Estate*, pp. 49–61.
12. Madden and Marcuse, *In Defense of Housing*, pp. 172, 173.
13. Gold, *When Tenants Claimed the City*, p. 242.
14. Christopher Mele, *Selling the Lower East Side: Culture, Real Estate and Resistance in New York City* (Minneapolis: University of Minnesota Press, 2000), p. 192; see Rodrick Wallace and Deborah Wallace, *A Plague on Your Houses: How New York Was Burned Down and National Public Health Crumbled* (London: Verso, 1998); Rodrick Wallace and Deborah Wallace, 'Origins of Public Health Collapse in New York City: The Dynamics of Planned Shrinkage, Contagious

Urban Decay and Social Disintegration'. *Bulletin of the New York Academy of Medicine* 66 (1990), 391–434.

15. Cari Luna, 'Squatters of the Lower East Side' (jacobinmag.com).
16. Madden and Marcuse, *In Defense of Housing*, p. 174.
17. Gold, *When Tenants Claimed the City*, p. 242; 'Housing in City Eroding Amid Housing Standstill'. *New York Times* (hereafter *NYT*), 8 February 1970.
18. Amy Starecheski, 'Squatting History: The Power of Oral History as a History-Making Practice'. *Oral History Review* 41 (2014), pp. 187–216, p. 190; Gold, *When Tenants Claimed the City*, p. 244.
19. Michael Dear quoted in Wallace and Wallace, *A Plague on Your Houses*, p. 29.
20. Wallace and Wallace, 'Origins of Public Health Collapse in New York City', p. 394.
21. Mele, *Selling the Lower East Side*, pp. 190–1; see Peter Marcuse, 'Triage: Programming the Death of Communities'. Report, New York: Working Group for Community Development Reform.
22. Jennifer Light, *From Warfare to Welfare: Defence Intellectuals and Urban Problems in Coldwar America* (Berkeley: University of California Press, 2003), p. 68; see for example Edward H. Blum, *Development Research of the New York City Fire Project* (New York: New York Rand Institute, 1972). I am indebted to Matt Farish for reminding me of the importance of the Rand Corporation.
23. Wallace and Wallace, 'Origins of Public Health Collapse in New York City', p. 394.
24. 'Why the Bronx Burned' (nypost.com).
25. Wallace and Wallace, 'Origins of Public Health Collapse in New York City', p. 398; see also Wallace and Wallace, *A Plague on Your Houses*; Madden and Marcuse, *In Defense of Housing*, p. 174.
26. Katie J. Wells, 'A Housing Crisis, a Failed Law and a Property Conflict: The US Urban Speculation Tax'. *Antipode* 47 (2015), pp. 1043–61.
27. Hannah Dobbz, *Nine-tenths of the Law: Property and Resistance in the United States* (Oakland, CA: AK Press, 2012), pp. 68–9.
28. Sarah Ferguson, 'The Struggle for Space: 10 Years of Turf Battling on the Lower East Side', in Clayton Patterson (ed.), *Resistance: A Radical Political and Social History of the Lower East Side* (New York: Seven Stories Press, 2007), pp. 141–65, p. 148.
29. Nicole P. Marwell, *Bargaining for Brooklyn: Community Organisations in the Entrepreneurial City* (Chicago, IL: University of Chicago Press, 2007), pp. 45–7; see 'Housing Aid Sought in Williamsburg', *NYT*, 24 August 1975; 'Tenants in Blighted Areas Restore Buildings and Hopes', *NYT*, 22 February 1978.

30. Peter Marcuse, 'Gentrification, Abandonment and Displacement: Connections, Causes and Policy Responses in New York City'. *Journal of Urban and Contemporary Law* 28 (1985), pp. 196–240.

31. David Harvey, 'Neoliberalism is a Political Project' (jacobinmag .com); Harvey, *Rebel Cities*, p. 5.

32. Eric Hirsch and Peter Wood, 'Squatting in New York City: Justification and Strategy'. *New York University Review of Law and Social Change* 16 (1987/1988), pp. 605–17, p. 614; Pat Lamiell, 'Squatting in New York', *City Limits*, October 1985.

33. 'Squatters and City Battle for Abandoned Buildings', *NYT*, 2 August 1985; 'On a Frontier of Hope', *NYT*, 4 October 1992.

34. David Boyle quoted in Ferguson, 'The Struggle for Space', p. 149.

35. Ferguson, 'The Struggle for Space', p. 151.

36. Ibid., p. 154.

37. Neil Smith, *The New Urban Frontier: Gentrification and the Revanchist City* (London and New York: Routledge, 1996), p. 24; 'A Housing Place for Artists Loses in Board of Estimates' *NYT*, 11 February 1983.

38. Rosalyn Deutsche and Cara Gendel Ryan, 'The Fine Art of Gentrification'. *October* 31 (1984), pp. 91–111, p. 93.

39. See James Cornwell, 'Villains or Victims: Are East Village Artists Willing Agents for Gentrification and Displacement of the Poor', in Patterson (ed.), *Resistance*, pp. 482–99.

40. Ferguson, 'The Struggle for Space', p. 152.

41. Ibid.; Cari Luna, 'Squatters of the Lower East Side' (jacobinmag.com).

42. Doug Turetsky, 'Rebels with a Cause'. *City Limits* (April 1990), pp. 12–15, p. 12.

43. See Amy Starecheski, *Ours to Lose: When Squatters Became Homeowners in New York City* (Chicago, IL: University of Chicago Press, 2016).

44. TL, TAM 335 (Squatters Rights Collection), flyer, 'The Squatters are your Neighbours', n.d., Kurt Reynertson papers, Box Number 1, Folder 1; TL, TAM 363 (Squatters Rights Collection), Morales quoted in untitled flyer, n.d., Fly Papers, Box Number 1, Folder 1.

45. Quoted in Ferguson, 'The Struggle for Space', p. 152.

46. Ibid., pp. 153–4.

47. Shelly Levine, 'ABC NO RIO' (bombmagazine.org); TL, TAM 313 (Squatters Rights Collection), brochure, 'Bullet, 1986–1989: An Act of Resistance', n.d, Jane Churchman Papers, Box Number 1, Folder 16.

48. Alan W. Moore, *Occupation Culture: Art and Squatting in the City from Below* (New York: Minor Compositions, 2015), p. 9.

49. Ash Thayer, 'Prologue', in Thayer, *Kill City: Lower East Side Squatters, 1992–2000* (Brooklyn, powerHouse Books, 2015), pp. 6–9, p. 9.

50. Starecheski, 'Squatting History', p. 203.
51. TL, TAM 313 (Squatters Rights Collection), brochure, 'Survival Without Rent', n.d., Jane Churchman Papers, Box Number 1, Folder 28.
52. Fly, 'Squatting on the Lower East Side', in Patterson (ed.), *Resistance*, pp. 213–18, p. 214.
53. TL, TAM 336 (Squatters Rights Collection), flyer, 'The War Against Spatial Deconcentration', n.d. Peter Spagnuolo Papers, Box Number 2, Folder 8; the term 'spatial deconcentration' remains controversial. For some squatters and other radical housing activists, it refers to a covert militarised response to the inner-city riots of the late 1960s which was predicated on the dissolution of urban neighbourhoods of colour. Activists point, in particular, to the death of Yolanda Ward, an African American employee at the Housing and Urban Development in Washington, DC who they believed was murdered to prevent her from exposing the true rationale underpinning 'spatial deconstruction'. There is little if any evidence to support these claims, though 'spatial deconcentration' is still one of the policy objectives set out in the US Code of Federal Regulations.
54. Dobbz, *Nine-tenths of the Law*, p. 89.
55. Smith, *The Urban Frontier*, pp. 3, 5; C. Carr, 'Night Clubbing: Reports from the Tompkins Square Police Riot', *Village Voice*, 16 August 1988; Sarah Ferguson, 'The Boombox Wars', *Village Voice*, 16 August 1988.
56. Ferguson, 'The Struggle for Space', p. 157.
57. Flash quoted in Cari Luna, 'Squatters of the Lower East Side'.
58. Smith, *The Urban Frontier*, p. 6; 'Tensions Remain High at Closed Tompkins Square Park', *NYT*, 17 June 1991.
59. 'Arson at Manhattan Bridge', *NYT*, 31 May 1992; 'For Homeless, A Last Haven is Demolished', *NYT*, 18 August 1993.
60. Luna, 'Squatters of the Lower East Side'.
61. TL, TAM 336 (Squatters Rights Collection), 'The City of New York, Peremptory Vacate Order', 20 April 1995, Peter Spagnuolo Papers, Box Number 1, Folder 3.
62. Miriam Axel-Lute, 'Battle over Thirteenth Street' (nhi.org).
63. Ibid.
64. Luna, 'Squatters of the Lower East Side'.
65. Ibid.
66. Spagnuolo quoted in ibid.
67. TL, TAM 336 (Squatters Rights Collection), Documents relating to 'Supreme Court Decision, East 13th Homesteader Coalition versus New Your City Department of Housing, Preservation and Development', July 1995, Peter Spagnuolo Papers Box 1, Folder 20.
68. 'Judge's Ruling Gives Squatters a New Shield Against City', *NYT*, 27

October 1995; 'Tension on East 13th Street as Squatters Await Eviction', *NYT*, 10 August 1996.

69. TL, TAM 335 (Squatters Rights Collection), flyer, 'Stop the Demolition of the 5th Street Squat', n.d., Kurt Reynertson Papers Box 1, Folder 1.

70. Fly, 'Squatting on the Lower East Side', p. 215; TL, TAM 335 (Squatters Rights Collection), flyer, 'Illegal Demolition Leaves 26 Homeless in NYC, and flyer, 'Giuliani Destroys Home in Violation of Court Order', n.d. Kurt Reynertson Papers Box 1, Folder 1.

71. On urban revanchism, see Smith, *The New Urban Frontier*.

72. Starecheski, 'Squatting History', p. 193.

73. Quoted in Luna, 'Squatters of the Lower East Side'.

74. Iain Boal, 'Prologue', in Iain Boal, Janferie Stone, Michael Watts and Cal Winslow (eds), *West of Eden: Communes and Utopia in Northern California* (Oakland, CA: PM Press, 2012), pp. xiii–xxv, p. xii.

75. Anders Corr, *No Trespassing! Squatting, Rent Strikes, and Land Struggles Worldwide* (Cambridge, MA: South End, 1999), p. 18.

76. Dobbz, *Nine-tenths of the Law*, pp. 104–5; see James Tracy, *Dispatches Against Displacement: Field Notes from San Francisco's Housing Wars* (Oakland, CA: AK Press, 2014), p. 29.

77. See Matthew Desmond, 'Eviction and the Reproduction of American Poverty'. *American Journal of Sociology* 118 (2012), pp. 88–133; Matthew Desmond, *Evicted: Poverty and Profit in the American City* (London: Allen Lane, 2016); Gretchen Purser, 'The Circle of Dispossession: Evicting the Urban Poor in Baltimore'. *Critical Sociology* 42 (2016), pp. 393–415.

78. Dobbz, *Nine-tenths of the Law*, p. 118.

79. See Smith, *The New Urban Frontier*.

80. Madden and Marcuse, *In Defense of Housing*, pp. 179, 180; see Kathe Newman and Elvin K. Wyly, 'The Right to Stay Put, Revisited: Gentrification and Resistance to Displacement in New York City'. *Urban Studies* 43 (2006), pp. 23–57; Jason Hackworth and Neil Smith, 'The Changing State of Gentrification'. *Tijdschrift voor Ecnomische en Sociale Geographie* 92 (2001), pp. 464–77.

81. Marianne Maeckelbergh, 'Mobilising to Stay Put: Housing Struggles in New York City'. *International Journal of Urban and Regional Research* 36 (2012), pp. 655–73, p. 663.

82. Right to the City Alliance (NYC Chapter), *People without Homes and Homes without People: A Count of Vacant Condos in Select NYC Neighbourhoods* (New York: RTTC-NYC, 2010), p. 1.

83. 'Living in Limbo in Manhattan's Ghost Housing', *NYT*, 11 May 1989.

84. Dobbz, *Nine-tenths of the Law*, pp. 97–98; 'Casa Del Sol Torched'. *The New York Rat* 2 (2004–5), pp. 1, 3.

85. Rana Jaleel, 'Into the Storm: Occupy Sandy and the New Sociality of Debt' (what-democracylooks-like.com).
86. Gold, *When Tenants Claimed the City*, p. 263.
87. I am indebted to Amy Starecheski for this observation. See TL, TAM 336 (Squatters Rights Collection), untitled document, Peter Spagnuolo Papers, Box Number 2, Folder 2 (List of Names).
88. Interference Archive, *We Won't Move: Tenants Organise in New York City*, exhibition catalogue (Brooklyn: Interference Archive, 2015), p. 6.
89. MoRUS, 'Reclaiming Space' (morusnyc.org).

Afterword

1. Quote in Sara Safransky, 'Greening the Urban Frontier: Race, Property and Resettlement in Detroit'. *Geoforum* 56 (2014), pp. 237–48, p. 237.
2. Quoted in Miguel A. Martínez López and Angela García Bernardos, *Okupa Madrid (1985–2011) – Memoria, reflexión, debate y autogestión colectiva del conocimiento* (Madrid, Seminario de Historia Política y Social de las Okupaciones en Madrid-Metrópolis, 2014), p. 218.
3. Detroit Resists, 'A Call to Action', in *Detroit Resists Catalogue* (issuu.com).
4. 'The Architectural Imagination' (vimeo.com); see also the website for the exhibition, thearchitecturalimagination.org.
5. See Andrew Herscher, *The Unreal Estate Guide to Detroit* (Ann Arbor: University of Michigan Press, 2012), digital online edition (quod.lib.umich.edu).
6. Detroit Resists, 'A Call to Action'. On 'austerity urbanism' see Jamie Peck, 'Austerity Urbanism: American Cities under Extreme Economy'. *City* 16 (2012), pp. 626–55; L. Owen Kirkpatrick, 'Urban Triage, City Systems and the Remnants of Community: Some "Sticky" Complications in the Greening of Detroit'. *Journal of Urban History* 41 (2015), pp. 261–78.
7. Thomas J. Sugrue, *The Origins of the Urban Crisis: Race and Inequality in Postwar Detroit* (Princeton, NJ: Princeton University Press, 2013), pp. xv, xviii.
8. Kirkpatrick, 'Urban Triage, City Systems and the Remnants of Community', p. 262.
9. Ibid., p. 266.
10. 'What Detroit Needs Now: More Squatters' (bloomberg.com).
11. Joshua M. Akers, 'Making Markets: Think Tank Legislation and

Private Property in Detroit'. *Urban Geography* 34 (2013), pp. 1070–95, p. 1090.

12. Ibid., pp. 1070–2.
13. Ibid., p. 1090.
14. Herscher, *The Unreal Estate Guide to Detroit.*
15. Safransky, 'Greening the Urban Frontier', p. 238; Kirkpatrick, 'Urban Triage, City Systems and the Remnants of Community', p. 265.
16. Ibid., p. 238.
17. Safransky, 'Greening the Urban Frontier', p. 239.
18. Don Mitchell and Nik Heynen, 'The Geography of Survival and the Right to the City: Speculations on Surveillance, Legal Innovation, and the Criminalisation of Intervention'. *Urban Geography* 30 (2009), pp. 611–32, p. 615.
19. William Bunge, *The First Years of the Detroit Geographical Expedition: A Personal Report* (Detroit, MI: Society for Human Exploration, 1969).
20. William Bunge, *Fitzgerald: Geography of a Revolution* (Athens: University of Georgia Press, 2011 [1971]).
21. William Bunge, 'The Geography of Human Survival'. *Annals of the Association of American Geographers* 63 (1973), pp. 275–95.
22. See for example, Antonis Vradis and Dimitris Dalakoglou, *Revolt and Crisis in Greece: Between a Present Yet to Pass and a Future Still to Come* (Oakland, CA: AK Press, 2011); Ada Colau and Adriá Alemany, *Mortgaged Lives: From the Housing Bubble to the Right to Housing* (Los Angeles: Journal of Aesthetics & Protest, 2014).
23. Dan Nemser, 'Pasado Compuesto' (thenewinquiry.com); *El Pais*, 8 January 2012.
24. Dan Nemser, 'The Other Occupy Movement' (thenewinquiry.com). On the history of squatting in Spain, see Antoni Batista, *Okupes, la mobilització sorprenent* (Barcelona: Plaza & Janes, 2002); Pablo Carmona et al., *Autonomía y metrópolis: Del movimiento okupa a los centros sociales de segunda generación* (Málaga: Cedma, 2008); Miguel A. Martinez López, *Okupa Madrid (1985–2011).*
25. Dan Nemser, 'The Other Occupy Movement'.
26. Dave Stelfox, 'How the Corrala Movement is Occupying Spain' (theguardian.com).
27. Dan Nemser, 'The Other Occupy Movement'.
28. Brenda Bhandar, 'From Proletarians to Proprietors' (jacobinmag.com); see Ada Colau and Adriá Alemany, *Mortgaged Lives.*
29. Antònia Casellas and Eduard Sala, 'Home Eviction, Grassroots Organisations and Citizen Empowerment in Spain', in Katherine Brickell, Melissa Fernández Arrigoitia and Alexander Vasudevan (eds), *Geographies of Forced Eviction* (London: Palgrave Macmillan, forthcoming).

30. I am indebted to Carlos Delclós for reminding me of this.
31. Miguel A. Martínez López and Ángela García Bernardos, 'The Occupation of Squares and the Squatting of Buildings: From the Convergence of Two Social Movements'. *ACME: An International E-Journal for Critical Geographies* 14 (2015), pp. 157–84, p. 177; see also Sophie Gonick, 'From Occupation to Recuperation: Property, Politics and Provincialization in Contemporary Madrid'. *International Journal of Urban and Regional Research* (forthcoming).
32. Ibid., pp. 170, 171.
33. See especially Pierpaolo Mudu and Sutapa Chattopadhyay (eds), *Migration, Squatting and Radical Autonomy: Resistance and Destabilisation of Racist Regulatory Policies and B/Ordering Mechanisms* (London: Routledge, 2016).
34. Miguel A. Martínez López, 'Squatters and Migrants in Madrid: Interactions, Contexts and Cycles'. *Urban Studies* (forthcoming).
35. López, 'Squatters and Migrants in Madrid'.
36. Jonathan Darling, 'Forced Migration and the City: Irregularity, Informality and the Politics of Presence'. *Progress in Human Geography* (forthcoming).
37. 'Welcome to Greece's Refugee Squats' (washingtonpost.com).
38. 'Occupy Turin: Refugees Find a Home in Italy's Abandoned Olympic Village' (theguardian.com).
39. See for example 'Un toit pour tout.e.s!' (calaismigrantsolidarity .wordpress.com).
40. Henri Lefebvre, 'The Right to the City', in Eleanor Kofman and Elizabeth Lebas (eds), *Writings on Cities* (Oxford: Blackwell, 1996), pp. 63–181, p. 173; see Mitchell and Heynen, *The Geography of Survival,* p. 615.
41. David M. Bell, 'Occupation From Below: Squatting Within, Against and Beyond'. *City* 20 (2016), pp. 507–11, p. 511.